MARKETS
AND
POWER

MARKETS
AND
POWER

The
21st Century
Command Economy

ERIC A. SCHUTZ

M.E. Sharpe
Armonk, New York
London, England

Library of Congress Cataloging-in-Publication Data

Schutz, Eric A., 1947–
    Markets and power : the 21st century command economy / Eric A. Schutz.
      p. cm.
    Includes bibliographical references and index.
    ISBN 0-7656-0500-7 (alk. paper) — ISBN 0-7656-0501-5 (pbk. : alk. paper)
    1. Capitalism. 2. Power (Social sciences). I. Title.

HB501.S434 2001
330.12′2—dc21   00-050505

To Cathy, Alex, and Megan, and to Mom, Dad, and Adrienne, with love

Contents

List of Tables and Figures

Table

Figures

MARKETS
AND
POWER

1

Introduction

For most people, "power" is so elementary an idea that, while it may be explicitly expressed only seldom, it infuses our every thought on human relations in one form or another. Sometimes it is a difficult concept to be very clear about, sometimes even taboo as well. When offered as explanation or description of the relationship between two people, or of any aspect of social life in general, power is rarely denied. Some do deny it, however, or at least deny that it is very helpful for understanding the most interesting or important things in human life. This book was written in an effort to counter the denial of power as a useful or meaningful concept by one particular such group: those in the mainstream of the field of economics. Because of the denial of power as a useful concept in mainstream economics, the study of that subject encourages the profound misconception among those who undertake it that modern market economies have somehow overcome the age-old problem of social power. I offer this book to students and others interested in economics as an antidote to that misconception.

While mainstream economists deny the usefulness of the concept of power, in the rest of the social sciences power is given much the same kind of attention as is the concept of the molecule in the fields of chemistry and biology. Indeed, those who study politics, sociology, anthropology, and history find themselves so repeatedly confronted with issues of power that for them one more book on that subject may be of little additional interest. Of course, even those already well acquainted with the idea of power might nonetheless find this book helpful, for it concerns the most important forms that social power takes in market economies *from the viewpoint of modern economics* —that is, in terms of the special comprehension that economists have of how markets work. Among all the social sciences, economics is the one most especially devoted to the study of market systems, and even though many economists might deny it, theirs is the field from which one would expect the most elucidation on how structures of power function in market societies. This book is intended to help fulfill such expectations.

Economics and Power

Where the concept of power has been an important element of inquiry, it has brought with it much controversy. Who has it and who does not? What are its bases? What are its possibilities—what does having it permit, what does lacking it prohibit? Of what exactly is it constituted—how does one know when one has it or lacks it? Is it "good" or "bad"? These are questions over which great argument has long coursed in all the social sciences, not to mention in philosophy and literature, but the mainstream of modern economics is uniquely silent on such issues. How can a social science not only avoid engaging in questions about social power but eschew its use as a theoretical construction altogether? Isn't power an essential element of all human relationships?

The term power carries three distinct but closely related meanings. We refer, first, to an individual's (or a group's) power to do some particular thing or to achieve desired ends in general, the capacity to act decisively in the world. This sort of power is closest in meaning to the physical power of the natural sciences, the ability to exert energy to accomplish things, and in humans may be directly related, of course, to a person's physical or intellectual strength. Second, in a more explicitly social sense of the term, we refer to power as the ability to influence other people, to get them to act or think in ways they would not otherwise. Power as the capacity to affect other people is indeed the very essence of social relations: Only to the extent that individuals affect each other can there even be "social relations" among them. Finally, we refer to power over people, in which an individual or group not only influences others but does so in a dominating way, getting them to do things that they do not wish to do or that are not in their own interest to do. This sort of power is, of course, strongly negative in connotation, and is the essence of power as a social problem as well as a philosophical and moral concern.

I will refer to these three sorts of power as, respectively, the power of accomplishment, influence or the power to influence, and dominating power. Perhaps not surprisingly, the last of these, the most problematic, will be the main focus of this book. One might ask, if dominating power is the main issue, why not then simply refer to it as "domination," an obviously much more precise term that immediately makes clear my intentions—why not just title my book *Markets and Domination*? I prefer to use the much broader term "power" because while domination is distinct in meaning from the other two kinds of power, it needs emphasizing that it is so closely tied to them that the three kinds of power are, in an essential way, all of a piece, they are essentially *one*. Having power of accomplishment generally implies having power to influence others—and conversely, of course, being able to influence people not only requires that one be able to accomplish specific things, it is itself a kind of accomplishment. Similarly, the power to influence people generally implies also the power to dominate them to one degree or another—and conversely, domination not only is a particular form of influence but also requires that one be able to influence people in certain ways. Using the term power inclines one to ask about what specific connections there are among its three forms, connections that, as will become evident in this book, I believe are absolutely essential in an inquiry the ultimate concern of which is domination per se. Alternatively, looking at "power," rather than at "domination," inclines one to consider at the same time the particular powers people may have that enable them to dominate others, as well as at the particular powers that those who are dominated lack.

How can any modern social science almost totally avoid both discussion about and analytic use of the concept of power? First, let me clarify that not all economists avoid considering power in their work—merely most of those working in the mainstream of the field.[1] In the writings of those representing the now dominant, politically conservative schools of economic thought—neoclassicals, monetarists, and new classicals—the concept of power virtually never appears, not even in analyses in which the presence of power is pretty obvious, for example, that of market monopoly. Those representing the most conservative of all schools of economic thought, the Austrians, do discuss matters of power, but virtually always restrict their discussion to issues of the dominating power of *government*. For them, significant power relationships among private individuals and organizations in the market economy simply do not exist.

Among the less conservative economists in the mainstream—traditional Keynesians and some "new" Keynesians—power in both the public and the private sectors is at least acknowledged. For example, some do recognize the importance of monopoly power and urge the use of state power in antitrust action against it. Yet even for some of these more liberal economists, avoidance of analyses of power relations sometimes seems almost studied, for example, in labor economics, where, as will be seen later in this book, major power relationships beg recognition.

It is only on the fringe of the field, outside of acknowledgment in the top-selling textbooks and in the "most reputable" academic journals—among a group sometimes referred to as political economists—that the concept of power is both employed as a tool of inquiry and considered as a topic of interest in itself.[2] There, among traditional institutionalists (the so-called new institutionalists really belong in the mainstream of economics) and radicals of various degrees and kinds (some new and post-Keynesians, Marxians and other leftists, and feminists), power is both a fundamental instrument of analysis and a basic concern of inquiry. For example, for most Marxist and feminist economists, domination by the ruling class, or by the male sex, is the primary issue of economic inquiry itself. And for traditional institutionalists, post-Keynesians, and many new Keynesians, power relationships are a major element in understanding how the economy works.

How can the broad mainstream of a social science ignore considerations of power? The answer is twofold. To begin with, the economic model most often employed by the mainstream largely precludes questions about power. Two features of that model militate strongly against any inquiry into power relationships, hence into how such relationships might be understood to affect things. First, the standard economic model relies on a radically simplistic utilitarian individualism for sorting through in an understandable way the enormous complexities of socioeconomic matters. The individual is depicted as totally self-concerned and dedicated to maximizing personal satisfaction ("utility")—real relationships with other people, power relationships as well as other kinds, do not impinge upon his consciousness, they simply are not part of his makeup. "Economic man" neither affects nor is affected by other people, and is, moreover, very much an automaton: Basically, his only activity is engaging in market transactions, and from these he seeks single-mindedly only one simple thing, again, his own pleasure. He owns and buys things, but exactly how he uses them is not of interest; he sells things, particularly his labor, but exactly how he labors, with whom, and in what sorts of social arrangements, are also not considered.

Pitiful and repulsive a character though he may be, economic man has been helpful for understanding markets, for he has greatly simplified what would otherwise be an enormously complex inquiry. Yet employing him in this capacity has had great costs: It may be possible to append to this rigidly simplified model of human behavior more realistic considerations of the social nature of actual human beings, but it has proved difficult to do so without complicating things to the point of obscuring definitive insights on issues of individual economic behavior. For example, in principle, we could preserve economic man's self-centered concern with personal satisfaction, while still allowing him to have some influence on other people by, say, his altering the constraints to which they are subject in their economic activities—an approach that I will consider in more detail later on in this book. In this way, we could relax our restrictive assumptions about economic man somewhat by supposing that he may have direct effect on other people, as opposed to the indirect and very diffuse influence he routinely exerts on them in his buying and selling in markets. But doing so, most mainstream economists would point out, would so complicate the already difficult analysis of individual welfare-maximizing behavior as to force an abandonment of that particular enterprise altogether.

The other feature of the orthodox economic model that has consistently militated against considerations of power has been the idea of "perfect competition," or somewhat more broadly, "perfect markets." The idea of a perfectly competitive market is one of the most fundamental in economics, and students from the very beginning of their studies are drilled with its characteristics—even if no such thing has ever or could ever exist, with its "indefinitely large" numbers of buyers and sellers who "freely" enter into and exit from the market at any time and who deal in a "perfectly" homogeneous product. Soon after, students may get the list of additional characteristics that would make for a perfect market—buyers and sellers having "perfect and free" information about all relevant aspects of the market, bearing "zero" costs of doing business with each other, and having "zero" external effects arising from their activities (i.e., effects on others not directly involved in production, consumption, or exchange). Farfetched as these notions are, they have contributed greatly to our understanding of certain aspects of how real markets work. I will look more closely at some of these characteristics of hypothetically perfect competition and perfect markets later on, but for the moment, suffice it to say that whatever benefits these ideas have brought to economic analysis, they have done so at great cost: As I will explain, there can be no power relationships among people exchanging in an assumed system of "perfect" markets, and the ramifications of power in economic activity simply cannot be considered in such a world.

Thus both the agents that populate the world depicted in the mainstream economic model and the market structures within which they interact according to that model disallow considerations of power relationships. Of course, economists do often inquire about the ramifications of "dropping assumptions" of the mainstream economic model—for example, what happens when there are only a small number of sellers in a market, or when there are sizable transactions costs or external effects, or when economic man does not completely maximize his welfare but merely "satisfices." Yet such inquiries virtually never venture into considering the power relationships that then become possible. Indeed, as I noted earlier, even where obvious and significant power relationships necessarily arise as assumptions of the conventional economic model are dropped, mainstream economists generally ignore them and eschew any use of the term power as well.

Given how important the concept of power is in the other social sciences, such an avoidance by economists seems altogether too studied. What could be wrong with giving some attention to power relationships where they obviously arise when dealing with exceptions to the model of economic man in perfect markets? What could be wrong with using other approaches than that model when it manifestly excludes analyses of major power structures extant in the economy? Where a particular mode of inquiry has limitations, other serviceable modes of inquiry should be taken up. Mainstream economics has not done so, but it is not because alternative modes of inquiry are lacking. Instead, the particular influences to which inquiry in the field has been subject from its social milieu, and the role economics has consequently played alongside the other social sciences, have inclined economists to stay comfortably within a mode of inquiry that precludes critical reflection on power.

Taken altogether, the social sciences are part of the same enterprise of the pursuit of knowledge for human progress as are the natural sciences and the liberal arts and humanities. As such they share the same traditions of humanism, enlightenment, and the modern movement for liberation. Thus the analysis and critique of established social power is a fundamental part of the *tradition* of the social sciences, and this is as true of economics as it is of the others. But the modern field of economics arose mainly not as a study of the economic aspects of societies in general but as the study of the economic aspects of *capitalism* (i.e., of the developing market system of Europe and Britain). Its critique of social power was mainly a critique of the then-established social power structures of European feudalism, against which it viewed the rising market system as the progressive opposition. Thus it allied itself very early with that system, as was so clearly manifest in the work of its "founding father," Adam Smith.

Along with that alliance, which was based on a principled antagonism toward older social forms that would hinder human progress, came another based on practical need. The new class of leaders of the rising market system greatly needed both advocates in the political and ideological struggle for a social environment conducive to markets, and help in understanding how this rising system worked and how to manage things within it. At the same time, the rising field in which economic matters were studied needed resources: places of study, libraries, and incomes for teachers, writers, and researchers. As leaders of the rising market system perhaps may have put it, an exchange was called for: their financial and other help in return for the support they needed. Very early on, the study of economics was influenced by the practical alliance of many economists with business.[3]

Today most academic economists work in departments organized as divisions of business schools or other business programs of one kind or another. The primary purpose of such an organization is not to facilitate the critical examination of business and the power structures of the business world from the viewpoint of the larger concerns of humankind, but to provide what *business* needs—management education, consultation, political and social advocacy, and other support for the business/market system. That is, in business schools the practical organization of economics as a field of inquiry has been centered mainly upon the requisites of business, not those of the pursuit of critical insight and truth in general. Moreover, even those academic economics departments that are independent of business programs—mostly in small, liberal arts colleges—are influenced in similar directions by their having to compete with the larger and better financed business economics departments for students, teachers, and research resources.

Of the social sciences then, economics is, by virtue of its deep practical alliance with business, far and away the least inclined toward critical inquiry about the power structures of the market system. This is not to say that the rest of the social sciences have completely escaped the influence of business as a source of the requisites for the work of study and teaching—far from it—but they have certainly been less subject to that influence than has economics. Thus while economics shares with the other social sciences the progressive tradition of a critical attitude toward established power in general, it is uniquely accepting of the relatively novel power structures of the business/market system of modern times. If the inclination in economics has been to develop a marvelously complex and involving model of economic activity in which social power plays no role whatsoever, it is because such a model enables an avoidance of critical inquiry into the power structures of modern business society.

Not only has economics therefore contributed very little to people's understanding of how power works in market societies today, but by avoiding the concept of power altogether in its inquiry into the nature of markets, it has actively fostered the grossly mistaken notion that such societies have, in their brief recent history, somehow escaped the problem of social power, or at least have put humankind on a path of such escape. The truth is, as I hope readers of this book will be convinced, that market systems, at least those seen predominantly in history thus far, are as much structured by social power hierarchies as are other major types of social systems. Markets do not really militate against structures of social power—they reinforce many such structures and add new ones of their own—they are themselves both constituted by and engendering of systemic power structures. To see this in a preliminary sort of way, and at the same time introduce the main themes of the rest of this book, it may be useful to consider in broad outline what the market system of today actually looks like.

Market Systems and Market Systems

A market is, of course, an ongoing and more or less routinized series of exchanges of some commodity for other commodities, especially for money, by significant numbers of people whose voluntary transactions determine the price of the commodity, or its exchange ratios in terms of the other goods for which it is traded. "Market system" sometimes refers to a collection of interrelated markets, but more often it designates a community or nation whose economic activity is mainly organized by markets—that is, with the allocation of productive resources among producers and the distribution of final goods and services among consumers being accomplished mostly by exchanges in markets. Mainstream economists are cheerleaders for such systems—they advocate them over all others in the name of the individual freedom of economic activity manifest in markets and the progressive liberation of humankind that market systems are supposed to bring forth over time.

But market systems are not all of a single, simple piece: Historically, there are market systems and there are market systems. Some market systems have clearly contributed to human liberation, while others have profoundly stifled it. As I will discuss further below, our own particular *kind* of market system is most accurately referred to as *capitalism*, a term with which most people are familiar but one that most conventional economics textbooks either omit entirely or else confuse by equating it with market systems in general. Whether this particular kind of market system has or has not contributed to human liberation is not a simple question—in some ways it clearly has advanced the cause of progress; in other ways it clearly has not. Treating it as if it were identical with all other kinds of market systems, with the dismissive judgment that all such systems are preferable to all other alternatives, as mainstream economists typically do, misses the important issues at hand in questions about power. To see this, before looking more closely at our own market system today, consider two other historic kinds of market systems quite different from ours.

Consider first the system of chattel slavery, such as existed in the American South and much of the rest of the world in the latter half of the last millennium, up to the nineteenth century. In its most advanced stage, this was a full-fledged market system, with land and capital goods being privately owned by individuals who could sell their properties in markets, with consumer goods being similarly distributed in markets, and, just as in our own market system today, with a well-developed labor market as well. But of course, there was this critical difference: Whereas in our system it is wage-labor that is exchanged in the labor market, in the slave system it was people themselves. In our system of wage-employment, people sell their own labor time to other people in contracts from which they are completely free to exit at any point; and the time that they forego to the buyer's command (i.e., the employer's) in return for a wage is only a fraction of the day, after which the employee is completely free for the rest of the day. In chattel slavery, on the other hand, working people are themselves bought and sold as commodities owned by other people: They cannot voluntarily exit from their contracted ownership by their masters, and every aspect of their entire lives, not merely their work days, is subject to the latter's command.

Both chattel slavery and our own present economic system are market systems, and an undiscriminating advocacy of these over all other economic systems would therefore be, to say the least, misleading. In their blanket advocacy of market systems, mainstream economists completely gloss over some profoundly critical questions of "detail": Certainly they must not mean to include the chattel slave market system as an example of a kind of system superior to all others in its promotion of human liberation!

Consider as a second example the case of the market system of the post–World War II economy of Yugoslavia before its disintegration in the last decade. Best known in the United States as a Communist nation (although by no means a part of the Soviet sphere of influence), Yugoslavia represented a kind of market system characterized by what may be called "democratic worker-owned or worker-controlled enterprise." While the Yugoslav government had formal constitutional ownership of most of the nation's means of production, virtually complete control over them was constitutionally designated to those who worked directly with them, as long as the workers organized their control democratically. Thus enterprises in Yugoslavia were, in effect, "owned" by their workers, who organized their firms however they saw fit as long as they fulfilled constitutionally stated requisites of democratic decision making. (Two other major examples of democratic worker-control systems, although not at a national scale, are the Israeli kibbutzim and the network of cooperatives in the city of Mondragon in the Basque region of Spain.)[4]

To clarify the issue here by some brief elaboration: All aspects of the operation of the Yugoslav firm were under the control of the workers as a group—from pay scales and job assignments to workplace technology, investment and disinvestment, and the disbursement of enterprise profit. Decision making was done democratically—by the group directly in smaller firms or, in larger firms, by managers appointed by elected and recallable representatives. While workers in a firm could not sell individually owned "shares" in their enterprise to others (tradeable shares were simply illegal), as a collective they could sell the whole enterprise or any part of it to another enterprise collective and use the proceeds as they wished. Wage-employment was illegal (except for the tiny sector of "mom and pop" firms), thus new workers taken on at an enterprise had to become full members of the firm's collective with full voting and other rights to participation in the firm's decisions.

In all respects the Yugoslav economy was a market economy: The worker-controlled enterprises produced goods for sale in markets, and bought their inputs from other such enterprises in markets. The government, unlike those of the Soviet-sphere Communist nations, interfered virtually not at all in producer- and consumer-goods markets (indeed government spending in Yugoslavia constituted a smaller share of the nation's gross domestic product (GDP) than even the U.S. government does in our own economy today). This was, moreover, a highly successful economic system: Yugoslavia experienced far better economic growth rates than the U.S. system for most of its existence.

Of course, we may safely presume that the Communist Yugoslav market economy is not exactly what mainstream economists in the United States mean when they advocate market systems over all others. On the other hand, a market system with worker-controlled enterprises would be extremely appealing in some critical ways, certainly from the viewpoint of working people. Indeed, what immediately distinguishes both the two cases just briefly described from our own particular market system of today is precisely the kind of *power structure* to which working people are subject in each case: in one kind of market system working people are chattel slaves, in another they are wage-employees, in a third they are participants in a democratic organization. Obviously these terms of difference, completely glossed over by an undiscriminating advocacy of market systems, are crucial for any pronouncements about the congeniality of such systems to human liberation. By highlighting and helping to clarify such essential matters, a sense of the importance of power in all social arrangements would certainly strengthen our understanding of the benefits and shortcomings of "markets."

Capitalism Today

Thus accuracy in referring to the particular kind of market system extant in most of the developed world today requires distinguishing it from other kinds of market systems. While I will often use the generic term "market system" in this book, in referring specifically to the system predominating in the world today, I will mostly use the more accurate term "capitalism." In a capitalist market system, not only are most economic activities organized by markets, but also, in particular, (a) means of production (capital goods and materials, buildings, land, and so forth) are privately owned by individuals with the right to exchange or sell their properties in markets, and (b) productive labor is done by wage-employees. As the greatly contrasting cases of chattel slavery and worker control make clear, in market systems in general, other kinds of private ownership of means of production and other ways of organizing labor are possible besides those which characterize capitalism. Similarly, different varieties of the capitalist market system itself are also possible. That which predominates today is probably best understood as a combination of three variations that analysts have distinguished since the early twentieth century: "Monopoly" or "corporate" capitalism, characterized by the predominance of very large private businesses with great economic and social power; "state" or "welfare" capitalism, characterized by the enlarged role of the state in economic activity and in counterbalancing the adverse social impacts of the capitalist private sector; and "global" capitalism, in which the boundaries of the separate capitalist nations of the world diminish in importance as their economic systems interweave into a single capitalist system that envelops the entire planet. While each of these three variations incorporates a different overall structure of power, their common core has remained relatively unchanged throughout the history of capitalism.

Even in global capitalism, where imperial power relations hold between the advanced and the undeveloped nations and where corporations are clearly transnational in scope, the primary organization of power nonetheless remains within the domain of the nation and involves the *national state* as traditionally understood (up to the present, at least). Mainstream economists, as I noted earlier, when they focus on power at all, consider only state power to be of much interest. Others who are better acquainted than they with the realities of power in the world today see the power structures of the national state, even in global capitalism, as absolutely critical for the whole system. Either way, state power must be a basic part of any complete account of power in the capitalist economy.

Yet for a number of reasons, it is not at all inappropriate to focus exclusively upon the private sector structures of power that are unique to the capitalist system, as I will do in this book. First, there is a critical need for some balance to the misconception promoted by mainstream economics today that significant power in market systems is *only* to be found in the state—a need that by itself should suffice for an investigation from an economist's viewpoint that focuses solely on private sector power. Beyond that, it may be argued also that state power in capitalism is distinct from that in other types of economies mainly by the particular kinds of power structures existing in the private sector with which the state is intertwined. Indeed, this can be said of all types of market economies, in which, by definition, the private sector necessarily predominates. Thus understanding the distinctive state power that rules in capitalism requires *first* understanding the structures of private power that characterize that system.[5]

In this book, then, I will examine the most important structures of power in the private sector in the capitalist economy, touching upon state power only where it is essential for the account. From the viewpoint of an economist looking at power in capitalism today, three major sets of private power structures stand out. First and perhaps foremost are those power structures constituted in relationships among capitalist firms. Business in capitalism today—especially in the form of the corporation but also in that of the proprietorship and the partnership—is certainly the most conspicuous organizational form of the system. Some even see it as the single distinguishing institution of capitalism, and while many political economists would argue that is a mistake, when one thinks of markets today, business is certainly the biggest player in any of them. I will consider several types of power structures extant in the relationships among businesses: *monopoly power* in markets, in which one or a few firms exert power individually upon customers or suppliers; the *power of finance*, in which financial firms—banks, insurance companies, and so on—exert power upon other firms with which they do business; and *network power*, in which collections of interrelated firms, knit together by both monopoly and financial power, in turn exercise power upon outsiders.

Second are those structures of power embodied in the relations among people within firms. These relations are, of course, completely nondemocratic hierarchical relations, with decisive powers resting at the top of the firm's hierarchy. Although most mainstream economists themselves have left the internal structure of the firm largely unexamined, political economists and others who have analyzed that structure emphasize most importantly the employer-employee relationships it embodies. However else such relationships may be perceived, what seems singular about them is the *employer power* possessed by those who command employees at work. It is by virtue of that power that each level of command in the firm's hierarchy is able to secure the compliance of all lower levels to its decisions, and that the firm may therefore, in some contexts, be safely treated as if it were a single economic agent, as it is in mainstream economics.

Third are those power structures constituted in relations among people insofar as they are endowed with greatly different amounts of *purchasing power.* The term purchasing power as generally used is actually inadequate for an analysis of the major power structures of capitalism, although I will use it for convenience nonetheless. The term conveys well enough the powers of accomplishment and influence on others that people exert as they purchase goods and services, but the real essence of purchasing power as a kind of power over people, I will argue, lies in the great inequality of its distribution that exists in capitalist market systems. In such systems, this very inequality of income and wealth in fact serves as the preeminent basis of all other social power structures, for those who have great purchasing power can both purchase superior positions in and avoid subjection to dominating power relationships. Thus purchasing power inequality not only arises from structures of domination, as those in power positions reap monetary benefits from those subject to their power, it also undergirds other power structures extant in the society. Economic inequality then is at the very heart of the issue of social power in capitalism.

One of the main conclusions to be drawn from this inquiry about power in the private sector of the economy is that capitalist market systems do not function merely anarchically, as if guided by an invisible hand that has nothing to do with hierarchical social structures. There is certainly a sense in which capitalist development has appeared as the natural or spontaneous outcome of the myriad decisions of individuals exchanging in markets. Yet in any social system that is importantly structured by power, the particular decisions of those at the top of the power hierarchy primarily determine at least the broad directions of things. The capitalist market economy is such a system, a pyramidal hierarchy just like those older systems of recorded history—indeed, just like its twentieth-century archrival, the Soviet Union. Essentially, people in power positions decide the broader contours or directions of economic affairs for those subject to their power. The latter decide for themselves their own economic activities *within the broader constraints set by those higher up*. Because the breadth of these constraints may seem relatively large for many people in the system (even though it remains quite constricted for those with little purchasing power), there may be more individual "freedom" in this system than in other hierarchical systems in human history. Yet the vast majority in this system are no more free from *dominating power* than in other systems. Alternatively, while there may be wider scope for unconstrained and autonomous individual economic activity in capitalism—especially in the affluence of advanced capitalism—there are nonetheless definite constraints, and these are as much determined by those in power in capitalism as in other systems.

There is, in this viewpoint, a definite judgment against capitalism. Dominating power is arguably not justifiable on any grounds of fairness, and societies that can do without structures of dominating power are definitely preferable to those that cannot, other things equal. Any analysis of social power must face the question of whether dominating power is present in the case at hand, and be prepared to make the necessary negative judgment if it is. Doing that requires an adherence to the principles of democracy, the ideal of equal access to participation in social life and decision making. The analysis outlined in this book finds that, while dominating power may not be a necessary feature of all market systems, it is an essential feature of the capitalist market system. On grounds of democratic distributive justice therefore, reforms of those institutions that constitute the power structures of capitalism are called for, and in the last chapter of this book I outline some of the more important of the reforms implied in earlier chapters.

Power and Practice

Thus the viewpoint of this book is not merely another way of looking at the system—an alternative view, less congenial than the predominant one (of mainstream economics), perhaps somewhat apt to cause disaffection or pessimism in readers, but otherwise of little consequence. Even for those who cannot imagine the breadth of reform that is called for at the conclusion of this book, the analysis of power offered here is of considerable significance for understanding how this market system actually works, hence for efforts, large and small, at making it work.

Regarding the ways in which power shapes the actual working of the economy, I have much to say in later chapters. On the role of power in efforts to *make* it work, consider briefly one of the most momentous issues of these times—the worldwide ecological and environmental resource crisis—a matter on which orthodox economics, while it has made major contributions in the past, can be of little further help if it continues in its aversion to questions of power.

Mainstream economists early on made at least one major contribution to our understanding of the environmental crisis, the idea of "negative externality." When a manufacturer's pollution damages another's property or person, the latter suffers a "negative external effect" of the former's production activity. The costs to the damaged party may be "internalized" by lawful compensation of some kind if he is able to successfully press the suit (although the compensation may not be at all an accurate reflection of the true costs he has suffered). But of course, in the most important cases of pollution or other types of environmental damage, no such suit is possible—for example, in cases like those of acid rain, ozone layer depletion, the greenhouse effects of fossil fuel use and deforestation, and species extinction the perpetrators are too many and the harm caused is too widely spread among the population for the external costs to be internalized.

The analysis of negative externality makes it quite clear that there is an absolutely essential public role in the resolution of all environmental problems: Markets, left on their own, cannot resolve environmental issues. Where possible, government is required to create appropriate private property rights and means of litigating damage suits. Where that is not possible—again, in all the most critical cases—government must create and enforce appropriate regulations, taxes, subsidies, or other incentives toward environmentally more congenial private behavior.

As I will discuss later on, power is fundamentally and unavoidably involved in negative externalities. For example, insofar as the victims of a manufacturer's pollution *must* suffer the damage the manufacturer causes to them or their property, they are subject to his "power." The fact that a power relationship of this sort invariably exists with negative externalities is virtually never mentioned in the conventional economic literature on the subject, but is critical for understanding how to resolve environmental problems. Simply put, where dominating power is present, it yields benefits; hence those who have it will take action to keep and exercise it. Resolving the harm caused by its use requires the exercise of some *countervailing power*.[6]

There are thus public issues involved in negative externalities. Major pollution, for example, is not merely an inadvertent side effect of the productive activities of firms whose owners and managers are invariably innocent of intending to do anything that would harm others. As countless individual cases have shown, polluting firms may spend big money on lobbying and public relations to maintain the legal right to continue polluting, and deliberate countervailing power on the part of the broader public must be brought to bear to satisfactorily resolve such cases in the public interest.

In a world in which power is not problematic, the kind of world with which mainstream economists generally concern themselves, the necessary public action would be forthcoming as a matter of course. But in reality, problematic power is the rule. Economists may prefer to leave issues of power in environmental matters to the political scientists and politicians, but the fact is that in such matters the most problematic of established power lies in the private sector, precisely the domain economists have staked out for themselves alone to legitimately study. For them to be silent about private-sector power in environmental issues is to leave untold just that story that economists, of all people, are best equipped to tell—and that is essentially what the mainstream of the field has done.

Rather than contributing to an understanding of how to build the necessary structures of countervailing power against those benefitting from environmental devastation, mainstream economics has, especially in recent decades, concerned itself with relatively minor aspects of the crisis and even thrown in with the business beneficiaries of environmental neglect. For example, economists have considered in detail the various alternative policy approaches to environmental problems: The "command and control" approach, to use their derogatory term for simple public regulation; the pollution-tax or -subsidy approach; and the supposedly "most efficient" marketable pollution-permit approach. All three approaches require close government regulation of the private sector, hence require that significant resources be taken by government for monitoring and enforcement, and for providing financial incentives if necessary; and they require also that the private sector relinquish some of its previous sovereignty in decisions about production and resource use. But in critical cases of environmental destruction like those noted above, the differences among the three approaches in cost and effectiveness pale to insignificance alongside the benefits of taking any serious action at all, and also pale beside the question of how best to accomplish the requisite seizing of public sovereignty from established private power in the first place.

On neither of these far larger matters have mainstream economists registered much concern—indeed, their propensity has been to belittle the environmental crisis as a public issue by reflexively advocating against government interference of all kinds in markets. First, because private power is essentially nonproblematic, in their view, there can be little reason for concern over the environment, since any crisis will in due course automatically precipitate whatever steps are necessary and sufficient to resolve it. Besides, how serious a problem can it be, alongside the immeasurable benefits of keeping government power appropriately curtailed? Thus orthodox economists have, in effect, withdrawn from making any constructive contribution to resolving what is certainly one of the greatest crises of modern times.

It must be acknowledged that to some extent economists have merely followed the broader trend these days toward laissez-faire public policy. On the other hand, to the extent that trend has been purely one of fashion and political convenience, economists, as "experts" on public policy, should not be excused from going along, and indeed may be justifiably charged with some responsibility for the fashion. In any case, their failure to accommodate the concept of power in their analyses of private economic behavior has greatly detracted from their contributions on a variety of other important public issues besides that of the environment. The health-care crisis, the developing monopolization of the media, the impending crisis of energy use in our transportation system, suburban overdevelopment, and the deterioration of our cities—in these and other important current economic issues, the problematic role of private-sector power simply cannot be ignored in any serious attempt at resolution. To take a reflexive laissez-faire policy stand on issues like these that clearly will require the exercise of countervailing state power for a satisfactory resolution in the public interest is at the least a major mistake. To suppose that in modern society the structures of power that most critically endanger democratic freedom lie outside of the market system itself (i.e., in government) when in fact problematic social power today is mainly centered in capitalist market structures, certainly impedes progress on these kinds of problems.

Again, this book is offered in the hope of helping to correct some of these broader consequences of the neglect of social power in the study and teaching of the economics of market systems. For those readers who are relatively ill versed in the subject of power, or who may even be approaching it for the first time, it is important to note that there is a voluminous literature on social power dating from ancient times to the present. I cannot do justice to even a small fraction of that literature in this book, but I do hope the book will serve as a decent introduction for those unfamiliar with the subject.

Given the breadth of the literature calling to be read on social power, I should state more explicitly what this book does not do. First, I do not attempt here a broad analysis of the general nature of power of the kind found extensively in the far more competent literatures of philosophy, sociology, and political science. Some general background is important, however—an elucidation of power in markets must at least be consistent with a general theory of social power applicable not only to other economic matters but also to all social relationships generally. Thus in the following chapter I outline the main ideas critical for my own particular approach to power in the rest of the book.

I also do not attempt here an in-depth *theoretical* analysis of power from the economist's viewpoint, either in general or in the particular context of the study of markets, since this too has been adequately done by now—albeit virtually unacknowledged in the mainstream of the field. Instead I hope merely to carry some of the insights achieved in the foundational work of other political economists to a broader audience than those typically concerned with political economic theory.

Finally, this book is about power in capitalist market systems, and I will not attempt here any extensive comparison of structures of power in such systems with those in other kinds of systems, such as feudalism or modern bureaucratic socialism. This too has been more than adequately done elsewhere, and I will dwell on comparisons only where they help clarify the nature of power in markets.

Instead, I will merely try to bring the portion of all this literature that I have become familiar with to bear in elucidating the most important structures of power distinctive of capitalist market economies today—business power, employer power, and purchasing power. While this kind of effort can by no means "prove" that systemic social power exists in modern market systems and is critical to understanding them, my hope is that it will at least provoke readers to investigate the matter further.

Notes

1. Readers may verify that this is broadly true of the mainstream of the field by looking at the contents of some of the more representative introductory and intermediate texts in macro- and microeconomics (especially the latter). A check of the text's index for the term "power" and perhaps other related terms, "domination," for example, and a reading of chapters in which issues of power might be expected to appear, should suffice. Among introductory texts, see, for example, N. Gregory Mankiw, *Principles of Economics*; Timothy Tregarthen and Libby Rittenberg, *Economics*; William J. Baumol and Alan S. Blinder, *Economics: Principles and Policy*. Readers might also examine some of the various dictionaries and encyclopedias of the field for references, such as, David W. Pearce, *The MIT Dictionary of Modern Economics*. Even John Eatwell et al., *The New Palgrave: A Dictionary of Economics*, a collection of considerable breadth by American standards, devotes relatively little of its total content to work on subjects related to power. See Douglas Mair and Anne G. Miller, *A Modern Guide to Economic Thought*, and David L. Prychitko, *Why Economists Disagree* for excellent accounts of the whole variety of different schools of thought—both mainstream and heterodox—in economics today. A fascinating apparent exception to the exclusion of power from economic theorizing is Mancur Olson, *Power and Prosperity*. His work, however, actually proves the point: It presents a quite mainstream economic viewpoint and analysis of the power of the *state*.

2. There are very few introductory texts still in print in the United States today that are representative of the various strains in political economy. Samuel Bowles and Richard Edwards, *Understanding Capitalism* was excellent; and E.K. Hunt and Howard J. Sherman, *Economics* remains so. See also Charles Sackrey and Geoffrey Schneider, *Introduction to Political Economy*; Hugh Stretton, *Economics: A New Introduction*; and Tom Riddell, Jean Shackelford, and Steve Stamos, *Economics*. Phillip O'Hara, *The Encyclopedia of Political Economy* gives an excellent broad survey of ideas of the whole spectrum of heterodox schools of thought. Douglas Mair and Anne G. Miller, *A Modern Guide to Economic Thought* provides excellent comparisons among the different schools in both economics and political economy. Among political economists, traditional institutionalists have been by far the most mindful of the subject of power; see Phillip A. Klein, "Confronting Power in Economics: A Pragmatic Evaluation"; William M. Dugger, "Power: An Institutional Framework of Analysis"; Warren J. Samuels, *The Economy as a System of Power* Vols. 1 and 2; and Eric A. Schutz, "Markets and Power." Pranab Bardhan "On the Concept of Power in Economics" is a good summary of how mainstream economists conceive power.

3. On the history of the close relationship between economics and the practical world of business and politics, see Ken Cole et al., *Why Economists Disagree*.

4. An excellent reference with bibliography and links on both Mondragon and the democratic cooperative sector in the United States is the ICA Group, Web site: http://www.ica.org. The authoritative book on Mondragon is William Foote Whyte and Kathleen King Whyte, *Making Mondragon*. There are large literatures on Yugoslavia

and the Israeli kibbutzim. On the former, see the somewhat critical Harold Lydall, *Yugoslavia in Crisis*; a more sympathetic view is Branko Horvat, "The Theory of the Worker-Managed Firm Revisited"; on the latter, Eliezer Ben Rafael, *Crisis and Transformation: The Kibbutz at Century's End.*

5. Of course, it may be argued that understanding the power structure of any modern society requires also an analysis of democratic political systems, since these have either challenged or prevailed in most nations of the world today. But that is a separate analysis that has been thoroughly undertaken in the field of political science, and moreover one which, again, if it is to be applied to the study of capitalism as a particular system, is best done on the basis of a prior comprehension of the private structures of power that define that system.

6. The critical importance of countervailing power as the remedy for structures of domination was one of John Kenneth Galbraith's major contributions to the modern discourse on social power. See his *Anatomy of Power*, chapter 8.

2

·

Power and Economics

Power is most definitely an important aspect of relationships between buyers and sellers in markets, and encompassing structures of power are preeminent among both those social institutions that underpin market systems and those that arise in the normal course of their functioning. The fiction that things are otherwise is lent credence by the neglect of the subject of power generally in economics, the field of inquiry most directly concerned with market systems. To clarify the reality behind the fiction we must first inquire at some length about the nature of power itself, to be particularly clear about exactly what power is.

Understanding Power

Consider again the three distinct connotations people usually attach to the term "power":[1]

- power to accomplish things,
- power to affect or influence people,
- power over people, or domination.

While it is the last of these that is of most concern as a social issue, it is appropriate nonetheless to use the term "power" rather than "domination" in order to highlight how closely intertwined are all three of these distinct meanings. To dominate, one must affect or influence people in certain ways, and to do that, one must be able to do or accomplish certain things. The converse holds as well: Being able to accomplish things may imply being able to influence people as well as having power over people to one extent or another. As a social problem, domination must be considered of a piece with the other two kinds of power—the problem of domination and the problem of power are one. But exactly what is the problem of power?

While power refers to a particular kind of relationship between two individuals in what has been called a "dyad," the relationship is virtually always constituted or determined by the actions of other people outside the dyad itself. That is, person A has power over B usually because of the actions or potential actions of C and D, who may or may not also be subject to A's power. The slave owner had power over the slave because a social apparatus existed to grant and enforce his ownership rights: Other individuals were prepared to act in a particular manner that gave the slave owner his power. Similarly, the power relationships pertaining between husbands and wives, teachers and students, managers and employees, and even parents and children are actually constituted by the larger social situation or context within which these relationships exist. Thus a "power relationship" is, in effect, an entire social arrangement of which the power dyad itself is merely a small part.

That relationship, understood either as the entire social arrangement constituting it or as the relationship between the two individuals themselves, is distinct from specific exercises of the power so constituted or from acts that the individual in power takes on the basis of or in making use of his advantage. Thus while "command" is sometimes taken as synonymous with power, for clarity I will use that term for reference to an exercise of power aimed at getting the other person to do some specific thing. Such an act may involve giving specific instructions, but the latter need be neither explicit nor face to face. For example, in a common usage in economics, one may be said to "command labor resources" without actually issuing instructions to laborers, indeed without necessarily having any association with working people of any kind at all.

In his exemplary effort to incorporate the concept of power into mainstream neoclassical economic theory, Randall Bartlett defined power as:

> The ability of one actor to alter the decisions made and/or welfare experienced by another actor relative to the choices that would have been made and/or the welfare that would have been experienced had the first actor not existed or acted.[2]

If, despite Bartlett's work, neoclassical economists continue to eschew the concept of power, it is not for lack of a comprehensive definition of the term suitable for their needs. For this definition is cast in exactly the same terms as the neoclassical model of "welfare-maximizing individual choice," and is moreover about as all-inclusive a definition as can be offered. It allows for all three of the distinct connotations of power and in no way restricts from consideration any kind of social relationships that might potentially involve power. Indeed, it specifies *only* that exercises of power over people must have either some objective behavioral effects upon those people (that is, upon their decisions) or else some subjective effects (upon their experienced welfare).

But for that very reason, Bartlett's concept of power is, for some important purposes, unhelpful or at least misleading: It takes no note at all of what kind of situation might give people power, nor of what it means to exercise power as a social act—it focuses upon the individuals involved in a power relationship, not upon the nature of their relationship. Like neoclassical economics itself, as has so often been said of it, Bartlett's concept of power too is "asocial." The real questions are, what is it about power that is distinct from other aspects or kinds of social relationships? What sort of social action is one taking when exercising power that distinguishes such actions from other things one might do in social contexts?

A more satisfactory approach would begin by noting that in neoclassical economics, individuals are actually understood to be not merely "maximizing welfare" but doing so in contexts that place constraints or limitations upon what they may accomplish: Individuals choose from among the alternatives available to them those that most improve their welfare. In terms of that model of *constrained* individual welfare maximization, one may then conceive of power as the ability to alter the constraints to which another person is subject in his/her decision making. Thus when the parent commands the child, for example, "Do this or else . . . ," the constraints within which the child makes her choices have been changed. Neoclassical theorists would say that the "costs" of some of the alternatives available to the child have been altered by the parent: If the child fails to clean her room, for example, she'll be denied playtime outside. The child now chooses a course of action, given these alterations in the constraints upon her or in the costs of her available choices, that is more likely in keeping with the parent's wishes.

Yet such a concept of power, although an improvement, is still not completely adequate. For in such a conception, power would be construed to be merely an ability to wield *threats or sanctions* upon another person. That is, one may threaten the other, for example, with loss of life or physical safety, or economic well-being, social status, affection, and so forth, if she fails to comply with one's wishes; or, one may instead promise the person some positive reward for compliance.[3] Thus Sam Bowles and Herbert Gintis, in their important economic analysis of employer power in labor markets, defined power as follows:

If *A* can, by using strategic threats or sanctions, command *B* to do something that improves *A*'s welfare, but *B* cannot similarly command *A* to do anything that improves *B*'s welfare, then *A* has "power" over *B*.[4]

It is vital to be clear that power so defined necessarily exists in labor markets (and I will make much use of Bowles and Gintis's exceptional work on power in later chapters), but there is another very important form of power that is not included in this definition: There are situations in which one may be able to get subjects' compliance merely by changing their *beliefs or attitudes* about things. Thus, one could convince them that it is in their interest to do one's bidding on the particular matter at hand—perhaps merely by making them aware of something of which they had been unaware, perhaps by deceiving them, perhaps by somehow affecting their emotional inclinations and attitudes about things.

In such cases, a subject's compliance is gained not by altering any of the actual constraints of which she takes account in making her choices, but instead by altering her perceptions of the constraints effective upon her or her evaluation of the choices available to her given those perceived constraints. That is, in principle, one may alter the *information* available to the person about the reality to which she is subject or one may alter the *values or preferences* she brings to bear in appraising that reality. In terms of neoclassical economic theory, power should thus be conceived more broadly as an ability to alter either the actual constraints of which the other person is aware—as in the exercise of threats or sanctions—or the other person's perceptions about the relevant constraints, or even her preferences about things given those perceptions.

Alternatively, one could simply take the term constraint more broadly to mean anything in the subject's environment that affects her decisions or well-being: Power then consists in one's being able to alter *any* of the constraints to which the other person is thus subject. Threats and sanctions, in this interpretation, involve constraints upon the subordinate's environment about which she is aware, but power may also involve constraints upon the subordinate's environment of which she is unaware, or upon her awareness itself, or even upon her attitudes or feelings about the things of which she is aware. In his careful reconsideration of the social theory of power, Tom Wartenburg conceives power in terms of this more comprehensive notion of constraint: "A social agent *A* has power over another social agent *B* if and only if *A* strategically constrains [or is able so to constrain] B's action-environment."[5]

Wartenburg's use of the verb rather than the noun "constraint" highlights yet another important aspect of the concept of power: "Constraining" usually means *further limiting* the subject's environment, relative to how it would be otherwise, or tightening the constraints effective upon the subject's actions and well-being. Thus it connotes doing something that is not in the subject's interest or does not improve her welfare. In his analysis, Wartenburg points out that one may well be able to use one's power over the other person to promote that person's interest or improve her well-being. Possibilities for such positive or "transformative" uses of power probably exist in all power relationships, and certainly are clear enough in such instances as those between parent and child, teacher and student, and husband and wife.[6] Yet if it is power as *domination* that is of primary interest as a social issue, then it is the negative possibilities of the use of power that most matter: Power is most importantly something by which one who is subject to it may be hurt.

But focusing on power as domination in the negative sense requires making some further clarification both of the nature of the "constraints upon people's action-environments" that are at issue, and of people's "welfare" as that which is affected by power relationships. First, those subject to such power, even in very oppressive power relationships, are "free" to make at least some choices and presumably make them in ways that improve their welfare relative to what it would be otherwise: Their choices are, practically by definition, welfare-improving. But while a subordinate's welfare is thus improved by the choices he makes from among whatever alternatives are offered by the dominant individual, the *situation* of subordinacy in such a power relationship must be presumed detrimental to the subordinate's welfare. Slaves, for example, were often induced to comply with commands of their owners by being offered positive rewards to assure compliance. In offering a reward, of course, the owner alters the constraints to which his slave is subject, or changes the costs and benefits of various alternatives available to the slave. The slave then decides whether to accept the terms of the offer, and his choice makes him better off than he'd be had he chosen otherwise, but not better off than he'd be were he free. Even if, with some particularly beneficent master, all commands given to a slave were in the form of such positive offers of reward, by no means would we then conclude, merely because the slave has positive choices, that he is not subject to the power of the owner.

Thus there are two distinct sets of constraints upon the slave that are at issue: Those that the owner immediately alters in his command of the slave, and those present in the larger social context that constitutes the slave's subjection. This distinction—between situational constraints and constraints immediately subject to the dominant individual's discretion—is supremely important for our considerations later on about power relationships in market exchanges. When one decides to sell something, for example, one does so because accepting the buyer's offer makes one better off than one would be otherwise: One's welfare is then improved when one carries out the decision to abide by the buyer's wishes. Yet such freedom of choice does not in itself imply that one is necessarily free of subjection to a buyer's power: A monopsony, for example, is a clear-cut case in which sellers have freedom of choice but are nonetheless subject to a buyer's power.

Second, the "power of belief" alluded to above implies that it is possible for a subordinate in a power relationship to be unaware of the social arrangements or situational constraints that constitute the relationship to which she is subject. Or if she is aware of these arrangements, she may accommodate or otherwise reconcile her values, attitudes, beliefs, and preferences to them, for example, by accepting them as "appropriate" or affirming their value or desirability "in the larger scheme of things." Subordinates in obvious power relationships must rationalize their status in one way or another, often coming to the conclusion that they are, after all, as free and sovereign "as possible." Of course, this goes both ways: The person in the position of power may not be fully aware of his advantage, or, especially in light of the fact that a position of power is preferred to one of subordinacy, he may reconcile his values to the situation by rationalizing its appropriateness. Thus both individuals in a power dyad may mistakenly equate their "welfare" in such a relationship with what their welfare would be in other, more congenial circumstances.[7]

Especially for the subordinate therefore, on whom the onus of proof is most likely to be placed when there is any question about the burden of the power relationship, it is critical to distinguish between her welfare as she experiences it in the actual circumstances in which she lives, and what may be called her *interest*—that is, what she would consider to be to her benefit were she completely free to choose and act with full knowledge of all possible alternatives. Obviously this distinction may not be an easy one to draw. Yet certainly people may misperceive or rationalize all sorts of things, and presumably may misperceive or rationalize power relationships as well, even those of which they are part. The distinction between welfare and interest is therefore essential for sustaining even the possibility of an accurate study of such relationships.[8]

How might we conceive of power then, in light of these considerations? Clarity and the requisites of an inquiry into power as a social problem suggest that power be conceived something like this:

> If person A can get person B to do something in A's interest by taking advantage of some situation or acting in some manner to which B, were she free to choose with full knowledge from among all possible alternatives, would not give her full consent, then A has "power" over B.

Power, Exploitation, and Alienation

The definition just given is appropriate for analyzing power as a social problem partly because it highlights the essence of what is negative in domination: In a power relationship, the dominant person may get benefits from the subordinate at the expense of the latter. The nature of the benefit taken consists in his having the subordinate do things for him or *act in his interest* rather than her own. In general, the benefit that the dominant person may take from the subordinate may be constituted in the form of some specific material "good" or perhaps merely some "service" provided by the subordinate; and it may be either directly taken from the subordinate or taken by some indirect or circuitous means. But in every case, according to this conception of power, what the superior takes from the subordinate is, in the most critical sense, the latter's *activity itself*, which the dominant person, in effect, redirects from whatever purposes the subordinate would have chosen for herself to those of his own.[9]

This aspect of power relationships—the subordinate's potentially being made to act on behalf of the superior's interest rather than her own—is usually referred to ? *exploitation* of the subordinate by the dominant individual. Since any activity one performs for another without giving one's full consent may reasonably be called work or labor, the exploitation of labor, a central concept in many heterodox economic theories of capitalist systems, is actually involved in all power relationships as here defined.

It might be thought that the concept of exploitation resolves a major problem some theorists have noted in analyses of power, specifically, the problem of *reciprocity* in power relationships. In principle, every such relationship is to one degree or another reciprocal: While one individual more or less clearly dominates the other, still the subordinate most often has at least some power over the dominant individual. Even chattel slaves were able to influence their owners to some extent. But if this is so, then the question becomes, precisely how is it determined that the power of one of the two dominates that of the other? It might be thought that in most cases one could effectively measure the power of each over the other by considering quantitatively "who works for whom": Whichever of the two expends activity on the other's behalf (as measured, e.g., by hours of labor) is exploited, hence must be the subordinate.

But "working for" someone does not in itself constitute exploitation: Parents work for their children, for example, and younger generations work for retirees, without being thereby necessarily subject to exploitation. Working for someone implies an exploitative relationship only when it is done without full consent by, or contrary to the interests of, the person doing the work—that is, when it is done in the context of a power relationship. Thus one must determine first whether the relationship involves an imbalance of power before one can infer exploitation.

In principle, the only way to make that determination is to examine the relationship in detail, taking account of all the relevant social arrangements that constitute it and considering the scope of possible activities of each individual and how they may be affected by the other individual. One must ascertain who may do what to whom, what specific benefits each person can thereby solicit from the other, and which of all these may be reciprocated and which may not. If an asymmetry in the amount of effort each individual expends for the other exists, then that imbalance is explained by the power relationship, but one cannot take a shortcut and infer the power relationship from a mere asymmetry in effort expended. It is not from the quantity of work the slave expends for the slave owner that we conclude the latter is dominant, but from a detailed qualitative understanding of all relevant aspects of their relationship.[10]

Closely related to exploitation as an essential characteristic of all power relationships is another key concept of many critical heterodox economists, especially followers of the tradition of Marx and Veblen, *alienation*. In the classic legal definition of the term, one alienated one's property by giving or selling the rights to its use to someone else. In that usage, some properties or rights were, in principle, "inalienable"—that is, one could not forego them, nor could anyone else legally or rightfully take or purchase them from one (e.g., the right to free speech or religion). But in a power relationship, some portion of the subordinate's life-activity itself, being directed by and for the purposes of the dominant individual and not the subordinate's own, is alienated in something like that classic sense of the term: The subordinate has, in effect, foregone that portion of her life-activity, and it is now literally "not her own." Alternatively, the subordinate is, in a quite objective sense, not fully in command of herself, her life-activity being not completely her own but partly someone else's.

Marxist and other heterodox theorists have analyzed extensively the effects of this alienation upon people's psyches and behavior.[11] Thus, insofar as a person's life-activity has been alienated from her by her subordinacy in a power relationship, she may also be said to be alienated from her own ends and interests, and from her own self-initiative and self-direction. Depending upon how important the power relationship is in her life, feelings of misdirection, confusion, impotence, and passivity follow straightforwardly to one extent or another. Insofar as people's full comprehension of reality may depend upon their being able to act as they choose in pursuit of their own preferred ends, the subordinate's intellectual development must be to that extent stunted. Feelings of meaninglessness would seem to follow directly from the alienated person's being unable to intellectually construct her own comprehension of things by means of her own free intellectual and other activity. She may adopt various compensatory behaviors or other distractions from such feelings as well—religion may indeed be the "opiate" of people subject to oppressive power, or in more current times, consumerism may serve as the requisite distraction.

Moreover, because the subordinate is necessarily in fundamental contention with the dominant individual—unavoidably so, since their purposes concerning the direction of a portion of her own life-activity itself are radically at odds—she may thus certainly be said to be alienated from the dominant individual. A manifest attitude of estrangement and antipathy toward him and others involved in the power relationship follows directly. And an essential indifference may extend even more broadly to people not involved in the relationship at all, especially to the extent that the subordinate is not able to freely develop relationships with others because of the power relationship to which she is subject. This stunting of her social capacities may compound the more direct effects of alienation on the subordinate's intellectual development, insofar as the latter depends on the breadth of her social interaction. Competitive and even predatory behavior would also seem to follow, as well as various other strategic behaviors, like dishonesty and social inauthenticity, to the extent that people's social selves are thus stunted.

Thus the concept of alienation is, at the least, an important key to understanding not only the psychology of subordination in individuals but also the nature of social behavior and relationships more broadly in all social contexts structured by power. It is a theory of "meanness" in social relationships, and indeed for many commentators on the human condition more generally, it amounts to a kind of secular theory of the "original sin" or "fallen-ness" of humankind in the history of civilization.

To continue in the terminology of heterodox economists of the classical tradition, the exploitative and alienating characteristics of power relationships imply that such relationships tend to reproduce themselves, that is, to persist more or less, and that they do so in what may accurately be called a dialectical process, that is, a historical process of conflict and contention. Subordinates generally seek to change or escape from their situation to achieve the autonomy and individual sovereignty necessary for them to pursue paths of development more of their own choosing and in their own interest. To the extent that subordinates seeking autonomy then succeed in resisting or escaping their subordinacy, power relationships dissolve over time, for example, as in the normal case of the adolescent's development vis-à-vis his parents. But in general the dominant individual has at least some immediate interest in maintaining or expanding the scope and benefits of his dominance. And since he may exercise his power with that specific intention in mind, he may command his subordinate to perform actions whose particular purpose is the continuance or expansion of the power relationship itself. Even if the superior does not do so, the subordinate's effort expended for the dominant person is effort that might otherwise be expended on resisting, escaping, or overturning his subordinacy. Thus, insofar as subordinates are acting at least partly for their superiors' purposes rather than for their own, their activities actually serve the purpose of sustaining their own subjection. Conflict and contention between superior and subordinate ebb and flow over time, then, as subordinates act to resist those who dominate them and as the latter succeed in getting them to act in ways that reproduce their own subordinacy. These ideas, writ in the larger context of social history, suggest for heterodox economists, especially traditional institutionalists and Marxists, a way of understanding enduring social structures and institutions as historically evolving—rising, developing, and falling in a dialectic of contention over the power relationships they constitute: As Marx said, "History . . . is the history of class struggle."[12]

Power in Complex Social Relationships

Analyses of power relationships generally involve considering social arrangements that are complex to one degree or another. Indeed, the social structures constituting a power relationship may be complex enough to be far more interesting than the power dyad itself. For example, the set of relationships involved in a power structure may include a whole hierarchy of transitive power relationships, with A having power over B, who has power over C, who dominates D, and so forth. Of course, many other people may be involved who are not themselves directly part of the hierarchy but whose various actions determine the structure of the constraints effective upon the subordinate or others higher up in the hierarchy. The actions of these outsiders may themselves be conditioned by other power structures or hierarchies to which they are subject—distinct power structures thus bolster and reinforce each other by restricting the alternatives available to their subjects. There may be whole organizations of intricately interconnected and mutually reinforcing power hierarchies that coordinate greatly varied activities of many people toward the ends of those in command, for example, in the modern state or business corporation. And in modern times the social arrangements of power are all the more complex with progressively advancing social specialization and the division of labor in production.

Social complexity itself does not essentially alter the exploitative and alienating relationship between those at the apex of a power hierarchy and those at the bottom, nor the nature of their relationship as one of an evolving dialectic of opposition. But it may greatly alter the quality of power relationships. For one thing, increasing specialization and complexity means greater interdependence among people in a society, a thicker web of interconnections among individuals. Thus it would seem to imply a greater likelihood that significant reciprocity may exist in power relationships: Subordinates may be able to take advantage of a greater variety of offsetting or counterbalancing structures of constraint upon their superiors, and increasing complexity then may actually have the effect of attenuating power relationships.

On the other hand, increasing complexity may alternatively imply that a broader variety of external constraints exists upon the subjects of any hierarchy, hence make them all the more enmeshed in the power structure. Increasing complexity also suggests a greater need, and presumably a greater opportunity as well, for organization, that is, the gathering together of related specialized activities into a coordinated whole aimed at some single end. Insofar as organization may be said to dramatically increase people's power to accomplish particular things—by deliberately bringing to bear on that accomplishment the interrelated activities of many people—it strengthens both people's power to influence other people outside the organization and their power over those other people as well. Thus organization may be said to be the essence of social power in modern societies.[13]

Finally, from the viewpoint of the social scientist, increasing complexity may make quite difficult the determination of the exact structure of a power relationship at a point of time, and even the determination of whether power exists in the relationship in the first place. For the same reasons, it may equally serve to hide that structure from the subjects of the power relationship themselves, who cannot then be counted upon for an accurate understanding of the complexities of their own situation. Of course, the *deliberate* hiding of relevant information by those in power positions may also be an important element in the maintenance of their positions. Especially in that case, social complexity may make the question of who ultimately rules in a power relationship nearly impenetrable, and especially so in modern market systems in which specialization and the division of labor in production are far advanced.[14]

Yet difficult though it may be to answer that question, it is possible at least to clarify the issues by improving somewhat on how we conceive of power itself. As I have defined it thus far, power is determined to be present on the basis of a hypothetical decision made by the subordinate individual B in what may be called a "counterfactual" situation: If, in more congenial circumstances of "freedom of choice with full knowledge of all possible alternatives," *B* would not consent to the actual situation or to the command given by *A*, then *B* is determined to be subject to *A*'s power. So stated, however, *B*'s hypothetical decision of whether to consent or not may be construed as occurring completely outside of any complex social decision-making context. That is, first, *B* decides completely independently of what all other individuals who may be concerned in the matter might also choose. Second, *B* does not consider what she thinks the broader social arrangements of her society ought to be, but only her own individual position *given* those arrangements.

Such a characterization of the counterfactual situation may suffice well enough when the broader social structures involved are not at issue, but in complex situations such structures are very likely to be at issue. And even a hypothetically free decision that *B* might make regarding whether to consent to the actual situation must be understood to occur in a social decision-making context, that is, in which all other affected individuals' preferences should also appropriately be taken into account. Without going into the details of just how such a social decision-making process might be conceived, it ought to suffice to say that the appropriate counterfactual must be one of *consensus decision making in a fair and democratic setting*.

Power and Democracy

In light of these observations then, the definition of power given earlier ought to be modified to one something like this:

> If *A* can get *B* to do something in *A*'s interest by taking advantage of some situation or acting in some manner to which *B*, in a completely fair and democratic, consensus decision-making process, would not give her full consent, then *A* has power over *B*.

Obviously for simpler contexts this definition is merely the equivalent of the preceding one. And by generalizing also for more complex situations in which the difficulties of social decision making are clearly present, it should help illuminate power relationships in a great variety of possible cases, not only in nondemocratic societies but also in democratic societies extant in the capitalist world today. Like the preceding definition, this one too makes explicit the moral dimensions of an inquiry about power—by highlighting the essential fact that dominant individuals may treat subordinates unjustly. This definition, however, also brings to the fore the nature of the injustice of power in social contexts involving more than merely two individuals: Since in a more congenial setting the subordinate would not give her consent to the command or situation, she is, in effect, being excluded from decisions that bear upon her—including not only those decisions made by the dominant individual himself that affect her, but also those decisions made in the larger community by virtue of which he is empowered over her. Thus since the subordinate is being excluded from decisions made in her community that affect her, the unfairness lies in an unequal sharing of community decision making among people, that is, in social decisions made undemocratically.

As it is characterized here then, "power"—that is, power over people, or power as domination—may be understood to be the diametric opposite of democracy. While there has been great controversy on the exact requisites of democracy in such advanced and highly complex societies as those of modern times, it may be argued that the general principles of what constitutes democracy are agreed upon by nearly all commentators, even those with fairly conservative views of what is "practical." Among the latter should be counted Robert Dahl, who suggests the following principles as necessary for democratic decision making:

1. *Effective participation.* . . . All members [of the affected group] must have equal and effective opportunities for making their views known . . . as to what the policy should be.
2. *Voting equality.* . . . Every member must have an equal and effective opportunity to vote and all votes [must be] equal.
3. *Enlightened understanding.* . . . Each member must have equal and effective opportunities for learning about the relevant alternative[s] and their likely consequences.
4. *Control of the agenda.* . . . Members must have the exclusive opportunity to decide how and what matters are to be placed on the agenda . . . [and their decision must determine the action taken].
5. *Inclusion of [all] adults* [who are affected by the decision-making process].[15]

Briefly then, suppose a (counterfactual) social decision-making process in which these principles hold: If, in such a process, B would not consent to A's command or to the broader situation by virtue of which A gives his command, then B must be subject to A's "power."

On the other hand, of course, this democratic counterfactual would pertain for relationships between people that do *not* involve power as well. That is, a correct determination of whether a relationship involves power requires those who are involved in or affected by the relationship to deliberate and decide on that question in a (counterfactual) situation in which *no such power exists*: A power-free social structure would be one in which universal democratic decision making prevails. While the exact terms of democratic decision making in large social contexts are controversial and certainly far beyond the scope of this work, it is worth reflecting on the questions, what sorts of social relations would predominate in a truly democratic setting? What would human behavior be like in a world without power?

Real equality in human relations in a world of unalienated individuals may, in fact, be difficult for many people to imagine. Yet spaces often open up in the social fabric, even in modern power-saturated societies, in which the sort of human relations that would be expected to prevail in power-free situations actually do appear to prevail and endure. In such cases, which Ricardo Blaug refers to as "breakouts of democracy,"[16] what may be perhaps most striking about social relations is the degree of *honesty and mutual respect* with which people relate to each other. Perhaps where people see others as true equals of themselves, they relate to others as if the others were as important to them as they are to themselves. Unalienated relations imply a casting off of the many layers of "social face" which people deploy in their relating to each other, an extreme degree of openness and honesty in the projecting of oneself and one's ideas and perceptions to others, including one's perceptions of those with whom one is relating. Blaug describes how, when such a "breakout" occurs:

> [A]ll accounts note that speech becomes animated and debate heated. . . . Now people are keen to be heard, they listen to others with interest, and concern is expressed to elicit all views. Exclusionary tactics are directly challenged, as are attempts to distort the needs and interests of others. Whatever the common interest under discussion, all salient facts are actively explored, and the group, now pooling its cognitive resources, confronts the matter at hand in its full complexity. . . . [P]articipants in deliberation broaden their tight focus on individual interests, first to seeing things from the point of view of others, and then to those interests the group has in common. As the group continues to meet, friendship, vitality and rapid learning all draw people in. . . . There *are* disagreements, and these are acted out—often in highly dramatic ways. . . . [P]articipants seek ways to deliberate that are seen as right and fair . . . no matter how ingeniously egalitarian the procedure being used, it is the subject of almost constant assessment and complaint. . . . [L]eadership is no longer based on social roles, but becomes more fluid: its functions divided and shared. Where it does accrue to particular individuals, it is because the *group* benefits from that individual's abilities.[17]

One enduring social institution sometimes thought to be free of power relationships is the family. While that may be potentially true, in the reality of most families power is ever present and critically structures the relations between spouses and between parents and children unless strong efforts are continually made by family members to sustain a democratic setting, preferably with support from others in the family's larger social environment as well. A perhaps predominant portion of the whole feminist movement is, of course, directed at men's power over women in family relations. As a particularly apt illustration of the ideas developed here thus far, consider for a moment the power of parents over children.

An Illustration: Parents' Power

That parents have power over children should be all too obvious. Adults' physical size and strength, their intellectual capacities for reasoning, their knowledge and experience relative to those of children give them many advantages by virtue of which they may command children. These realities alone enable them to threaten children or, alternatively, to offer positive sanctions; to hide or distort information available to children; and to influence children's preferences by manipulating their emotional and cultural environment—and to do so in pursuit of the parents' own interests, if they wish, rather than the children's.

What may be less obvious is how critically parents' power depends upon constraints effective *outside* of the immediate relations between parents and children in the family itself. Perhaps first among these is the legal environment: Age requirements for property ownership, contracting, and employment; regulations on automobile and equipment operation; codes on participation in politics and culture; requirements for school attendance and behavior; curfews and so forth—all have the effect of constraining children from alternatives to at least a minimum of obedience to their parents. Cultural and religious restrictions on children's permissible activities have the same effect. Legal, cultural, and religious restrictions are, all together, enforced by adults specializing to one degree or another in activities aimed at assuring children's compliance with those codes; but even adults who are not so specialized—relatives and neighbors, for example—enforce or encourage children to follow the basic code of obedience to parents. All cultural institutions, finally—the media, schools, churches—work to influence children's thinking and behavior by example and persuasion, and most likely accomplish more along these lines with children than with adults, whose critical capacities are more developed. The direction of acculturation by these institutions nearly invariably favors the traditional family as the primary social structure for raising children and helps assure then that the basic rightness of parents' power is widely accepted.

This larger environment of constraints bolsters parents' power quite significantly, and without it that power would likely become irrelevant at a fairly early age in the child's life. As is, many of these constraints operate for a significant time even after the child has reached legal maturity, and the family's economic constraints effectively continue to bolster parents' power even then as well: For young people with a prospect of property inheritance from parents there is the threat of disinheritance. And for the vast majority for whom wealth inheritance is irrelevant, having a lower earning capacity and less secure job tenure in one's early work-life effectively continues a young person's vulnerability to elders' offers of financial help.

This is not to say that all of these constraints are necessarily "bad." Many of them are, of course, designed precisely for protecting children from dangerous environments for which they are unprepared or from exploitation by others outside the home or for better assuring their earning power later on, for example, auto drivers-license age requirements, child-labor laws, required school attendance. The point is that this environment serves as the larger set of background constraints by virtue of which parents may command their children, since these constraints not only limit the available alternatives to children's obedience but also actually influence children's values.

On the other hand, many of these constraints may well be gratuitous and in need of major deconstruction, for they may function to unnecessarily close children's alternatives to the point of inhibiting their development. School, for example, should be a place of growth and liberation, not a training in regimentation and a largely mind-dulling conformity to an imposed competition for status. Weekend curfews, for another example, aren't necessary where there is sufficient adult monitoring and guidance of and participation in young people's activities. Even restrictions on child labor can certainly be overdone, for when it is appropriately structured in the right kinds of setting, "child labor" is actually essential for the development of children's physical and mental capacities. (Of course, employment in unrestrained profit-maximizing enterprises or other institutions not directly and solely committed to the child's interest itself is not an appropriate context!)

The criterion for determining whether such constraints are appropriate should be the long-term interests of the child, that is, protection from harm and contribution to learning and development. Insofar as these constraints do not satisfy that criterion, they actually work against those parents who would use their "transformative power" over their children for the ultimate end of liberating them to determine and pursue as best as possible their own interests.[18] The transformative purposes to which parents' power may be put constitute, of course, the only ultimate justification for its use. Parents then may rightly use their ability to threaten or positively sanction children to control the information available to them and to influence children's values in ways that channel children's activities away from harmful situations and into directions that facilitate exploration of their capacities and encourage their intellectual, emotional, and social growth.

As any conscientious parent can attest, however, this is much more easily said than done, and indeed exercising transformative parent's power may be so difficult that many parents may simply give up on the effort. For one thing, exercising parents' power in the positive ways in which conscientious parents would prefer may be especially difficult in these times, when the external constraints and inducements working upon their children appear more and more to be beyond their influence. Schools seem increasingly subject to control by remote bureaucracies and political forces all too interested in cheaply mass-producing a certified and properly sorted workforce, and teachers, whose transformative power over children merits another analysis in itself, are thus severely constrained in their own exercise of such power. The mass media seem increasingly closed to influence on behalf of parents' and children's needs, and are, in any case, less devoted than ever to fostering a balanced and careful public consideration of public issues of any kind (as I will discuss in later chapters). Political and quasi-political decision making that involves parenting issues seems inaccessible or ineffective as parents are increasingly strapped for time and resources, and as corporate business influences expand and grassroots organizations like parent-teachers associations increasingly become merely ceremonial.[19]

In fact, it may be taken as a general rule—applicable in most times and places—that the larger society within which the family must live has priorities or necessities of its own with regard to the upbringing of children that may conflict with a commitment by parents to using their transformative power for the liberation of their young. The background constraints effective in the larger society outside the family may so strongly direct young people's development that even the most conscientious effort to use transformative parents' power may have little clear effect. Poverty, as an obvious example, especially in underdeveloped countries but in advanced nations as well, so severely constricts parents and children that the best parents may hope for is to give their children the strength to endure a life of more or less certain harsh adversity. Similarly, working-class families in advanced market economies may find that the schooling available to their children functions primarily as a means of socializing the latter for work-lives in semiskilled, skilled, or technical wage-employment rather than as an institution in which young people may explore and develop the unfolding possibilities of their lives.[20]

Thus the background constraints of the larger society that condition parents' power are critical both for providing the fundamental basis of that power and for determining the directions and purposes for which it may be used. And conversely, because parents' power is critical in the socialization of young people, it helps bolster other power structures extant in the larger society and indeed may be an essential element in those structures. Clearly, as long as children must be conditioned and guided into acquiescence with other power structures later in their lives, the possibilities of successfully exercising transformative parents' power are thereby limited.

There is another difficulty in the attempt to use transformative parents' power, one that may hold even in the most congenial of social settings, that is, the problem of the parents sorting out the child's real long-term interests from their own. Even without adverse constraints in the larger society, parents may use their power to channel children's activities in directions that enhance parents' emotional or social needs, rather than the children's, and may be quite unaware they are thwarting those explorations the children need for developing their own capacities. Thus parents may reap psychological benefit from the use of their power at the expense of their children's actual development—for example, nurturing an overachieving child may serve to compensate for a parent's feelings of his own inadequacy. The psychological analysis of such cases must be challenging. They represent a form of exploitation in the fullest sense of the term developed earlier—the child's activity is not expended for his own purposes but for his parent's—yet neither the child nor the parent may be fully or even partly conscious of that fact, and the parent may well believe he is exercising his power transformatively rather than in conflict with the child's real interests. The consequences of this kind of "psychological exploitation" arising with parents' power may be a virtual model of alienation.

This sort of psychological element may be present in other kinds of exploitative uses of parent's power as well. That is, when the parent gets the child to act or "labor" in his material interest rather than the child's own, he may be at the same time trying to resolve some unfulfilled emotional or social need as well. But while the psychological aspects of exploitation may be difficult to ascertain and analyze, the exploitative use of parents' power as an economic phenomenon, that is, for parents' material interests, is not at all so. When parents take advantage of the child's capacity to work in the home doing cleaning or cooking, for example—if it is above and beyond what is necessary for the general development of the child's intellectual and physical capacities and if there are other choices available to the parents—they are clearly exploiting the child for their own ends. Whether the child is being "adequately paid," for example, with an allowance, is arguably irrelevant, since the child's irreplaceable *time* has been foregone and cannot be made up with any compensation. Outside the home, employing children in family-owned and -operated businesses may be a fairly common form of parents' exploitation of their children, excluded as it is from full coverage by child-labor laws. And of course, sending children out into the legal or illegal labor market while claiming a portion of the child's earnings when other options are available is clearly exploitative also.

On the other hand, the fact that parents may employ children's labor or earnings to help support the family does not in itself necessarily constitute their exploiting their children. The parents of a family in poverty may, in good conscience, find that the family's very survival, certainly a requisite for the child's own long-term development, depends upon their children's working more than would otherwise be in the child's interest. That is, they may exercise transformative parents' power as best they can, *given the constraints to which they, the parents, are subject,* and find that they must employ the child's labor for the sake of the family's survival considerably more than would be good for the child otherwise. In effect, the parents are then clearly not responsible for the abuse of the child—they are doing the best for the child that can be done in their situation. Blame for the child's mistreatment, if anyone can be blamed, must fall upon those whose exercise of exploitative power upon the parents places the latter in such a situation, for example, in low-wage employment. Thus, like power itself, exploitation too is "transitive" (i.e., if person A has power over B, who has power over C, person A can, by exploiting B, in effect, indirectly exploit C as well)—and the larger social context within which parenting must occur is, again, critically important.

Obviously it can be difficult or impossible to successfully use transformative parents' power on children's behalf when the broader circumstances, especially those of the structures of power extant in the larger society, conflict with it. Thus in broad terms the requisites of a supportive environment for the transformative use of parents' power are fairly clear: (1) Schools appropriately devoted to a liberating education (and appropriately funded as well, of course) rather than to other ends, for example, merely "baby-sitting" children or reproducing a cheap labor force. (2) Sufficient numbers of adults in the community at large who are willing and able to help oversee and share in children's and young people's activities, along with sufficient amounts of the other resources required, for example, easily accessible recreation spaces and facilities of all sorts. (3) Access by young people to explorations of and a gradually increasing participation in the adult worlds of citizenship and work—and an accommodation of the latter to the curiosity, presence, and especially the participation of youth. (4) A support network of other adults at all levels of experience in child raising and social participation who are sufficiently close and accessible to parents that the latter may easily turn to them for counseling and deliberation on the many challenges of successful child rearing. (5) And so forth.[21] It does indeed "take a village to raise a child."

Power and Market "Imperfection"

Thus power is perhaps the most troubling of concepts in the social sciences. Yet unsettling though it may be for those who would understand social relationships, it is unavoidably fundamental to all efforts at objectively comprehending the realities of human life. As I noted in the last chapter, in political science, sociology, and history the concept of power has an unassailable and indispensable theoretical status. Why and how can the mainstream of economics, alone among the social sciences, eschew considerations of power? Is its demarcated subject matter, market systems, an exceptional realm of social activity that is in fact largely untainted by power relationships?

In the traditional view of neoclassical economics, power as described here is not an essential feature of the relationship holding between market transactors. Buyer and seller meet equally free to choose with full knowledge from among all possible alternatives, deciding whether to exchange, and at what terms, fully voluntarily. Each gets the other to give up something of value, to forego something the other would not choose to forego otherwise, but neither of them foregoes anything without being compensated with something at least as desirable in return. On net therefore, neither person loses anything, in his/her own estimation, an estimation that is, again, completely freely made with full knowledge of the alternatives.[22] Each individual influences the other, but only beneficially—neither can negatively influence the other, since the other may refuse the exchange—thus both end up unequivocally better off. Market transactors exercise upon each other at worst what Bartlett calls merely "positive power," not power in the sense we understand it here.[23]

Strictly speaking, this holds only in well-functioning and competitive markets—indeed, only in markets that are *perfectly* so. Yet while neoclassical economists recognize that it is an imperfect world, of course, their presumption has been that markets either naturally conform, or by enlightened policy may be made to conform, closely enough to the terms of the "perfect markets" model that the conclusion is nonetheless roughly true. In that view then, significant power relationships between market transactors are better seen as the exception than the rule. Alternatively, there may well be important and even critical such exceptions in reality, perhaps in dire need of correction by appropriate public policy, but even so, they do not concern what is essential in the market system itself. Moreover, since their correction requires public interference, the benefits to be attained thereby must be weighed against the potential damage of resorting to public power for interference in a system that is essentially benign.

A good part of the remainder of this book will be about just how "imperfect" a world this is, in need of just such correction. Some preliminary illustration, however, of major market imperfections acknowledged by neoclassical economics will help introduce the issues to be developed later on, at the least by casting some doubt on the neoclassical view on power in markets. As a first example, consider the archetype situation of power in markets that is recognized in traditional neoclassical economics, that of *monopoly*. The monopolist or similarly privileged supplier (e.g., an oligopolist or dominant firm), exploits a situation in which buyers have no (or few) alternative sources of the good, by extracting extra profit from them. The case is a perfect example of power as described here, and is referred to as such by many neoclassical economists. Obviously, pure monopoly, without some government role in granting the privilege, is rare, but near-monopoly markets abound, and as most neoclassicals have acknowledged, the problem of monopoly power is by no means confined to the pure case. I will elaborate on the problem in the next chapter, but here it might suffice for readers to consider merely a few commonplace examples: How many local daily newspapers does one have access to in one's city? How many manufacturers of low- and mid-price range auto's are there in the world today? How many passenger airlines serve the major cities of the United States? How many local and long-distance telephone companies are available in one's city? How many television cable and satellite companies, electric power companies, mass transit companies? Familiar anecdotal evidence suggests that monopoly or near-monopoly power may be a considerable problem indeed.

Yet neoclassicals are nonetheless typically fairly sanguine about it, most importantly because they feel that while power may be exercised by a monopoly, the situation cannot last long if its market is anywhere near well functioning. According to "contestable markets theory," the monopolist must either lower its commodity price toward a competitive level, and hence lose its excess profit, or else be put out of business by new entrants that, attracted by the prospect of extra profit, then underprice it.[24] If the monopoly is able to exercise significant power for some length of time because of a failure of such new firms to enter, then it must be because of either some unusual imperfection in the market itself or else some artificial interference by government. Such a view dovetails nicely with the extreme notion that "markets can never be part of the problem, they must be part of the solution," and ignores the fact that major barriers to the potential entry of new competing firms are, as I will discuss in the next chapter, widespread in all concentrated industries today.

As a second illustration, consider the case of information asymmetry, a problem by now extensively analyzed in mainstream economics, although rarely in terms of the power relationships inherently involved. An individual who has information that another lacks can often use it to get the latter to do things that she would not otherwise do: Information asymmetry *is* a kind of power situation. On the other hand, the person potentially subject to power based on information asymmetry may sometimes be able to buy the information, and when she can, in the ideal case, no power can be exercised based on the former asymmetry: In a transaction in a well-functioning and competitive market, the buyer forgoes something to get the information, but the value to her of the information attained more than compensates what she pays, and in the end no one can be a loser on account of the buyer lacking the information prior to the transaction.

There are, however, some problems with information as a commodity. For one thing, a potential buyer of information usually cannot know what it is really worth to her until after she's acquired it—yet after she's acquired it, of course, she no longer has any incentive to pay for it. For another thing, because information is difficult to contain, or exclude other people from acquiring, third parties may be able to get it without having to pay for it, hence neither buyer nor seller in an information transaction can know what its real market value is. These and other difficulties have made the subject of the connections between information and markets a major topic of investigation in modern economics.[25] The issue of power arises in the course of that inquiry mainly not insofar as information is difficult to value but insofar as it may be *withheld*, *misrepresented*, or *fabricated*.

The primary instance considered in mainstream economics is that of principal-agent relationships, in which an individual (the principal) hires another (the agent) to advise and make decisions for him about things important to his well-being.[26] Major examples abound in modern economies: patients and doctors, clients and lawyers (or clients and accountants, realtors, auto mechanics, and so forth), students and teachers (or, students and schools), corporate owners and managers, and so forth. In each case the agent is hired for his expertise, and since the principal cannot perfectly monitor the agent's actions, and the latter is free to make his own decisions for the principal, the agent may exploit the principal by withholding or misrepresenting information which only the agent has. Thus the doctor gets the patient to return for frequent visits, the auto mechanic gets his customer to agree to unnecessary repairs, and the electrician gets the homeowner to agree to additional work. Alternatively, the agent merely asks an excessive contract price from the principal, who pays the excess on the hope that it is sufficient to buy the agent's trustworthiness, a kind of economic rent like that attained from monopoly. All of the agents just listed are known for their relatively high incomes—the CEO extracting an excessive compensation from his company's board of directors is merely one of the most notorious cases.

Obviously the agency problem is widespread and serious in modern, information-dependent economies. Mainstream economists have given it much attention, yet continue by and large to eschew the vocabulary of power in their analyses of the matter. One gets a strangely distorted picture of things because of this omission, for example, in analyses of the principal-agent characteristics of employer-employee relationships. Employees of all kinds are, to one extent or another, agents of their employers, hence pose more or less serious "agency problems" that employers address by various organizational means and incentives. But posing the matter as mainly a technical question of the best use of managerial resources for allocating labor, rather than as one involving a *power relationship*, glosses over the important insight that, as agents, workers actually do have some power over their bosses. By ignoring a major aspect of that power relationship, such an approach evades other issues as well—in particular, it leaves completely unremarked those important aspects of the relationship between worker and employer (to be discussed in a later chapter) on account of which the employer is, despite whatever agency power workers may have, after all "the boss."

As a third illustration, consider the case of *externalities*, a form of market imperfection universally recognized among neoclassicals, although, like information asymmetry, practically never treated in terms of the power relationships necessarily involved. In fact, power is inherent in all situations involving externalities, as the well-known case of pollution costs illustrates. In the context of a well-functioning and competitive market system, a person could not do detriment to another by harming the latter's property with some pollutant without appropriate compensation agreeable to both parties. That is, in a well-functioning market such compensation would be institutionalized as a routine transaction and would be power-free or would involve only positive power. According to the famous Coase theorem, given well-defined property rights and assuming no transactions costs involved in reaching and sustaining a contract, compensation would have to be made to one party or the other such that *both* parties, the polluter and the "pollutee," would end up benefiting on net by the act of pollution and the accompanying compensation.[27] Harm can only be done to one or the other of them—that is, "negative" power can only be exercised in their relationship—if appropriate rights have not been defined or significant transactions costs exist, since only then might a mutually agreeable compensation not be possible. In such a case, for example, the first person might pollute the second's property without sufficient compensation to the latter for damages or cleanup. Or perhaps, instead, the polluter might be forced (e.g., by a court) to refrain from whatever activity causes the pollution but then might not be given full compensation from the pollutee or the state for the costs incurred in doing so.

The neoclassical account of the pollution problem focuses on the lack of adequately defined property rights: Generally, the problem is that appropriate *private rights* have not yet been set up—perhaps it is impossible to set up such rights, more likely (according to the neoclassical account) society has merely been slow in accepting the necessity of doing so. In this view all that is required generally to resolve the pollution problem is to define such rights, thereby creating a full and well-functioning market, where before there had been only a partial and ill-functioning one. Society can then turn things completely over to whatever private parties are involved to resolve such pollution problems themselves by means of more or less routine, mutually satisfying market transactions. Again, it is the *lack* of a market or an *imperfectly formed* market that is the problem.

Of course, most students of environmental issues know better than to think that the creation of novel private property rights and markets can in themselves have much positive effect on the major industrial pollution crises of these times. It would be a daunting task indeed to try to resolve such problems as the greenhouse effect, ozone destruction, and biodiversity depletion merely by creating new, well-defined and easily enforceable, marketable private rights. Most importantly for our own purposes here, even were such a solution possible, it would still not settle the problem of power. For the creation or alteration of property rights, be they private or public, well- or ill-defined, is itself necessarily an exercise of power from which some gain while others lose.

The example of private property rights in land and natural resources is perhaps one of the easiest with which to see this point. The development of full rentable and marketable private land-ownership rights in Europe, where in earlier feudal times no such rights existed, involved an entire history of political and martial struggle within the landed nobility and between the nobility, the monarchs, the church, and the common people. The right to expel nonpaying tenants, for example, clearly a critical element in modern land-ownership rights, was accomplished historically only on the forced exclusion of numberless serfs in the course of the enclosures of the common lands to which, in earlier feudal times, the serfs had had full legal claim. And of course the creation of new private property rights in land in the Americas was accomplished by what can only be called a wholesale piracy of the lands already owned, albeit in other ways than those customary in Europe, by

Native Americans. In fact, these processes of expropriation continue down to the present as well, in the same sorts of violations of treaties and renegotiations of mineral and forestry rights, housing, territorial boundaries, and so forth, as occurred in earlier times.[28]

One of the most significant examples of the role of power in property rights in current times may be found in the former USSR, where one of the most massive transformations of property rights ever accomplished peacefully in a short time has occurred in the form of the privatization of state-owned productive capital. Even were it conceivable that the resultant economy of private markets could be anything like well functioning and fully competitive, the process of its creation has been an obvious exercise of power by a class that has, in effect, merely rebuilt the foundations of its former rule in the Communist system. For both the initiators and the beneficiaries of the entire process have clearly been none other than the former nomenclatura, that is, the former class of bureaucratic and Communist Party member decision makers in the Soviet Union who now own the entirety of privatized property and remain in full control of that which is not yet privatized as well—even as other options have been available in the privatization process (for example, distribution of productive capital to worker self-managed enterprises).[29]

The immediate beneficiaries in all such instances are easily identifiable and invariably derive their gains at the expense of easily identified rivals by means of obvious exercises of power upon the latter. Later on, other benefits may accrue in the course of market exchanges of the rights so created, where again winners and losers are generally easily identified, although the delineation gets cloudier over time as exchanges continue. Power is thus the very basis of property rights, and even if the latter were well defined in a well-functioning and competitive market system, identifiable market transactors in those rights would be the beneficiaries, while others would be the subjects, of the exercise of that power.

Thus aside from those significant power relationships that would seem to be widely extant throughout markets in the real world on account of "imperfections," even hypothetically perfect market systems must necessarily rest upon social power structures in which market transactors are therefore inescapably also involved. One last illustration of the neoclassical orientation concerning the concept of power pertains to what is perhaps an even more critical matter, that of the formation of the tastes and preferences on the basis of which individuals make their decisions in markets and elsewhere.

Economists habitually deduce their theoretical and policy conclusions on the assumption that individuals' wants and needs—their "utility functions" or preferences—are given and immutable. They do so often ostensibly to avoid overstepping the bounds of their own competence, but more often merely because it facilitates more straightforward and definitive conclusions than might be gotten otherwise, that is, were it accepted that people's feelings and attitudes about things actually do change. This simplistic assumption has led to some real curiosities, for example, the notion, widespread among neoclassical economists, that corporate advertising and marketing efforts have no effects on people's tastes and preferences regarding goods and services but instead merely notify people of what is available.[30]

Taken at its face value, the notion of given and unchanging preferences suggests a *geneticist* view of human nature: If individual wants and needs are not at least partly formed in the course of life experience, then they must originate in, and be constituted solely by, individuals' genetic endowments. There are, of course, some major problems with geneticism as a theory of human reality. Aside from some of the company in which it puts its believers, it implies a deterministic world without human freedom, and makes it difficult to comprehend human learning and all of the social activity apparently devoted to it.[31] On the other hand, acknowledging that human preferences are formed at least partly by life experience, immediately and necessarily raises the issue of power, not merely that of parents over children but that of all socializing and cultural institutions, from schools and churches to the mass media and, of course, corporate advertising and marketing.

Just how striking it is for an entire field of social science to omit studying power may be seen alternatively by considering the question Randall Bartlett posed in his critique of the neoclassical view: Precisely what sorts of things must be true in order for power relationships *not to be present at all* in social reality? The logical conditions that must hold, he argued, for power to be completely absent from human interactions are these, which I list in much abridged form:

1. All individuals must have either perfectly complete information, or else perfectly equally distributed information; or else, perfect and universal honesty must prevail; or else, perfect and freely enforceable legal rights must exist to "full truth in all discourse."
2. Property and contract rights must be (a) perfectly and exhaustively defined; (b) perfectly freely enforceable, (c) created by unanimous consent in completely democratic decisions, and (d) unchangeable except by the unanimous consent of all affected.
3. Individual tastes and preferences must be completely free of all social influences.[32]

Taking these conditions altogether or even singly, it is difficult to see how one could maintain that power relationships are absent or insignificant in *any* realm of social activity. Of course, granted that therefore markets too embody power relationships, one may still argue that power is somehow less critical in market systems than in other kinds of economies or in other realms of social life. The issue then may be resolved only by a closer look at the nature of the particular power relationships and structures most distinctive of market systems. That then is the task undertaken in the remainder of this book.

Notes

1. Adequately defining power is a critical part of any inquiry about it. Some comprehensive studies of power in recent years include Keith Dowding, *Power*; John K. Galbraith, *The Anatomy of Power*; Steven Lukes, *Power: A Radical View*; Lukes, ed., *Power*; Bertrand de Jouvenal, *On Power*; Thomas E. Wartenberg, *Rethinking Power*; Wartenberg, *The Forms of Power*; and Dennis Wrong, *Power*. See Pranab Bardhan, "On the Concept of Power in Economics" on how economists have defined power.

2. Randall Bartlett, *Economics and Power*, p. 30.

3. "Sanction" is sometimes used as synonymous with threat or promise, but here it refers instead to the actual carrying out of either of these.

4. I have paraphrased somewhat. See Samuel Bowles and Herbert Gintis, "Contested Exchange," p. 173.

5. Thomas Wartenberg, *The Forms of Power*, p. 85.

6. Ibid., p. 184. Wartenburg defines it as power that "seeks to bring about its own obsolescence by means of the empowerment of the subordinate agent." In teaching, for example, ideally the teacher's power is deliberately exercised "in such a way that the subordinate agent [the student] learns certain skills that undercut the power differential between her and the dominant agent."

7. In particular, in such circumstances the subordinate may accept positive offers from the dominant individual, for example, and also believe that she would do so even were she not subject to power.

8. Note that I am not suggesting that anyone but the individual herself may determine "ultimately" what her interest is, of course. See Stephen Lukes, *Power*, and his *Power: A Radical View*, for an extended discussion of interest-based, counterfactual approaches to power like that taken here.

9. Consider what may appear to be an exceptional case, like that of a simple theft—a burglary, or a street mugging. The (momentarily) dominant individual takes from his victim some material good, and the benefit he gains from his dominance appears to be the welfare or utility he gets from the good rather than from some activity per se on the part of his subordinate. But the subordinate may have put in some significant time and effort creating or acquiring the good she foregoes to the thief, or accumulating the money used to purchase it. If not, but she nonetheless values the good, then she values it in terms of time and effort similarly required to replace it. In either case it is time and effort she had already expended or would have planned on expending, for her own purposes. Of course, the good taken by the thief may be of no value whatsoever to the victim, in which case he has not really "taken" anything from her at all, and may even be said not to have actually exercised his (momentary) power over her.

10. Thus, in cases of "slavery" found today, the subordinate is "enslaved" by

virtue of there being no way to escape from practically complete control by his master, who does not own him in the legal sense but does own him de facto. In these terms, much sweatshop labor and sharecropping are slavery insofar as the subject is so ensnared in a web of debt, poverty, or other constraints that he basically belongs to his employer. See Kevin Bales, *Disposable People*.

11. The classic original on alienation is Karl Marx, "Economic and Philosophic Manuscripts of 1844"; Erich Fromm, "Marx's Concept of Man;" and Bertell Ollman, *Alienation*, are essential reading on the subject. Walter A. Weisskopf, *Alienation and Economics*, is a classic on the subject from an economist's viewpoint. Also, Samuel Bowles and Herbert Gintis, "Alienation and Capitalism."

12. See Karl Marx, *Manifesto of the Communist Party*, Part I, in Robert C. Tucker, *The Marx-Engels Reader*. Traditional institutionalists, while not particularly adherents of the dialectical view of history, considered the evolution of institutions as fundamentally involving power and changes in power relationships. See John K. Galbraith, *The Anatomy of Power*, chapters 8 and 9, and Geoffrey M. Hodgson, "Evolution and Institutional Change."

13. John K. Galbraith. *The Anatomy of Power*, chapters 6 and 7.

14. Thus the literature on who rules the United States today is contentious. See G. William Domhoff, *Who Rules America?*

15. Robert Dahl, *On Democracy*, pp. 37–38. While Dahl's discussion is mainly focused on "political units" or states, it is obviously widely applicable, as he insists, in any "association." See also Robert Dahl, *A Preface to Economic Democracy*. Note that no claim is made here that *practical* democracy (i.e., as found in its many imperfect forms in the real world) is itself without problems of power—only that *ideal* democracy should be the model counterfactual for identifying power relationships. David Held, *Models of Democracy*, gives an excellent comparison of the whole variety of conceptualizations of democracy, both practical and ideal. Peter Bachrach and Aryeh Botwinick, *Power and Empowerment*, gives a more radical theory of participatory democracy in particular.

16. Ricardo Blaug, *Democracy Real and Ideal*, p. 135.

17. Ibid., p. 138. Blaug continues with the *demise* of such "breakouts" as well—they are all too fragile in larger social contexts in which real democracy is merely a utopian wish.

18. Thomas Wartenberg, *Rethinking Power*, p. 85.

19. See Nancy Folbre, *Who Pays for the Kids?* and Sylvia Ann Hewlitt and Cornel West, *The War against Parents*, on the difficulties of parenting in these times.

20. See Samuel Bowles and Herbert Gintis, *Schooling in Capitalist America* for an account of how the pressures of the broader society impinge on education in capitalist market systems.

21. Again, see Nancy Folbre, *Who Pays for the Kids?* and Sylvia Ann Hewlitt and Cornel West, *The War against Parents*.

22. Milton Friedman's *Capitalism and Freedom*, although it does not use the term "power" to characterize anything but the state, is the classic and most succinct statement of this view of market transactions.

23. Randall Bartlett, *Economics and Power*, p. 41.

24. On contestable markets, see William J. Baumol, "Contestable Markets." William G. Shepherd, "Contestability vs. Competition" is a critique.

25. Indeed, in its delineation of the subject fields of economics, the *Journal of Economic Literature*, the flagship of mainstream economics, devotes a whole section to the economics of information.

26. Charles Perrow, "Economic Theories of Organization," gives an excellent overview of principal-agent theory, and its relevance and shortcomings for understanding power.

27. The Coase theorem appears as a basic element in the coverage of any textbook on environmental economics; the original article was Ronald Coase, "The Problem of Social Cost."

28. The process as it is now occurring on indigenous lands all over the world is well described in the very readable book by Jerry Mander, *In the Absence of the Sacred*, Part Four. See Randall Bartlett, *Economics and Power*, chapter 8, for a discussion of the role of power in the creation and maintenance of rights, in general.

29. See, for example, James Angresano, *Comparative Economics*, chapters 15 to 17, on the transition from the Soviet Union toward a capitalist nation.

30. See any textbook on the economics of industrial organization for a discussion of this and other views on advertising, for example, Stephen Martin, *Industrial Economics*, chapter 11; William G. Shepherd, *The Economics of Industrial Organization*, chapter 12.

31. Randall Bartlett, *Economics and Power*, pp. 24–26, describes the essentially genetic determinist view implicit in the assumption of "given" preferences.

32. Ibid., p. 66.

3

Business Power I: Monopoly

Market systems are usually depicted as a kind of anarchy in which large numbers of unorganized and completely self-concerned buyers and sellers intermingle in what appears to be an utterly random and chaotic fashion, like the haphazard movement of gas atoms. Order arises out of this process, ironically, almost despite the intentions of its participants: Resources needed for production get allocated to their various uses, and the goods and services produced get distributed to participants in accord with their expressed needs of consumption. What appears to be an atomistic anarchy, in effect a competition of the self-interest of each against all, actually organizes society's economic processes in a marvelously effective manner, "as if by an invisible hand," it is said.

This book will argue, however, that what happens in capitalist markets is better understood as essentially involving the exercise of hierarchical power. Even the most atomistic and competitive of markets in reality must be understood to implicate a power hierarchy, and most markets are nowhere near so atomistic. The extreme opposite of atomistically competitive markets is monopoly, the very embodiment of a power structure and far more important therefore for discerning the reality of the "invisible hand" than is the myth of the anarchic market system. Indeed, monopoly power broadly understood, rather than being merely a special theoretical case, as in neoclassical microeconomics, is actually a cornerstone in the foundation of real-world market economies.

The Monopoly Model

In a monopoly market, the seller of the commodity can completely deny buyers access to the good because of a situation in which buyers lack alternative sources, unlike in competitive markets, where many other suppliers are readily available. In the basic textbook account, the threat of complete lack of access suffices to get buyers to pay a premium on the price if they want the product—and the profit-maximizing monopoly price exceeds the hypothetical competitive-market price by a determinate margin. Alternatively, the textbook monopoly takes advantage of the situation by placing further negative constraints upon buyers in the form of increases in their costs of obtaining the good. Since competition prevails on the buyers' side of the monopoly market, no individual buyer can similarly alter the constraints to which the monopoly seller is subject—there is complete nonreciprocity in the relationship—hence monopoly is a clear-cut case of power as defined here.[1]

It should be pointed out that the converse case of *monopsony*, in which a single buyer dominates sellers, is equally important. While the economic theory of monopsony differs in other ways from that of monopoly, as a power structure it is simply the reverse of monopoly: A single buyer occupies the power position instead of a single seller, and by the threat that sellers would completely lack access to a buyer otherwise, compels them to part with their commodity for a lower price than they would otherwise be able to ask. In what follows, I will discuss monopsony as a distinct case only when necessary.

Note that *given* a monopoly price, everyone involved may be said to be satisfied with the situation of monopoly in a market: usually no potential customer who would willingly pay the price ends up being denied access to the product, and all parties adjust to the added constraint of having to pay a monopoly price by altering their purchases in a utility-maximizing manner. Within the constraints the monopoly has placed upon its customers, the latter remain free to buy whatever quantities of its product they wish, or not to buy at all. As in all cases of the exercise of power, choice on the part of the subordinate has not been in any sense completely denied, but merely constricted to one degree or another from what it would be otherwise.[2] Moreover, assuming no other inhibiting factors at work, given the equilibrium price, there is a balance between the demand and supply sides of the market—neither side is dissatisfied with the terms of the exchange, that is, with what each is able to get from the other at the given price. However, considering the alternative structures potentially available for producing and distributing the good, by no means is everyone involved satisfied with the situation of unfettered monopoly per se, as the history of state-constituted restrictions and regulations of monopoly indicates.

In the textbook account, the benefits taken by the monopoly are in the form of a transfer of real income from buyers to the firm: Buyers pay a higher price and get altogether a smaller quantity of the commodity, while the firm gets an excess of profit. Actually, the real income lost by buyers is easily shown to be greater than the amount gained by the monopolist; the difference is referred to as an "allocative efficiency loss." The effect of monopoly then is twofold: There is both a simple redistribution from buyers, and an additional complete loss of the latters' real income as well. Mainstream economics has dwelled extensively upon the efficiency loss but remarkably little upon the redistributive effect, equally worthy of investigation though the latter may be. As an outright appropriation of a portion of the total earned income of the economy, that is, of the total product of labor in the economy, the monopoly's excess profit is the most important specific manifestation of its exploitation of people in the exact sense of the term used in the preceding chapter.[3]

The monopoly situation enables the privileged firm to exploit its customers in other ways as well. In price discrimination, the monopoly is able to attain even greater excess profit than otherwise by charging different groups of customers different prices in accordance with differences in "what the market will bear" for each group.[4] The firm may be able to raise its profit even further with lower production costs attained by cutting the quality of its product. On the other hand, its excess profit may permit the firm to sustain increased production costs in the form of "slack" on the part of managers or workers in the firm, what is called *X-inefficiency*. Those who are able to take such leisure-on-the-job are, in effect, sharing in some of the monopoly's excess profit—as are all others (besides the firm's owners) who may be able to extract higher incomes from their association with the monopoly than they might get otherwise, for example, creditors, material and equipment suppliers, labor union members, and so forth.

Again, all these real income transfers derive from exploitation by the monopoly, in that the firm, in effect, "extracts labor" from people by appropriating a portion of the aggregate product of labor in the economy. In principle a monopoly may also use its power to exploit by means of a more explicit command over people as well, that is, by means of specific commands or instructions given to customers that the latter must obey if they are to have access to the monopoly's commodity. Competitive retailers of a monopolist's product, for example, may be compelled to package or display the product not as they choose but as the monopolist chooses; wholesalers may even be restricted in whom they may sell the monopolist's product to. Firms taking what amounts to a managerial role in other firms with which they do business may be even more common in cases of monopsony, where, for example, a firm may even place some of its own managers in a position of overseeing the daily operations of subordinate parts or materials suppliers (I will discuss such cases further in the next chapter).

Just how important is this kind of power structure in reality? The basic model of monopoly holds a solid place in traditional economic theory from Adam Smith onward, but its bearing upon the real world has been subjected to an especially heated criticism from the recently ascendent right-wing of mainstream economics. One important concern raised in that criticism is that monopoly per se is rare in reality: aside from the rest of what appear to be quite competitive industries, the only markets that are even close to being monopolistic are cases either of *oligopoly* or of a dominant firm among other competing smaller firms. In both such cases, firms are arguably involved in competitive situations with other firms, and few opportunities for exercising power can exist: If any one firm attempts to exert monopoly power, customers may take their business to other firms. I will consider this question in detail below, reviewing what is known about the matter in the established field of the economics of "industrial organization." Briefly, it will be seen that, in fact, markets with oligopolies or dominant firms—concentrated industries, as they are called—are pervasive throughout market economies and behave sufficiently like monopolies per se as to constitute, for all practical purposes, just as great a public issue. As it is essentially monopoly-like power that is wielded in these widespread cases, the problem of monopoly, more broadly construed, remains.

Yet a couple of other important issues raised in the recent criticism of the monopoly model should be dealt with first, before considering how that model applies to the reality of oligopolies and dominant firms. For one thing, it may be denied that even a position of pure monopoly could actually give a firm any significant power in the first place. The circumstance that gives a monopoly power over its customers is its ability to deny them access to its commodity on account of an absence of other suppliers. According to the theory of *contestable markets*, however, as long as the monopoly is taking excess profit there will be incentive for other firms to enter its market as additional suppliers of its product.[5] Such potential new entrants pose a threat to the monopoly, which it can counter only by reducing its product price enough to eliminate its excess profit. Since its product price would have to be reduced to a competitive level, even though the firm has a monopoly position, it is not able to exercise its monopoly power—which is, of course, equivalent to saying that it has no such power. All of this applies by extension, naturally, to whatever other means the monopoly firm might attempt to employ in order to gain excess profit or otherwise exploit customers—product quality cutting, price discrimination, restrictive agreements, and so forth, all would be similarly ineffective. Thus as long as such entry by new firms is possible, the monopoly's potential power over its customers is completely thwarted by the threatened competition of such firms. Note that this obviously applies equally in markets with oligopolies and dominant firms as well.

This is all merely theory, however, since most economists acknowledge that *barriers to entry* exist that, in general, prevent such a happy scenario. That is, there are things that bar potentially competing firms from entering a monopolized (or concentrated) market, thereby enabling the established firm(s) to charge a higher-than-competitive price or otherwise extract an excess profit.[6] Right-wing economists would emphasize barriers created by the state. Patent rights, for example, while certainly important for stimulating technological development, eliminate or reduce the threat of potential rivals of the privileged firms for a time. A variety of other exclusive licenses, privileges, and noncompetitive contracts granted by the state have the same effect, even if most are ostensibly granted for valid reason in the public interest (e.g., in electric power production, sanitation, national defense contracting). Other less direct state policies have a similar effect as well—for example, tariff and other import barriers and export subsidies. Government is certainly a prime source of monopoly power wherever the latter exists.

Yet even subtracting state interferences, other entry barriers in real-world markets are quite substantial enough to make the case. Consider some of the more important of these. First, exclusive or concentrated *ownership of available necessary resources* automatically rules out potential competitors. The Aluminum Company of America's virtual monopolization of known bauxite (aluminum ore) deposits prior to World War II is merely one of the more extreme and better known cases, resolved at least somewhat in the public interest by a breakup of the firm into the three independent aluminum producers that now dominate the industry. Many dominant firms and oligopolies, like the aluminum industry today, have secured their positions against possible outside competitors precisely by concentrating the ownership of major resources in their own hands.

Second, *transport costs* of product supplies may give firms regional monopoly power by eliminating or reducing customers' access to other firms elsewhere. When firms in a market have *scale economies* in production (an issue to be dealt with more thoroughly below), the effect of the cost of transporting the firms' product may be such that only one or a few firms can produce cheaply enough to provide for customers in a region encompassed by transportation for which customers can afford to pay. Such a firm then takes excess profit at least equal to the amount of the transport cost that would be incurred by customers were they to deal with other firms outside the region. Where transport costs of resources are significant, a similar relationship may hold between firms using the resources and providers of the resources: Firms using the resources, if they have scale economies, may have regional monopsony power over resource providers.

Third are *advertising and related costs* of achieving customers' recognition of a new entrant and its product. Established firms already have such recognition, and with it a clientele that is more or less loyal to the known product. A new entrant must win some of these customers away from the known product in favor of its own unknown product. To do so, its marketing therefore must be especially effective—and this is aside from having to compete with the established firm for scarce advertising space in the mass media (and monopolization or concentration in the media themselves may further compound the new entrant's difficulties).

Fourth, a great variety of *strategic preventive actions* is possible by established firms in monopoly or concentrated markets, given that the excess profit such firms are already reaping is available for financing or to cushion the costs of such actions. Thus if a new entrant threatens to move in, an established firm can undertake an intensive advertising campaign; or it can perhaps quickly offer a new, differentiated product more directly competing with the new entrant's product; or perhaps it can temporarily cut its prices, even to less than its costs. Excess productive capacity, widely observed in concentrated industries, may be constructed and readily available for established firms to compete in this manner with new entrants. Such actions taken during the start-up period of a new entrant make it difficult or impossible for the latter to build up a clientele. Moreover, if the established firm is large and well diversified it can subsidize some of these actions with profit taken in other lines of production; and if it has, in particular, access to large sources of capital, from outside or perhaps from one of its own subsidiaries, it can finance such actions that much more cheaply.

Finally, as if all that were not enough, there are premiums on the *cost of capital and credit* to new entrants in an established market—that is, such firms have access to less outside capital and must rely more heavily on their own internal funds. This is so because of the additional risk of lending to a new entrant that exists not only because the new firm and its product are still relatively unknown quantities but, more importantly, on account of all the other inherent disadvantages of new entrants already discussed.

The overall effect of such barriers to entry may be thought of as imposing additional costs upon new entrants, above and beyond what their production costs per se would be, upon entry. An established firm may therefore charge a product price that is accordingly that much greater than what it would have to charge to compete with the new entrant's production costs alone. If the new entrant's production costs are the same as those of the established firm, then the latter can charge a product price equal to its per unit production costs plus the per unit "entry costs" of the new firm, and thereby prevent the potential new entrant from finding it sufficiently profitable to enter. Of course, the new firm's production costs may well be less than those of the established firm—perhaps the new firm has a better technology, or perhaps less production "slack." But whatever advantages it may have over the established firm, these must be at least great enough to offset its entry costs in order for it to effectively compete with the established firm: Otherwise the established firm can set an entry-deterring price and still take a normal or above-normal profit. Thus the established firm's "limit price," as it is referred to in economics, may be something less than a pure monopoly price—or it may equal such a price—but it will, in general, most definitely exceed a competitive price.

Given the broad pervasiveness of barriers to entry throughout market economies, therefore, while the theory of contestable markets does add an important insight to the basic model of monopoly, it hardly constitutes more than a minor qualification of the model's essential message about the reality of monopoly power. Yet granted that a monopoly situation does put the firm in a position of significant power, it might still be asked whether such a situation is necessarily of much concern as a social problem. One important consideration relevant to that question is that of *economies of scale*. Aside from barriers to entry such as those just noted, the only enduring advantage that can give a firm monopoly power is that of lower per unit production costs due to scale economies. If the production technology used in the industry is such that only one or a few large firms may produce most cheaply for the scale of demand in the market, then normal competition over time will eliminate all but one or a few firms producing the product. And of course, since new entrants are similarly eliminated, scale economies may be thought of as a special type of entry barrier. But if that is the case, then the monopoly's domination of its market occurs merely because monopoly is the most *efficient* manner for production to be structured in the industry. The whole issue of domination, it may then be argued, loses significance beside the social benefits of cheaper production.

There can be no question that scale economies are widespread and important as a determinant of the existing degree of concentration of many industries. For example, all sorts of materials transport and container technologies have scale economies deriving directly from basic physical necessities. In combination with relatively low product transportation costs, such economies are responsible for major regional "natural" monopolies (e.g., in electricity, water, sewerage, and other utilities), and are partly responsible for many of the most outstanding oligopolies and dominant firms (e.g., in chemicals and oil refining). And a variety of information-processing, decision-making, and coordination costs are such that economies of scale are probably considerable in management as well as research and development, accounting for a good portion of the bigness of all sorts of businesses. Considerable scale economies exist in advertising also, although these cannot be argued to justify monopoly power or bigness (one cannot maintain that a firm benefiting from scale economies in advertising is thereby better able to fulfill consumers' wants cheaply, since, as was noted in the last chapter, the point of advertising is not to fulfill consumers' wants but to create them).

But given the pervasiveness of significant barriers to entry in real-world markets, it would be a mistake to suppose that wherever monopoly power exists in free markets (i.e., aside from cases of state intervention) it must be due to economies of scale. And scale *diseconomies* are known to be as effective as are scale economies in all production activities, and invariably predominate at some point. For example, at some scale of size and complexity, managerial cost economies disappear, and diseconomies set in due to diminished organizational flexibility and rising information processing and flow costs. While the empirical evidence of the importance of scale economies is strong, there is equally strong evidence of scale diseconomies that are allowed to persist behind barriers against the entry of potential competitors that are at least as widespread as are scale economies.[7]

Moreover, even if scale economies are present that fully account for a firm having a monopoly, the firm still will certainly exploit its position of power to the fullest, and it makes little sense therefore to suppose that it will pass on to its customers the social benefits of its greater productive efficiency. Instead, whatever cost reductions it attains due to scale economies would merely be taken by the firm as an even greater excess profit than it would otherwise take. Insofar as such benefits are thus expected to be appropriated by the monopoly itself, greater production efficiency certainly cannot justify its domination over customers from their viewpoint, and the need for regulatory action by the state in such cases is universally acknowledged (subject to appropriate public goods cost-benefit criteria, of course).[8]

Monopoly Power in the Real World

But how applicable can this model of monopoly power be, when so few real monopolies exist in reality? While "concentrated" industries may appear to be similar to monopolies, in fact aren't the firms in such industries—either oligopolies, or else dominant firms sharing the market with many smaller firms—forced to compete considerably for customers' business? Besides, how widespread are concentrated industries anyway? Aren't most industries relatively atomistic, especially in these times of increasing competition worldwide?

The conclusion must be acknowledged from the economics of industrial organization, the field in which these questions are studied, that market concentration poses a social problem that is of at least equal significance with that of monopoly per se. Concentrated industries pose for their customers pretty much the same problems as do pure monopolies, hence constitute the same kind of threat to the public interest. And they appear to be the norm rather than the exception in modern market economies.

To begin with, collusive behavior is much easier and more to be expected in concentrated industries than in others. Policy coordination is a most effective means for otherwise competitive firms to behave in concert as a single entity, improving their total profitability and hence that of each of them singly. Of course, such coordination can often be achieved even in atomistic situations, for example, by member associations such as those that dominate medicine, law, accounting, and real estate. Some means of assuring members' compliance is always necessary, since individual members have great incentives to "cheat" on the arrangement by pricing their own product below that set by the group, bringing the whole group down if too many others then join the flight. In medicine, law, and so forth, the means of compliance is by a certification of the individual member without which, because of the nature of the industry, the member finds it difficult or impossible to do business. Consumers of medical and legal services need such certification to assure adequate quality of the service, and it is considered in the public interest that the state sanction the certification process. The medical and legal practitioners' associations then employ their certification power to limit entry into their professions (with entrance exams, lengthy and difficult schooling, and so on), thus raising the prices of their services and/or lowering the quality from what it might be otherwise, and improving members' incomes.

While obviously in other industries such a process would not work, alternative means for policy coordination are available when the industry is concentrated. In oligopolies, the number of firms is small, and assuring the compliance of individual firms to a colluding group may be relatively easy. Catching cheaters is easy insofar as there are fewer and more visible members to monitor; and disciplining them is easy to the extent that the colluding firms that remain can take strategic action together against the cheater (e.g., with an advertising campaign or a price war). United in compliance with the whole group then, colluding oligopolies can together restrict output, raise prices, divide up the market, sustain entry barriers, and so forth.

Except where it is explicitly held to be in the public interest (and there are a number of important such cases), this is all quite illegal in most advanced market economies, of course.[9] But antitrust authorities are not necessarily very well supported by their governments, nor strict enough even when they are, to prevent collusive conspiracy, especially in politically business-friendly times such as these today. Moreover, collusion need not take conspiratorial form: Merely tacit collusion may work just as well, and in that case antitrust action is far less likely to be effective.

For example, a single large firm may be implicitly recognized by fellow oligopolies as the "leader" in pricing, whom the rest merely follow when price changes are made. Knowing the rest will follow, the leader then may adopt a pricing policy that raises all their prices to a monopoly level. In such cases, the compliance of follower firms with the implicit agreement may be assured by the threat of retaliatory strategic action by the leader and the other firms, especially the threat of a price war or advertising campaign. Antitrust action is practically impossible, since in principle no evidence of conspiracy exists, there having been no communication among the participants other than by merely observing each other's pricing behavior.

In an industry with many smaller firms dominated by one or a few larger firms, the latter are the clear leaders and may often easily set the terms of the industry and be assured that the rest will follow, on threat of aggressive action by the dominant firms themselves. The dominant firms may normally allow smaller firms their niches in the market as a whole, but threaten to move into a smaller firm's niche and put it out of business (or else buy it out at a less than fair market price), if it begins behaving too competitively. Since the dominant firm can more easily absorb the marketing costs and price cuts necessary to do so than can the smaller firm absorb the costs of competing with a giant, the threat may be quite real. In such cases, then, just as in collusive oligopoly, the industry as a whole comes to behave just as a "pure" monopoly would.

Thus collusion of one kind or the other—explicit or tacit, fully voluntary or else under some sort of threat—is a likely mode of behavior for oligopolies or dominant firms. Of course, collusion is not the only possible expected outcome. It may be that conditions are not ripe for explicit or tacit collusion, and in that case the firms would be expected to compete with each other for customers' business, just as in atomistic markets. Yet the form taken by competition in such circumstances is quite different from that of atomistic competition—it has the nature of a "game" played by individuals, rather than a "struggle against nature" like that in which the small firm engages against an anonymous host of other small firms in an atomistically competitive market. That is, oligopolistic competition is a struggle of each firm against a *few* other firms, each taking into account, and strategizing in terms of, not just the state of the market as a whole but the character, situation, and expected behavior of every other individual firm. "Game theory" then becomes the conceptual tool of choice in the economics of competitive oligopoly behavior.

As elegant a tool as game theory is, however, and as important a part of economic theory as it is today, it has contributed relatively little to the study of real-world games of much interest, and the reason is particularly evident in the context of competitive oligopoly: There are simply far too many variables involved in the rivalry among firms to be able to make many interesting and realistic generalizations about expected outcomes.[10] Besides price competition (which can itself be quite complicated in modern multiproduct, multimarket firms), firms may employ competitive advertising or public relations in a variety of different media, aimed at a variety of different customer groupings; minor or major product innovations (the latter involving competitive research and development) or other changes in marketing strategy (e.g., reorganizations at the retailing end); changes in production technology (again involving competitive R&D); plant investment expansions or relocations; major product diversification; mergers, acquisitions, or divestments; and so forth.

Yet a few important conclusions have been drawn in the study of oligopoly games. Every reasonable model of competitive oligopoly concludes that, in terms of the product price and output in the market, having a few rival suppliers in a market is better for customers than having only one supplier, but significantly worse than having many. A competitive oligopoly price is less than what a monopoly would charge in the same industry, but is greater than what the price would be under atomistic competition—and the oligopoly output is greater than it would be for a monopoly, but less than in atomistic competition. Moreover, the smaller is the *number* of suppliers dividing up a market among themselves, everything else equal, the greater is the joint profitability of the competing firms.[11] Even if the conclusion is not intuitive, the power of a firm over its customers is, in effect, a function not merely of *whether* its customers have access to other competitive sources of the product, but also of *how many* such other sources they have access to.

Thus in theory, whether they are collusive or competitive, oligopolies and dominant firms constitute a social problem of comparable significance, even if of lesser degree than that of pure monopoly. The empirical evidence of the many studies that have been done on the connection between industry concentration and firms' profitability supports this conclusion. With some exceptions attributable to poor data or statistical methods, these studies show significant positive correlations between firms' profitabilities and both (a) the degree of concentration in the market in which they sell (measured by, for example, the industry four-firm concentration ratio—see below), and (b) their own individual market shares.[12]

Of course, correlation does not prove causation, and this evidence may instead be read as showing that *economies of scale* are responsible for market concentration: Scale economies lead to big firms with market power, and also lead to higher profitability. But such a conclusion ignores the importance of entry barriers and the lack of supportive evidence that scale economies are the sole explanation of bigness, as discussed above. Moreover, X-inefficiency or slack, as well as advertising expenditures and labor wage rates have also been found to be positively correlated with market concentration.[13] If scale economies are alleged to be the main cause of market concentration, then they must be quite great in order to apparently more than offset these other higher costs of firms in concentrated industries. It seems far better to conclude from all this evidence taken together that entry barriers permit both concentration and inflated costs, and that concentration, just as theory would have it, yields greater market power manifested in higher profits, some of which are spent on advertising and other strategic entry barriers as well as on workers' (and presumably managers') salaries.

How extensive a problem is market concentration in modern economies? Table 3.1, a selection of some of the most concentrated industries in the United States, gives some indication. Readers should not be surprised at many of the industries on this list, but may be unfamiliar with others—and some important, highly concentrated industries do not appear (e.g., the mass media, which I will discuss separately below). While there are many problems with this sort of information—not the least being the quality of the original data from which it is derived—at least some general impression may be taken from it. On average, in the manufacturing sector, the largest four firms in a given industry nationwide take about 40 percent of the industry's total sales, the largest eight take about 52 percent. Conservatively defining a concentrated industry as one with a four-firm concentration ratio of 60 percent or greater, concentrated manufacturing industries take about 21 percent of the total of U.S. manufacturing sales.[14]

These sorts of facts must be taken with some skepticism, of course. First, in general, many markets these days are international in scope, hence include foreign producers alongside the domestic U.S. producers that are taken account of in these data: the Census Bureau's measurement of concentration, to that extent, overstates the problem. On the other hand, many other markets are *local* in scope (e.g., urban or regional) rather than national, and national concentration ratios necessarily understate the extent of the concentration in local markets. Electric power, as an extreme example, has a national concentration ratio of 19 percent, but every relevant regional market is a strict monopoly. Moreover, these data are based on "4-digit" Standard Industrial Classification codes, and represent industry classifications that are broader than those in which firms actually produce. Data on finer classifications of industry types than these would be needed to make a more accurate estimate. For example, the motor vehicles industry actually consists of distinct industries producing passenger cars, small trucks, and cargo tractors and trailers; similarly, "batteries" consists of auto batteries, electronics batteries, and so forth. On that count too, these concentration ratios understate the problem (see Table 3.1).

Another kind of answer to the question of how serious a problem is concentration may be got by considering the extent of its effects on the economy as a whole: How much of potential aggregate output is lost to consumers as a consequence of monopoly power? Recall that what consumers lose directly, as a result of monopoly, consists of two parts—that which is lost to the monopoly itself, plus the additional "allocative efficiency loss." A great many attempts have been made to estimate the latter of these losses: The results give a loss that ranges from about 0.4 percent to about 4 percent of national income. If one adds to the allocative efficiency loss the additional costs of the resources expended by monopolies and oligopolies in defending their market positions (e.g., advertising expenditures intended to prevent potential rivals from entering), the estimates of the total costs of market power due to concentration range from about 7 percent to about 13 percent of total national income.[15]

Only a single estimate has ever been published by an economist of the redistributive effect of concentration, that is, the "ripoff" of consumers that monopolies and oligopolies take in the form of excess profit. The study considered the extra wealth (net worth) accumulated by the wealthiest 0.25 percent of the households in the United States on account of market power deriving from concentration (that is, wealth accumulated from monopoly excess profit). It also considered the wealth lost by the poorest 28 percent of all households (due to real income losses from higher monopoly prices for goods and services bought). The poorest household group actually had (and continues to have) negative net worth, but were there no market power due to concentration, their wealth *would be* 1.4–2.0 percent of the total of all household wealth. The richest actually owned about 19 percent of all wealth at the time of the study (in chapter 6, I will discuss their share today)—but *would have* owned only 3–10 percent of it, had they accumulated no monopoly profit.[16]

Besides the unavoidably great imprecision of quantitative findings like these, interpreting such evidence depends considerably upon one's viewpoint: Is the glass half-full or half-empty? One may be unimpressed by the importance of concentration in modern capitalist economies. But clearly there is a fairly strong argument to be made for popular perceptions about the

Table 3.1

Selected Concentrated Industries, 1992

| | Percentage of total industry sales made by industry's largest | | | |
Manufacturing Industries	4-firms	8-firms	20-firms	50-firms
Manmade cellulose fibers	98	—	—	—
Primary copper	98	100	100	100
Household laundry machines	94	—	—	—
Cigarettes	93	—	—	—
Malt beverages	90	98	99	99
Vegetable oils	89	97	100	—
Asbestos products	88	99	100	—
Military tanks	88	94	99	100
Tobacco (chewing and smoking)	87	98	100	100
Batteries	87	95	99	100
Aluminum (roled and drawn)	86	95	99	100
Electric bulbs and tubes	86	94	98	100
Breakfast cereals	85	98	100	100
Refined cane sugar	85	99	—	—
Greeting cards	84	88	95	99
Secondary glass products	84	93	100	na
Small arms ammunition	84	95	98	100
Motor vehicles and car bodies	84	91	99	99
Military ordinance and accessories	83	89	97	100
Hard-surface floor coverings	83	99	—	—
Household refrigerators and freezers	82	98	100	—
Flat glass	81	—	100	—
Malleable iron products	80	95	100	100
Turbines and generators	79	92	98	100
Aircraft (all)	79	93	99	100
Macaroni and spaghetti	78	85	93	96
Industrial gases	78	91	96	99
Photographic equipment	78	83	89	93
Aircraft engines and parts	77	84	90	95
Chocolate and cocoa products	75	88	98	99
Tire cords and fabrics	75	98	100	—
Chlorine and alkalies	75	90	99	100
Manmade fiber and silk fabrics	74	89	100	100
Corn products	73	93	100	100
Beet sugar	71	93	100	—
Soybean oil products	71	91	100	100
Plumbing fixtures (vitreous)	71	94	99	100
Guided missiles and space vehicles	71	93	100	100
Tires and inner tubes	70	91	98	100
Household appliances (water heaters)	70	91	9	100
House slippers	68	89	99	100
Aluminum (sheet, plate, and foil)	68	86	99	100
Malt and by-products	65	97	100	—
Cottonseed oil	62	81	100	—

(continued)

Table 3.1 *(continued)*

	4-firms	8-firms	20-firms	50-firms
Food containers (sanitary)	59	82	98	100
Aluminum (ingot and billet)	59	82	100	100
Household vacuum cleaners	59	86	100	100
Weighted average—all manufacturing	40	52		
Retailing services				
National chain dept. stores	100	100	100	100
Discount and mass merchandising	79	88	98	100
Conventional dept. stores	56	78	94	99
Home and auto supply stores	44	48	52	56
Athletic footware stores	69	75	80	84
Bookstores	41	45	50	56
Hobby, toy, and game shops	65	71	76	79
Sewing, needlework, and piecegoods stores	48	59	65	70
Financial and other services				
National commercial banks	32	42	49	77
Personal credit institutions	50	64	81	90
Securities brokers (dealer and flotation)	33	47	67	77
Title insurance	71	88	96	99
Land subdividers and developers	7	10	16	26
Investment offices	40	56	75	87
Credit reporting services	53	63	70	77
Computer facilities management services	53	69	80	90
Truck rental and leasing (without driver)	57	64	72	78
Passenger car rental	47	69	76	82
Amusement parks	64	77	86	91
General hospitals (for profit)	53	71	84	92
Transportation and utilities				
Local and suburban mass transit	24	31	48	63
Sightseeing bus services	34	48	70	87
Intercity and rural bus services	—	61	74	89
Garbage and trash collection	35	38	42	48
Trucking terminal facilities	75	92	100	100
Air transportation (2–digit SIC)	100	100	100	100
Crude petroleum pipelines	60	80	97	100
Telephone	46	71	92	94
Television broadcasting	48	55	67	80
Electric utilities	19	32	58	78

Source: U.S. Census Bureau, 1992 Census of Manufacturers, Table 3.

Note: Except where indicated, all manufacturing industries are 4–digit SIC codes, while some finance, retail, transportation, and other are 3–digit SIC codes. "Weighted Average—All Manufacturing" give the average concentration ratios for all 4–digit SIC industries—weights are the industries' value of shipments—the author's calculations.

dominance of "big business": Concentration is arguably the *preeminent* market structure in modern economies at every level of market definition today—international, national, regional, and local, and constitutes a social problem of no small moment for modern capitalist societies.

A Tendency Toward Greater Concentration?

The urgency of that problem is greatly increased when one considers the possibility that a systematic tendency of rising concentration may be inherent in market systems. In one of his few prognostications widely acknowledged by mainstream economists as worthy of their lofty respect, Karl Marx offered that a "tendency of concentration of capital" exists in capitalist history, that is, that the ownership and control of society's productive capacity tends to rest in relatively fewer hands over time.[17] The concentration of capital is a somewhat broader concept than is concentration in markets, and a thorough evaluation of Marx's idea would be beyond the scope of this book. Yet there are strong grounds for accepting that at the least a tendency toward rising concentration in markets does exist.

Over the decades that market concentration has been systematically and routinely measured, most economists would allow that it increased prior to the period 1960–80. The significant decline in measured concentration that occurred during the latter decades, however, lent weight to the argument that there is no consistent tendency toward concentration.[18] At this point in the new millenium, the empirical evidence is less clear on what may have happened since the 1980s—partly because of an erosion of the usefulness of the traditional Standard Industrial Classification codes, an overhaul in those classifications by the Census Bureau, and the lack of any careful study to date using both the old and the new classifications. Still the major boom in corporate mergers and acquisitions that occurred in the 1990s suggests a resumption of previous trends, and the issue is raised once again.

The main argument concerns whether any tendency toward concentration must necessarily be countered to one extent or another by tendencies of the opposite kind. For one thing, certain technological changes have had the effect of reducing the "minimum efficient scale" of production in some industries, hence the average business size has declined. Second, technological developments in transportation and communication have, especially recently, expanded the geographical scope of most important markets: interregional and international competition have increased even if regional or nationally based measures of concentration have risen. For example, the automobile industry in the United States was highly concentrated until the advent of a market for imports in the 1960s and 1970s brought into the market a host of Japanese and European producers.[19]

Yet there are clear limits on the effectiveness of these countertendencies against increasing concentration. Regarding interregional and international competition, once a market expands to include producers from across the entire world, no further such countertendency can exist, and any tendency toward concentration then must predominate, as it obviously has, for example, with mergers in the auto industry wordwide. And clear limits exist also on the extent to which technological changes can reduce the minimum efficient scale of production as well: As long as major economies of scale are effective, production units can profitably be shrunk only so far. Among the most critical sources of scale economies are physical laws that cannot be easily avoided if at all. Consider, for example, that the surface-area-to-volume ratio of fluids' and materials' containers declines with their size, thus reducing the per unit cost of containing and transporting the materials with increasing scale (e.g., in pipes or on freighters). While the resulting scale economies hold only up to a point determined by the strength requirements of the container structure, as stronger new materials and structures are developed, larger sizes are permitted.

Similarly, major scale economies arise from the specialization of labor permitted in larger production establishments, everything else equal—for example, due to improvements in workers' skills at specific tasks that develop from repetition, reductions in the time wasted moving processed materials from one production task to the next, and especially the increased use of nonhuman energy sources that is allowed with the division of labor. Certainly many important new technologies have had the effect of *increasing* the minimum efficient scale of organization in many industries. And while new technologies in communication and transportation have expanded the geographic area encompassed in many markets, thus increasing the amount of competition in them, those very same technologies have also permitted larger scale *firms*. For example, new communication and information processing technologies have revolutionized production process monitoring, control, and coordination, including the control over and coordination of labor of all kinds, and have dramatically expanded the scale and scope of production activities that may be subjected to any given centralized management.

By no means does this imply that technological changes leading to expanding scale economies must be fully to blame for increasing concentration. As pointed out earlier, considerable "excessive scale" above and beyond firms' minimum efficient scale is widespread: Scale economies apparently account for only a portion of the size of many major firms. Yet certainly when new technologies permit scale economies, firms will be quick to take advantage of them, partly because they are generally quick to take advantage of cost reductions whatever may be their source, and partly because there are special additional advantages deriving from greater firm size. These latter then—which have more to do with simply *doing business* on a large scale than with *producing* on a large scale—must be considered the real source of a tendency toward increasing concentration.

First, because of enormous scale economies in the mass media, larger firms spending any given fraction of their revenues on advertising their products have access to a disproportionately larger audience than do smaller firms. Second, larger firms often have access to cheaper production inputs, not merely because of scale economies in input-producing industries, but because of buyers'-side bargaining power—that is, monopsony market power. This is especially so in labor markets, where larger firms may be able to deal more effectively with even the strongest labor unions. Third, larger firms often have cheaper access to credit and capital—their size reduces their perceived riskiness (particularly that of longer-established firms) and gives them additional name recognition among banks and investors. This is especially so insofar as larger firms experiencing financial difficulties have broader impact on their communities, and are therefore more likely to be bailed out one way or another by government. On account of their broader impact on the public, moreover, larger firms have greater political influence at higher levels of government. Last and by no means least, greater size is more likely to yield increased market power, that is, monopoly, oligopoly, or dominant firm power, the economic profit from which serves both as an incentive to expansion and as the source of the financing or leveraging of strategic actions that in turn bolster or expand that market power even further—for example, by increasing spending on advertising and political lobbying, by facilitating short-term "predatory pricing" against rivals, by expanding excess production capacity to be used in the event of competition by a new entrant, and so forth.

Thus, business involves an incessant quest not merely for profit, as in the mainstream economics account of the firm's prime motivation, but more particularly for expansion, whether it be by means of simple growth in the firm's production capacity—preferably at the expense of that of other competing firms—or by means of merger and acquisition. That this quest translates directly into a tendency toward increasing market concentration is widely appreciated outside of mainstream economics, and even an intelligent layperson may safely observe, as did Albert Einstein, that:

> [P]rivate capital tends to become concentrated in few hands, partly because of competition among the capitalists, and partly because technological development and the increasing division of labor encourage the formation of larger units of production at the expense of smaller ones.[20]

A Most Critical Example: The Media

The threat posed by the accretion of "social" as opposed to economic power resulting from concentration in markets has been widely felt as well, albeit too little among economists. In his observation on concentration, Einstein continued,

> The results of these developments is an oligarchy of private capital, the enormous power of which cannot be effectively checked even by a demo-cratically organized political society. Moreover, under existing conditions, private capitalists inevitably control, directly or indirectly, the main sources of information (press, radio, education). It is thus extremely difficult, and indeed in most cases quite impossible, for the individual citizen to come to objective conclusions and to make intelligent use of his political rights.[21]

For the primary benefit accrued by firms with power in markets—excess profit income—gives them power also in politics and in the cultural institu-tions that structure people's values. Especially important among the latter are the mass media, which may serve then as a fitting example not only of market concentration itself but also of its larger social ramifications.

Perhaps nowhere else has increasing market concentration in recent years been as visible and as threatening to public values as in the mass media industries—broadcast and cable television; radio, music, film, and video pro-duction; newspaper, magazine, and book publishing; and the newest addi-tion, the Internet. Together these constitute the means (outside of the education system) by which the vast bulk of information about the larger society is made available to people—the mass media are, in effect, the very "ether" of our cultural space. As such, it might be thought that they are essentially neu-tral with regard to the content of the information they serve to convey, that they are merely the means by which that information is transmitted and can therefore be of no consequence for the nature of the information conveyed. That is not at all the case: The social structures that form the media critically shape the kinds of information people may get from them.

Thus, for example, a monolithic media system controlled by a single na-tional state organ could hardly serve the needs of a democratic society, dis-couraging as such a structure must be for essential democratic values such as minority rights and diversity, local participatory self-governance, egalitari-anism, and so forth. But even far short of such an extreme, the mass media as actually constituted today pose serious problems in their role of providing the cultural requisites of democracy, problems that are enormously com-pounded by increasing concentration in the market structures of the media. While this is not the place for an extended analysis of the mass media, a brief introduction to these problems will help clarify just how critical an issue is that of market concentration in the media industry.[22]

One most fundamental problem is that the mass media convey only *one-*

way communications: The viewer, listener, or reader cannot respond, either immediately or after a reasonable time, to the producers of the messages they receive. Audiences' lack of access to means for responding to or querying message producers—particularly for doing so in ways that include the rest of the affected audience as well—may put them at a disadvantage in calling those messages into question, leaving audiences vulnerable to misinformation or manipulation by message producers. Of course, it may be impossible for audiences to have such means of response—if so, then the cultural requisites of a democratic society absolutely require that by some other means as great a diversity of contending perspectives be conveyed in the mass media as exists among its citizens.

Two other fundamental problems of the mass media in a market system are posed by their *private ownership in capitalist enterprises*. First, their private ownership, like that of the vast bulk of productive capital in market societies, is held virtually exclusively only by the wealthiest classes of people. Since ownership means being able to exert one's preferences upon that which is owned, one would expect that the viewpoints extant in messages conveyed by the media would tend to reflect, or at least not greatly contradict, those most preferred by their owners. Since the latter tend to be of a distinct social group, a great bias may therefore exist in the content of the messages conveyed in the media in market societies—for example, against messages greatly sympathetic to a major redistribution of private wealth and income, or messages considering the possible advantages of public or worker ownership of media enterprises themselves.

Second, being mostly pure free-market institutions, media enterprises have sought sales wherever they may, and accordingly find themselves at this point in their history primarily in the business of selling *advertising space*. That is, the vast bulk of their revenues derive from selling to other private enterprises access to the audiences the media firms serve for the purpose of persuading audiences to purchase those enterprises' products. That means that it is not first and foremost audiences' preferences about media content, for example, in entertainment or news, that matter most in media firms' determination of what content to provide, but advertisers' preferences.

The latter must be presumed quite distinct, in general, from audiences' preferences, of course. From audiences' viewpoint, media content is news and entertainment, while from advertisers' viewpoint, it is "packaging" for their commercial messages, and they care greatly about that packaging, for it may greatly influence how their commercial messages are received. Thus for media firms, the guiding principle of all their production effort is to provide content that appeals to audiences (so that they have something to sell to advertisers!) without violating advertisers' need for attractive packaging. The upshot is entertainment and news content that tends to exclude messages that may well be quite appealing to audiences but might alienate them from advertisers—for example, messages criticizing particular advertisers' business policies or messages criticizing material consumerism and commercialism in general.

All of these most critical problems of the mass media in capitalist market societies—that they provide only one-way communications, that they are mainly privately owned by the affluent, and that they are predominantly commercially driven—are greatly if not completely mitigated by *market competition* in the media industry. The more independent media firms there are in business, the greater is access to at least some of them by a broad range of potential message producers—that is, the easier is access by even the least of those in their audiences who would respond to or question messages conveyed, and the less critical is the one-way nature of mass media communications as a whole. Similarly, the greater is the number of media firms competing for audience attention, the more likely it must be that even relatively nonaffluent people have ownership of at least some of them, and that at least some media firms therefore convey messages more attuned to the political and social agenda of the nonaffluent—thus the less glaring must be the bias in media content overall toward the preferences of affluent business owners. Finally, the greater is the number of media firms vying for audiences, the more likely it is that at least some will find ways of doing business without great dependence upon advertising revenues, and the more likely it is that a sizable portion of the mass media will not be commercially driven.

Briefly, then, in a democratic society a highly competitive media industry is absolutely essential for providing audiences as broad a diversity of views as possible. Yet to the extent that in market systems a tendency toward rising market concentration predominates, the opposite is the most likely development. A survey of the mass media in U.S. history shows pretty clearly such a tendency at work in that industry all along, but recent decades have brought the matter to what may be a point of crisis—most importantly because of deregulation and the laissez-faire orientation toward antitrust in government in these times. Virtually all major cities in the United States today are served by monopoly daily newspapers; and most of those newspapers are outsider-owned, usually by one of the half-dozen largest media conglomerates. All daily newspapers, and all the major Internet news providers as well, now get the major portion of their international news from only two news services. There are perhaps several hundred cable television channels in the United States, but only six corporations dominate their programming, with 80 percent of the national market. About half of all book retailing is done by the Borders and Barnes & Noble national chains. In the music recording industry, the top-five firms get 87 percent of total industry sales, with their ownership of the overwhelming majority of the several hundred or so separate "labels" that exist. In music, the connection with commercial advertising is indirect, but present nonetheless in the close relationship with radio broadcasting, where among the thousands of stations operating across the nation, four firms take a third of all the revenues generated. (A recent issue before the Federal Communications Commission has been whether to allow many thousands of "microstations" to compete, a turn of events that could certainly help matters. Still, the problem remains of where all these small operators will be getting their news, programming, and music content.)[23]

In fact, there is even less variety and diversity in the media industry than this brief count of firms would indicate, since large media firms now dominate or at least have a sizable presence in many different parts of the industry at once. Partly this is so merely because of the extensive technological changes occurring in the industry, for example, in cable and digital broadcast television, in the "digitization" of all the media, and in the Internet—the industry is simply in flux. But mergers across sectors in the last decade or so have been simply astonishing. By now, all in all, about ten firms dominate all of the media today, the largest of them with major interests in newspapers, radio, television and cable networks, video rentals, film and television studios, theaters, music, magazines, book publishers, retailers, and various Internet services. Indeed, many "media" firms are significantly diversified beyond the media industry itself, for example, in theme parks, restaurants, and cruise lines, while many "industrial" or other firms have taken major stakes in the media, for example, Sony's movie theaters in the United States and GE's ownership of the NBC television network.

This kind of conglomeration raises a whole additional set of concerns about business power beyond those of concentration itself. For conglomeration in the media allows cross-promotion and coordinated advertising that proceeds on several interrelated fronts, and also gives nonmedia firms with large media interests major advantages over others without such diversification. There is, moreover, the additional problem of *integration* among independent media firms. That is, not only are firms conglomerated but there are interconnections among the conglomerates in the form of joint ventures (activities in which several firms combine participation), and interlocks of various kinds (for example, mutual stockholdings, directors sitting on the boards of several firms, and so forth). This sort of integration in the media implies, of course, less competition among the firms involved and even greater opportunities for coordinated cross-promotion and other kinds of collusion. Concentration per se then is merely one element of the structure of business power in the media: The social problem constituted by concentration is compounded by the conglomeration and partial or informal integration of media firms. Conglomeration and integration are equally critical in other industries as well, and to these and related matters, then, I now turn.

Notes

1. It is possible, of course, for the monopolist to face the countervailing power of a single buyer or monopsony. In this case of "bilateral monopoly," the equilibrium price is not determinate in any simple way, but depends on the relative bargaining power of the two contenders.

2. Alternatively, monopoly need not be overtly oppressive—although, as I will explain, it could be. Also, note the counterfactuality of the referent case of competition, which contrary to widespread mythology is not a "good" thing in itself but merely insofar as it provides buyers with sufficient alternative sources of the commodity to prevent their subjection to market power.

3. While today's mainstream economists would *never* use the term, Joan Robinson, in *The Economics of Imperfect Competition*, one of the original foundation pieces on today's neoclassical theory on the subject, found the term "exploitation" precisely descriptive of the benefit of a monopoly market position.

4. Interestingly, in the modern theory of price discrimination, it is the elasticity of demand that determines the price the monopolist will charge a segment of the market. Price elasticity is, of course, a reflection of the intensity of buyers' need or demand for the commodity, which is, in turn, a measure of the buyers' potential vulnerability to the monopoly.

5. The seminal reference on contestable markets is William J. Baumol, John C. Panzar, and Robert D. Willig, *Contestable Markets and the Theory of Industrial Structure*.

6. While contestable market theory was created for and remains in the world of pure theory, the literature on entry barriers is thoroughly grounded in extensive empirical work beginning with Joe S. Bain, *Barriers to New Competition*; see William Shepherd, *The Economics of Industrial Organization*, pp. 209–214, for a remarkable list and description of types of entry barriers.

7. See William Shepherd, *The Economics of Industrial Organization*, chapter 7. As another example, while containers' and pipes' surface-area to capacity-volume ratio necessarily declines with increases in size, thus leading to scale economies, their wall strength must be increased more than proportionally with their capacity, which of course leads to scale diseconomies.

8. That is, public utility-type or rate-of-return regulation, or else public ownership or similar oversight.

9. One such legal cartel that is widespread but perhaps unfamiliar to most people is that among milk producers in each of over sixty large cities in the United States under the oversight of the Department of Agriculture (William Shepherd, *The Economics*, pp. 264–265).

10. Typically, industrial organization textbooks today devote at least a chapter to game theory, for example, Lynn Pepall, Daniel J. Richards, and George Norman, *Industrial Organization*, chapter 5. Indeed, many are more or less *based* on game theory, such as, Oz Shy, *Industrial Organization*—highlighting what seems to be its most important contribution to the subject: It is absolutely essential to consider the

nature of competition in oligopoly as a strategic behavior in complex interaction with similar behavior among rivals.

11. Lynn Pepall, Daniel J. Richards, and George Norman, *Industrial Organization*, chapter 5.

12. For example, Stephen Martin, *Industrial Economics*, pp. 158–178.

13. On concentration and X-inefficiency, see William Shepherd, *The Economics*, p. 105; on advertising, Stephen Martin, *Industrial Economics*, p. 172; on labor compensation, ibid., p. 175.

14. Author's calculation, using the data in U.S. Census Bureau, *1992 Census of Manufacturers*, Table 3.

15. Stephen Martin, *Industrial Economics*, pp. 29–40. Note that these estimates do not include the additional losses to the economy as a whole due to X-inefficiency.

16. William S. Comanor and Robert H. Smiley, "Monopoly and the Distribution of Wealth"; a more recent simulation study is Irene Powell, "The Effect of Reductions in Concentration on Income Redistribution."

17. Karl Marx, *Capital*, pp. 776–777.

18. William Shepherd, *The Economics*, pp. 161–164.

19. Ibid.

20. Albert Einstein, "Why Socialism?" pp. 157–158.

21. Ibid.

22. On what follows, see Robert W. McChesney, *Rich Media, Poor Democracy* and *Corporate Media and the Threat to Democracy*; Edward S. Herman and Noam Chomsky, *Manufacturing Consent*; Ben H. Bagdikian, *The Media Monopoly*; and Michael Parenti, *Inventing Reality* and *Make Believe Media*.

23. Robert W. McChesney, *Rich Media, Poor Democracy*, chapter 1.

4

Business Power II:
Networks and Finance

Traditional indicators of concentration such as those discussed in the last chapter significantly understate the actual extent of concentration, for they fail to show the *informal integration* often existing among legally independent firms. Firms may formally integrate, of course, in legal mergers or acquisitions. In informal integration, firms that are legally independent cooperate, behave in concert, coordinate their policies to one degree or another, as if they were, to some extent, merely separate divisions of one single firm. In effect, there are fewer organized "units" of production than the number of legal firms chartered as corporations, proprietorships, cooperatives, and so forth—and statistical indications of concentration that are based on numbers of firms understate the actual extent of concentration. Thus it is possible that measured concentration may be falling over time, even as actual concentration, counting that constituted by informal integration, is rising.

The critical implication of informal integration is, of course, that firms do not necessarily behave as the autonomous and independent "atoms" assumed in standard economics, occasionally bumping into each other at random to do business but otherwise oblivious, self-contained, having no enduring relationships with other firms. Instead they often form lasting cooperative relationships that allow one degree or another of policy coordination and to which they may commit resources to sustain. These relationships are not at all the equivalent of mere market exchanges between participating firms, nor are they necessarily equally voluntarily entered into. They often involve the exercise of power on the part of one or more of the firms involved, and they frequently enable the participating firms to jointly exercise power upon outsiders and share the benefits thereof.

The tacit or conspiratorial collusion among oligopolists discussed earlier is an example of such a relationship, of course, what may be called informal *horizontal* integration. Instead of setting their prices and output levels independently, with each firm trying to maximize its own profit regardless of what others do, the participating firms cooperate on the setting of price and output to maximize their joint profit, dividing the latter in some fashion to which they all agree. Each firm could perhaps take some quick profit in the short term by dropping out of the cooperative agreement and lowering its price, but in the longer term, the other participants would be able to lower the dropout's profit considerably by meeting its competition with retaliating price cuts. Of course, they would prefer not to have to do that, since all firms would be hurt by the competition, but the consequences of failing to take appropriate retaliation against a "cheater" would be even worse in terms of the business lost to the cheater. Far better then for each firm to go along with the group, cooperate, and take their share of the monopoly profit to be had by behaving in concert as if they were a single firm. This may hold well enough among oligopolists that are more or less equal in size, and such arrangements may be even easier to maintain if a single participant greatly dominates the others in size and can threaten them into cooperation, for example, with the prospect of what, for them, might be a devastating price war.[1]

There are other things than price and output on which otherwise rivalrous firms may cooperate. For example, firms may collude as buyers of an input, perhaps dividing a pool of some natural resource and excluding others from it, or cooperating on stifling a labor union seeking to organize their employees. They may pool some of their resources in joint ventures, for example, oil companies jointly constructing a pipeline or auto companies jointly producing a car model or firms jointly funding an advertising campaign or political lobbying effort to advance their common cause. Other possibilities exist too of horizontal integration of one degree or another, as I will discuss below. In each such case of partial, informal integration, the participating firm's profit from giving up some of its decision-making autonomy by cooperating with other firms exceeds what it could take in normal competition with its rivals (i.e., in noncooperative, atomistic independence). And again, power on the part of one or more of the participants may serve to sustain the relationship, and exercising power upon outsiders—for example, input suppliers, labor unions, rival outside firms, or the public at large—is likely the whole point of cooperating in the first place.

Aside from horizontal collusion, other instances of informal integration are often referred to as *business networks*, of which two broad types may be distinguished. In *vertical* integration as traditionally considered, firms in buyer-seller relationships with each other—that is, firms upstream-downstream from each other in the flow of production—may form cooperative relationships, coordinating policies on some or all aspects of their production activities. In what I will refer to, for lack of a better term, as *conglomerate* integration, firms that are not closely related to each other either horizontally or vertically—for example, firms producing completely different final consumer goods—similarly enter cooperative arrangements. Like horizontal integration, informal vertical and conglomerate integration have bearing on the extent of concentration in the economy: They imply that the actual extent is greater than it appears. They also have specific implications for the role of power in markets, and this chapter will focus on those implications. However, consider first a critical question: If the firms participating in a close informal cooperative arrangement could accomplish the same goals, in principle, by legally merging together into a larger whole, why maintain a merely informal relationship?

Formal vs. Informal Integration

Vertical integration, both formal and informal, is a major feature throughout the economy. Extensive formal vertical integration is widely found: A single firm in the mining and extractive industries, for example, may own deposits of a mineral and employ facilities for extracting it, refining it, transporting both the extracted mineral and its refined products for use in production or to wholesalers or retailers, and manufacturing and retailing the final products to consumers as well. It may also have wholly owned subsidiaries that manufacture tools, facilities, or materials used at various of these stages, for example, a construction subsidiary specializing in building its mining facilities, or a manufacturer of chemicals used in its mineral refinement processes. Historically, most extensive vertical integration has been accomplished by firms merging with or acquiring independent firms with which they previously did business, thus incorporating into themselves suppliers of various inputs (in "upstream" vertical integration) or users, wholesalers, or retailers of their products ("downstream").

Alternatively, however, instead of formal vertical integration a firm could allow the other firms with which it does business to retain their legal independence and merely continue buying from or selling to them. Indeed, whatever may be the reasons for formally integrating them into itself, it might instead choose to leave them independent if it can find other ways of *managing their operations*—for example, by placing some of its own managers in positions of continual or periodic oversight at the other firm (there are other possible approaches too, as I will discuss later on). In such cases, of course, the de facto integration does not appear in any statistics based on numbers of firms. Thus, for example, while a materials or parts suppliers' market may appear, on the basis of its concentration ratio, to be quite competitive, appearances would be greatly deceiving if many or all of the suppliers are actually de facto subsidiaries of one or a few firms to which they sell their product.[2]

In the traditional industrial organization literature, the reasons for seeking formal integration with, for example, supplier firms included such things as the need to assure more regular delivery or better quality of the input, or wanting to close out rival users of it from access to its supply. In the "new institutionalist" economic theory of business organization, a firm may choose to incorporate into itself a supplier firm if there are "agency problems" in their relationship—that is, to put it in more straightforward language, if the supplier would otherwise be able to exercise some *agency power* over the buying firm in the course of their business.[3] Independent parts suppliers, for example, are contracted to do whatever work is involved in producing components, but may, within the terms of the contract, exercise considerable discretion in how that work is done—they are, in effect, agents of the buying firm in a principal-agent relationship. As such they may have both the incentive and the opportunity to skimp on aspects of product quality that are not easily verified or not well specified in the contract. To prevent being taken advantage of in such an exercise of agency power, the buying firm may simply incorporate the supplier into itself (by acquiring the latter's assets or controlling interest in its stock), thereby allowing a continual and closer scrutiny over the formerly independent supplier's production.[4]

But clearly, formal vertical integration of this sort is only one possible solution to the problem of agency power: For example, the buying firm may instead simply place permanently or periodically some of its own managers alongside the supplier's managers to oversee the latter's production. Creating a network like this between the two firms (or incorporating the supplier into an already existing network) may amount to the buying firm's exercising *power of its own* over the supplier without formally incorporating the latter into itself, and using that power, in effect, to counter the supplier's agency power. A position of monopsony power (or oligopsony or a dominant buyer position) would obviously suffice to enable the buying firm to do this.[5] Note that since a firm in such a position may choose either formal or informal integration with the supplier firm, the decisive power would appear to lie not in the supplier's agency power but in the buyer firm's ability to incorporate the supplier into its domain one way or the other.

I use the term *conglomerate* integration to suggest a similar parallel between the other main type of business network and the corresponding formal legal structure of a single firm, the conglomerate corporation. Formal and informal conglomeration is widespread, and is of perhaps even greater significance than vertical integration. The formally conglomerated corporation is, of course, ubiquitous in capitalist economies today. Its rise in recent times manifests a new form of market power that requires a broader conceptualization of the idea of market concentration, as well as of its measurement.

Insofar as its subsidiaries are involved in completely unrelated production activities, the special power of the conglomerate corporation derives partly from the risk pooling that occurs in diversification.[6] The fact that it has many different production activities ongoing at any time means that the ups and downs of profitability of the firm as a whole are less than those of any single subsidiary, whatever may be the sources of profitability fluctuations of the latter (since the profitability variations of subsidiaries tend to offset each other). It is thereby able to obtain outside capital and credit more cheaply than any of its subsidiaries could individually, since it is less risky. Alternatively, the conglomerate is able to shift some of the risk of lending and other financial investing from banks and other investors onto itself, thus allowing its subsidiaries to pay a lower risk premium on their borrowings and capital than they would were they unconglomerated. Consequently conglomerate subsidiaries may have a competitive advantage in their respective markets against rivals that do not also belong to other conglomerates.

The conglomerate corporation also has special power deriving from its ability to cross-subsidize its different activities. Its direct control over a variety of activities enables it to employ the above-average profits of some subsidiaries to subsidize other subsidiaries that may need temporary help. For example, if a subsidiary is subject to some competitive threat by a potential new entrant into its market, the parent conglomerate can cross-subsidize whatever strategic preventive action may be necessary (e.g., an advertising campaign or other marketing ploy or a price war), thus bolstering the subsidiary's position in its market. Making such an investment out of other subsidiaries' profits may bolster the parent company's overall profit and power as well, insofar as it may then be able to reap some monopoly profit from the protected subsidiary that the latter may not have been able to reap on its own. Thus buttressed by each other, conglomerate subsidiaries may move as new entrants into established markets more effectively as cross-subsidized entities (with access to cheaper capital as well) than can firms lacking the advantages of conglomeration. Note that cross-subsidization too amounts to an alternative and sometimes superior financial arrangement that is provided by the conglomerate: Nonconglomerated firms with income surpluses have the latter transferred to other firms with deficits in their funds (relative to their needs) via the banking system and financial markets; conglomerate subsidiaries, on the other hand, have their surpluses transferred via the conglomerate firm's headquarters.

Risk-diversification and cross-subsidization account for a good part of the success of the conglomerate corporation. The other important source of its economic success lies in what has been popularly called the "synergy" that may arise when more or less distantly related production activities are brought together under common management (i.e., activities that are related but not closely related either horizontally or vertically). For example, conglomerate subsidiaries using similar processes to produce different products may be able to benefit from sharing their technical know-how more easily than could independent firms that may have separately owned patents, or that may be competitive rivals in hiring the technical employees that operate the production processes. Or perhaps a conglomerate may be able to tie the marketing of two different but related products together in ways that benefit the sales of both subsidiaries relative to what they could achieve as independent firms marketing their different products separately. Cross-advertising and -promotion in media conglomerates, for example, as discussed in the last chapter, has this effect.

Thus the conglomerate firm brings to bear in markets what amounts to another form of market power distinct from but compounding that which exists due to market concentration. Despite the occasional ebbing of conglomerate merger activity during the last several decades—due to a periodic need to "slough off the excess" acquired during merger waves—the long-term trend is most definitely toward more corporate conglomeration, at least as reflected in the measured degree of diversification of large firms.[7] The degree of market concentration may appear to be unchanged or even declining over time, that is, as traditionally measured by industry concentration-ratios, for example. But if conglomeration is occurring, then market power —when understood to include the multiplicative powers brought to bear by conglomerated firms—may actually be increasing nonetheless. For this and other reasons, measures of *aggregate* concentration, the portion of aggregate rather than industry production done by the largest firms, must also be taken into account in order to get a clearer picture of the overall extent of the problem of concentration (Figure 4.1).

And, just as is true of horizontal and vertical integration, the goals of conglomerate integration too may be achieved informally. That is, legally independent firms in unrelated or only distantly related production activities may be interconnected in networks by a variety of informal relationships that permit risk-diversification, cross-subsidization, and synergetic collabo-

Figure 4.1 **Aggregate Concentration**

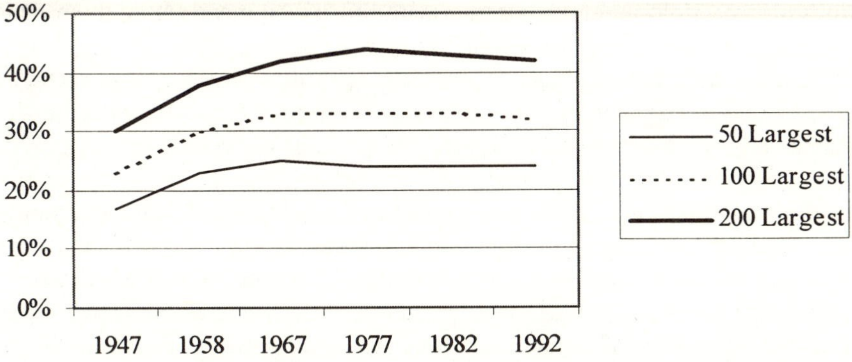

Source: U.S. Census Bureau, *1982 Census of Manufacturers: Concentration Ratios in Manufacturing* (MC82–5–7); and U.S. Census Bureau, *1992 Census of Manufacturers: Concentration Ratios in Manufacturing* (MC92–S-2).

ration or policy coordination of one degree or another. Insofar as this type of business network is found in the economy, the extent of real conglomerate power is actually greater than what is indicated by the number of formally incorporated conglomerates.

Recall that formal conglomeration is actually a kind of *financial* mechanism: It shifts the risks of capital and finance from investors to the firm itself, and also sometimes allows for a closer supervision of the movement of investable funds from surplus production units to deficit units. Thus, in parallel with formal conglomerates, informal business network structures would be expected often to appear as "communities of interest" under the aegis of banking or financial firms. Before turning to the subject of vertical and conglomerate networks per se then, it will be helpful to consider first the nature of the power of financial institutions, a topic of critical interest in itself.

The Power of Financial Institutions

Banks and other institutional lenders are, in an important sense, at the apex of the structure of power in modern capitalist market systems, a fact widely appreciated intuitively but virtually never considered by mainstream economists with anything like the kind of rigor they routinely bring to other matters of finance. As buyers and sellers of investable funds, financial institutions may appear to be merely intermediaries between the suppliers and users of these funds, and it might be thought then that if any power is wielded in financial markets, it must be mainly by the suppliers of funds themselves: After all, it is with those individuals and corporations who own accumulations of investable funds, rather than with those who merely hold them, that ultimate spending power would seem to lie.

I will consider the subject of personal spending power itself in a later chapter. Here the point may be made that the power of banks and other financial intermediaries lies in their being institutions with vastly greater power resources in the form of spendable funds than most equivalent sized nonfinancial corporations, as well as even the very wealthiest individuals or families. That does not mean that nonfinancial businesses or individuals may not themselves have power *over* these institutions, but where they do, the power such individuals and businesses are then able to wield is the special and considerable power of financial institutions. That power is composed of at least three essential elements: The vast purchasing power over the disbursement of which financial institutions have control; monopoly or concentration in the financial sector; and lenders' short-side power arising from special characteristics of finance as a commodity.

By centralizing the accumulation of the funds of many individuals, businesses, and other organizations, banks and other financial institutions hold vast amounts of spending power. This they disburse to borrowers who are enough in need of funds above and beyond what they already have to pay for them. Nonfinancial businesses are particularly needful of reliable access to outside money for investment in the many, various, and pressing requisites of competition, from plant expansion and relocation, to special materials inventory purchases and strategic marketing campaigns. In capitalist market systems, liquidity is the ultimate source of flexibility, maneuverability, and the capacity to expand, and financial institutions are the source of most of the outside liquidity available to firms for these needs. In a world of perfect markets, that fact would not give them any special powers, but in the real world it is otherwise.[8]

For one thing, concentration in the financial sector is at least as great as elsewhere in the economy. The largest five U.S. chartered commercial banks hold 30 percent of the assets of the approximately 3,400 such banks in the United States with $100 million or more assets, and the top ten hold 40 percent.[9] Concentration at the local level is far greater: The average three-firm concentration ratio for urban area markets in the United States is 67 percent, while that for rural markets is 80 percent.[10]

Moreover, not only is concentration per se great in the financial sector, but there is also a special kind of hierarchical organization among financial institutions that implies their effective concentration exceeds their apparent concentration. Large banks typically tend to do business with large financial and nonfinancial firms, both in lending and holding deposits, while small banks tend to do business with small firms. But large banks also tend to serve as *bankers* for smaller banks and other smaller financial institutions—that is, they lend to them as well as hold deposits for them (not only for convenience but also by law). In effect, large banks thus exert some lender's power upon small banks, and the system as a whole is to that extent informally integrated.

Equally important is the short-side power that banks and other institutional lenders have on account of the nature of credit as a commodity, a topic that merits some closer attention. Short-side power is that which a market transactor has by virtue of being on the "short side" of an excess supply or demand situation, that is, on the side opposite that of the excess. If there is an excess demand in a market, then sellers are on the short side. They have power over buyers insofar as they are able to pick and choose among buyers' offerings, or among buyers themselves, and can thereby threaten a buyer with whatever losses the latter would take were he unable to buy—for example, losses due to related investments the buyer may have made elsewhere that would have to be written off were he excluded from access to the commodity. It is this threat of loss that, in the textbook account of market "reequilibration," induces buyers to raise their offer prices, even to the point, if necessary, of canceling out whatever gain they may otherwise have expected to make from their purchases (in order to minimize long-run losses).

In the basic textbook account of market disequilibrium, no such situation can long endure in a market unless there is some kind of unusual interference with the free movement of prices, for example, by government. Excess supply or demand is nearly immediately eliminated by a price movement favoring the short side of the disequilibrium that brings the market back to equilibrium—that is, yielding benefits, even if only temporary, to short-side power holders. A power relationship based upon a sustained disequilibrium between market supply and demand is quite possible, however, and indeed exists in what may be considered the two most important kinds of markets of all in capitalist systems: labor markets (which will be considered in detail in the following chapter) and financial capital markets.[11]

In the latter, it appears, there is a systemic shortage of the commodity being traded—credit—and credit rationing is arguably a routine feature of the behavior of lending institutions.[12] The reasons are twofold. First, on the demand side, in "normal" times, the need for capital in firms competing for position in their markets is practically obsessive: As stated above, firms require liquidity for maneuverability and "first mover" advantages in an expansionist rivalry with competitors that may rightly be called compulsive. For this, of course, their own retained funds plus direct sales of stock and securities to the public will not suffice: they need more yet.[13]

Of course, in itself this would merely imply that in the market for finance, firms must pay for their compulsion: The equilibrium price of credit and capital would simply be higher than it might be otherwise. But the price does not equilibrate the supply of funds with this obsessively great demand, second, because of the nature of the commodity being exchanged in finance markets. That commodity is spending power over which lenders can have no direct control once they part with it to borrowers: Lenders thus need strategies for assuring that borrowers take the best possible actions necessary to repay. The upshot is that lenders give borrowers premium terms on their credit (low interest rates, easier repayment schedules, and so forth) as part of a broad strategy aimed at eliciting credit-worthy behavior from them and insuring against unworthy borrowers. These premium terms or low borrowing costs engender a perennial excess demand in the market for credit, thus putting lenders on the short side of finance capital markets.

To elaborate briefly: Creditors can have at best inadequate information about the specific actions of borrowers that determine the latter's ability to repay their credit, and realize that some borrowers in need of cash may exaggerate their own honest evaluations of their creditworthiness or be dishonest or engage in excessively risky investment projects. For that reason creditors insist on monitoring closely their customers' credit histories, incomes, and assets; current operations and plans; and specific uses of the borrowed funds; and also insist on suitable collateral. Moreover, in order to avoid the losses that noncreditworthy borrowers may bring, lenders offer their customers premium credit terms that reduce the incentive for regular borrowers to behave this way: In effect, the lower are the rates borrowers must pay for credit, the less incentive they have for "taking long shots," and the fewer uncreditworthy borrowers there will be who are applying for any given amount of funds.

In addition, providing easier terms than what would clear the credit market—that is, than what would eliminate the excess demand manifest in those "waiting in line" for credit—assures that regular borrowers will behave appropriately by creating a situation in which there is a real threat of loss to them if they do not. They may be threatened with a loss of maneuverability and "first mover" advantages derived from continuing and relatively cheap access to credit because with excess demand, lenders may pick and choose among borrowers, and may with impunity subject at least some of them to such a loss of credit, knowing that other borrowers with whom they may instead do business are waiting in line. It is this threat that assures borrowers will behave appropriately, that is, by complying with lenders' insistence both on monitoring and on occasionally interceding in policies affecting their use of the borrowed funds.

Institutional lenders use this short-side power over borrowers—compounded by the power they derive from concentration in finance capital markets—to exploit borrowers in various ways.[14] Thus some portion of financial institutions' profit derives not from providing the service of financial intermediation between savers and investors but instead from lenders' exercise of power over customers. One particularly important piece of evidence on lenders' power for present purposes is that in financial institutions' lending to nonfinancial corporations, even very large ones, financials' insistence on various kinds of access to decisive influence in borrowing firm's policy making is common, while a similar degree of influence of nonfinancial corporations in financials' decision making is not.[15]

Financial institutions thus exercise their power by actually exerting influence upon subject firms' policy making. The upshot is a degree of informal integration of nonfinancial corporations under the aegis of financial institutions that loosely knit together whole cross sections of both horizontally and vertically related firms, as well as only distantly related firms, into common policy-coordinating networks. The threads by which this knitting together is accomplished include not only financial connections per se, but also such devices as directorship interlocks, stock control, and the encouragement of joint ventures. Manifest in it is another important kind of power residing in financial institutions, what may be called "planners' power."

Networks and Planners' Power

Business networks have been studied extensively in recent decades, albeit not by economists but by business organization theorists and sociologists. Using case studies as well as sophisticated statistical network analysis tools, these theorists have found that groupings of firms having enduring relationships with each other are common throughout the economy. There is a sense also that as a form of business structure, networks are becoming an increasingly important way for firms to improve their competitiveness in markets (of course, from the economist's viewpoint they actually detract from competition by reducing the effective number of competing units in an affected market). In the classic Darwinian notion of competition, firms without the advantages of formal or informal integration in larger units do poorly in these times, it is said, and pass away or get absorbed by larger integrated units, which then come to be predominant.

Why does it pay firms to form or join networks more in these times than in earlier times? One possible reason is the new technologies that have arisen in transportation, communication, and information processing. As noted in the last chapter, these have permitted an expansion of markets to include geographically more widely dispersed producers and customers, and have also allowed for better monitoring, control, and coordination of diverse production processes, including labor, by any centralized management. Thus hierarchical networks like those presided over by financial institutions may be both larger, tighter, and better planned on account of these technologies that have universally had the effect of better connecting diverse and distant organizational units. Even nonhierarchical networks can coordinate their activities more closely using these new technologies. To that extent increased informal integration has arisen on account of the same technological changes as those that have promoted the increased formal integration of larger and larger firms.[16]

The informal vertical integration that I discussed earlier is a kind of business network, but variations on informal conglomeration are at least equally widespread. Some of the most studied examples are in the computer and software industries, where the flow of production between firms doing business with each other is multidirectional. For example, software and hardware producers may buy from and sell to each other regularly, even in roughly equivalent amounts, in addition to consulting with each other so extensively that one sometimes may not distinguish employees of one firm from those of the other. Since they generally network together with other firms (e.g., advertising and marketing firms involved in promoting their hardware-software packages), they appear more like sister subsidiaries of a conglomerate than like the classic "upstream-downstream" case. Economies of scale and the benefits of collaborative planning are considerable in computer and software production, and the networks of firms in those industries can be quite large.[17]

In general, the kinds of connections that may hold firms together in networks go far beyond simple buying and selling. Mere contractual exchange repeated over a long time can be sufficient to establish an exclusive cooperative relationship between firms, especially when there is also some sharing of management, technical personnel, or consultation in one direction or the other. However, firms may also establish stronger relationships by means of joint ventures, stockholdings, directorship interlocks, and credit. These stronger types of relationships may go in both directions between networked firms. For example, mutual stockholding even in small amounts may tie the interests of the firms or their managements together far more than were they merely doing business with each other,[18] and if they also share directorships on each other's boards, the connection may be even closer. Joint ventures have the same effect. These sorts of things are often found among networked firms and clearly indicate a level of integration at least sufficient to cast doubt on the notion that autonomous firms in merely atomistic relationships with each other predominate in market systems.

Particularly interesting for present purposes are one-directional connections. A firm that has an unreciprocated stock holding of another, if it has a sufficient share, may be able to exercise some influence on or control over the other's policies, of course. The share required for such influence may be quite small, moreover, if the other firm's remaining stockholders are widely dispersed.[19] A firm with some directors or top managers on the board of another similarly has influence in the latter's policy making—of course, simultaneous stockholding and board interlocks, if unreciprocated, certainly indicate significant influence. If in addition it has loaned funds to the other, then there may be the special influence also of lenders' power. Lenders' power may by itself lead to one-directional stockholding and board interlocks—the lender thereby having some influence over the borrowing firm's behavior. Thus banks, while not permitted to own nonfinancial firms' stock, do have control over most of the stock held in their trust departments (for private individuals, pension funds, etc.), often in amounts that may give them virtually controlling interest, in the issuing firms. They also often have one-directional board interlocks with their clients.[20] In monopsony too, as discussed above, there may be a basis for one-directional stockholdings or interlocks, and the monopsonist moreover may provide credit or investment capital to its supplier firms, making them all the more dependent upon it and subject to its control.

In statistical analyses of business networks generally, a network invariably has a "hub," a single large firm or small group of large firms with which all the rest in the network are connected by buying or selling and/or stronger ties like stockholdings and interlocks (Figure 4.2). In the cases of producer-supplier vertical integration discussed earlier, the hub is the buying firm, of course—for example, the automobile manufacturer around which extends a network of various materials, parts and service providers. Another example, again from the computer and software industries, would be a diversified big-name hardware producer surrounded by materials and components suppliers as well as producers of both final and intermediate software (i.e., both end-use applications software and software specifically used with the hub's hardware products). Other networks have a financial firm or group as the hub, and there the surrounding network of firms is typically less closely related in production, although they may be related regionally. These I will refer to as financial-hub networks, distinguishing them from producer-hub networks, that is, those with nonfinancial firms as hubs.

In each case, the hub generally has special power vis-à-vis the rest of the network. In producer-hub networks, the hub may have monopsony power over much of its network, and in financial-hub networks the hub has lender power over its networked firms. Moreover, in both cases the hub may have

Figure 4.2 **Business Networks and Interlocks**

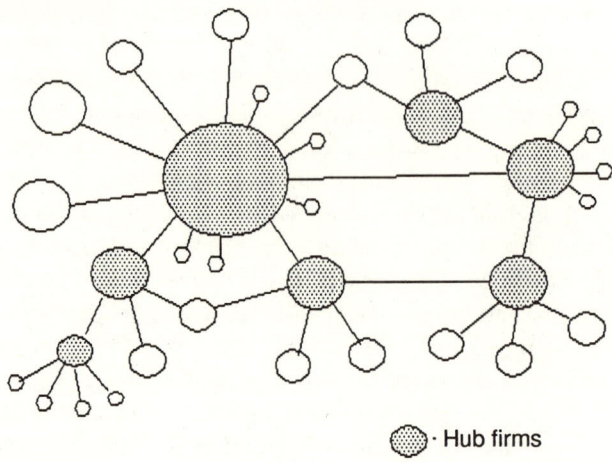

⬡ · Hub firms

another kind of power deriving from its role as planning center for the rest of the network.[21] Just as in a large firm with a diversified but interrelated set of formally integrated production activities, so too in an informal network, a critical coordination of the whole set of activities takes place at the top of the hierarchy, at the planning center. The planning center derives power over the rest of the network because of the latter's need for access to two things that only the planning center has: *information* and the capacity to make *key commitments*.

Because it deals with all of its networked firms, the hub has information about the production activities, capabilities, and plans of each, as well as about the various production relationships among them and how they are tied together. Each other firm, to one extent or another, depends upon that information for its own production and investment planning purposes: It cannot decide which specific kinds of production activities in which to invest without it. A single firm supplying an input for another might perhaps be able to coordinate with only the buyer firm in order to decide what to produce, how much, and so forth, but the buyer firm's plans may depend upon the plans of many other firms: In a set of interrelated activities, the interdependencies may be complex. And if each interrelated individual product itself requires minute technical specification in order to be properly fit with the others—for example, like those produced by firms in computer and software production networks, or in auto industry networks, or in the large building construction industry—a producer then may need to coordinate with many other firms. In such cases, the totality of the information on products and specifications that each firm requires for its own decision making may accrue only at the planning center. Each firm then must turn to the hub for the information it needs, a situation of which the hub can take advantage by insisting that the rest of the network, in effect, "pay" for that information in various ways (for example, in lower prices received for products sold to the hub or higher prices paid for services bought from it)—in effect, foregoing to the hub something more than its share otherwise of the profit to be made on the final products.

Along with information, however, networked firms also need *commitments*—that is, promises from each other or other indications that can be accepted with confidence on whatever projects involve them. Even with good information, a firm would balk at committing itself to investing in some production activity without a similar commitment from the other firms involved, for example, input suppliers, buyers of its products and others with which it must jointly cooperate. When the production activities are interrelated, a whole web of such commitments is required. Moreover, frequently there must be some key commitment made to assure that the project as a whole has some prospect of success, for example, a commitment to make the end-product marketing expenditures necessary, or a commitment to extend a major portion of the investment funds required by all the participants together. Since the hub is usually the largest firm in the network, especially in its spending power, it is the most likely to be able to make the kind of major commitment necessary to bring the whole network along on any given project.

Based on its strategic position, moreover, the hub is usually able to decide among various possible key commitments that may be made at each point in time, and each possible commitment will have different effects on the profitabilities of different firms in the network. That is, some commitments will benefit some firms and hurt others, while other possible commitments will have the opposite effects on those firms. Each firm then "hangs" on the particular decision made by the hub, that is, it is subject to the threat that the hub will decide on a particular commitment that yields it relatively little compared to its yield were the hub to make other possible commitments—the hub may even decide on a commitment that may put the firm out of business. The success or failure of each firm then is at the mercy of the specific decisions to which the hub commits, and the hub then can exploit that dependency—getting the other firms to do things they might not otherwise choose, and/or extracting some "pay" for the "service" of choosing to make commitments that benefit the "lucky ones" among them.

So described, planner's power, based on strategically useful, centralized information and the ability to choose among possible key commitments, is clearly present in all formal bureaucracies. For example, in capitalist corporations of any size, or governmental planning bureaucracies (from those of the former Soviet system to those of any level of government in the United

States today), subordinate departments are subject to the power of the home office on precisely such bases. Essentially the same thing is present to one degree or another in business networks in market systems. There the structure is not legally formalized in a way that completely melds the organizations together, but instead is only loosely built on regular buying and selling relationships, stockholdings, and directorship or management interlocks and joint ventures, and buttressed by whatever other power relationships pertain, for example, monopsony power or lender's power.

The upshot is the hub firm's ability to extract benefits from the rest of the networked firms, and to influence to a greater or lesser degree, and more or less at its own discretion, the directions of their activities. Thus the equivalent of what used to be called, in the days of the Soviet Union, "central planning" goes on not merely within large, diversified capitalist firms but also among them. Business networks are present at every level of economic activity, from the financial-hub network of small businesses organized around a small town bank, to those centered around regional or national banks and insurance companies, from the producer-hub network of the "one-company town" to conglomerate-centered international interest groups with radii that span the globe. This is not to say that networks now dominate all market activity to the point that it is best not even to refer to "markets" any longer in the traditional sense of atomistic decision making and supply-and-demand determined prices. However, networks do appear to be sufficient in scope and power that the traditional concept of the "market system" is grossly deficient as a description of how things actually work.

Planners' Power and Local Development

This is perhaps nowhere better exemplified than in urban and regional development, where the role of both financial- and producer-hub networks has been extensively studied by sociologists and business organization theorists and historians. Even a relatively small local development project may be an extremely complex economic process, with a vast variety of different activities needing to be coordinated. Seldom is the process left willy-nilly to the anarchy of atomistic markets.[22]

Consider a sector of truly atomistic, that is, more or less un-networked, market activity, consisting of locally based small businesses in both services and manufacturing, that may be presumed to be present in a city of any size in an industrial nation today—a sector of firms whose economic activity is not primarily determined in networks to which they directly belong. Extending the range of observation somewhat, consider also the surrounding rural area, now including agricultural, forestry, or mining businesses, and so forth, into which this atomistic sector also extends. Some of these businesses may have one degree or another of monopoly or monopsony power within their markets, but presumably most do not. Some may deal in markets extending far beyond the local region, most may not. But even if this atomistic sector is large relative to the regional economy as a whole, it would be a mistake to suppose that the decision making that determines the development of this sector and its city and surrounding region is done according to the traditional model of atomistic markets.

This is so, to begin with, because in principle even a large sector of un-networked, atomistic firms in an advanced market economy must do business directly or indirectly with the *networked sector*. Atomistic firms must sell products to networked firms, or to their employees, managers, and owners, and they and their own employees, managers, and owners must buy goods from them. In fact, many firms in the atomistic sector, perhaps even most, may be completely dependent upon the business of the networked sector, and what is decided in the latter thus significantly influences the development of the atomistic sector, and may altogether determine the shape of much of it. Between the two sectors, the networked sector is the dominant one, and firms in the atomistic sector merely follow the directions of investment and production taken at the initiative of the local economic "powers that be."[23]

The typical urban financial-hub network, clustered around a major local bank (or, these days, a major local branch of a regional or national bank), includes other smaller financial firms (local insurance companies and branches, credit unions, and so forth), real estate developers, and major local construction companies, major local law firms, the local newspaper and other major local media, and major manufacturers. Such networks usually are the real powers that be in city development, although producer-hub networks rule in many cities, especially where the producer firm is a national or international firm employing many local residents. Also, networks' connections with government are extensive: Local, regional, and state government officials often are past or current (or prospective) managers or owners of networked firms or their hubs, and local government consults regularly with representatives of the hub firms, especially on local and regional development planning.

The bank at the center of a financial-hub network, with lenders' power serving to influence its client firms, and in consultation with them and with local government, serves as the center of decision making on local development. Suitable government cooperation with its plans is usually forthcoming: Government is involved early in consultations for one thing; moreover, the hub provides banking services to government, and government's political success depends significantly on the economic health of the hub and its network insofar as they provide a significant portion of its tax base, personnel, and political and financial support. Thus public expenditures, tax breaks, and other cooperation that may be necessary for some development project is already factored into the plans and will generally be forthcoming (barring unforeseen political difficulties such as rebellious neighborhood associations, which are usually more or less easily avoided by careful public relations). Deciding on key financial commitments then (including loans to government tied to the requisite government expenditures), the hub essentially sets the broad contours of local development—directly influencing the networked firms' directions of economic activity. The networked sector then influences the atomistic sector as well by determining much of the latter's business, and of course, the hub probably exerts some additional influence by strategic credit rationing in the atomistic sector.

Note that while I have used the term "influence" here, the sort of power wielded definitely has negative effect on many local businesses and citizens. Just as there are winners and losers among networked firms as the hub makes particular key commitment decisions (as discussed earlier), so too, whatever particular development plans may be made, there will be winners and losers in the atomistic sector. There is definitely an element of domination power involved in this process.

Thus the locus of the decision making that "rules" in urban and regional development is not the local sector of atomistic market activity—that sector is instead better understood to be subservient to the decisions made in the ruling networks. On the other hand, it would also be mistaken to suppose that the local powers that be rule completely at their own discretion. There is always much latitude in decision making among the alternatives available for local development by the hub in urban ruling networks, but the hub and its network are by no means all powerful. This is so because in market systems the local economy is inseparably connected with the larger national and international economies.

First, in general, both the atomistic sector and the networked sector locally have market relations with firms elsewhere: They or their employees and owners buy things from outside, and many local firms export to outside firms or regional markets. Second, networks may be interconnected. For example, a periphery firm in one network may well be a hub firm in another, or a periphery firm may belong to two distinct networks. Thus, local ruling networks are likely to be connected in turn with larger regional, national, or international networks. In particular, banks and other financial institutions, as noted earlier, are themselves knit together in a hierarchy of relationships structured on the lender's power of larger, higher-level banks vis-à-vis smaller, lower-level banks. At the peak of this hierarchy are the largest international institutions, lending to and holding the deposits of smaller institutions of national or regional scope, who in turn have similar relationships with locally based institutions. Indeed, the hub or other of the firms in a local network may well be a subsidiary of a national or international firm, for example, when the financial-hub is a local branch of a larger bank, or when a producer-hub or a network member is a plant subsidiary of a larger company. In either case—formal or informal integration of the local network into a larger entity—the local network's activities are constrained by decisions taken in the larger entity. The contours of the development of a city or region thus quite possibly may be fully determined by decisions taken at the highest reaches of national or international business networks, regardless of the preferences of any of the locals.

The picture that emerges of the capitalist market system in light of a consideration of networks is quite different from that of the atomistic markets model. Beth Mintz and Michael Schwartz have referred to the power of financial institutions as *financial hegemony* and argue quite convincingly and with extensive reference to case studies large and small as well as network, statistical, and other analyses, that the heights of the financial sector essentially rule the system as a whole—not with an iron fist but most definitely in terms of exercising discretion in deciding upon and setting the larger constraints within which the economy operates.[24] There is, in effect, a business hierarchy within which what John Munkirs called *centralized private sector planning* takes place.[25] The summit of the hierarchy is not confined to one specific place, as was that of the old Soviet central planning system, but instead dispersed among the headquarters of the top financial firms. The largest industrial firms are closely networked with them, and in turn, as I have described the hierarchy here, the rest of the economy is networked with these summit networks in a hierarchy descending down to the local level throughout the economy. Government is involved at all levels as well. There is great slack or flexibility in this system—it is after all a *market* system—but it is nonetheless also one of which "central planning" rules the broadest contours.

Afterword: The Corporation and Social Power

A major part of the progressive left movement in the United States has traditionally focused on the economic, social and political power of the private business corporation as a primary source of the social ills of modern times.[26] The indictment of the corporation brought by this movement is serious and grievous, especially today: With its growth in size, adherents are saying, the corporation has gotten way out of hand, and is now in need of radical reform. In the United States, the legally chartered corporation is endowed with most of the rights of the individual citizen, it is a "person" with basically the same rights of free speech and political participation. Thus it may "promote its own thing," that is, advertise its products and lobby in politics for its own interests, with complete impunity, despite its considerable advantages in size and resources over private citizens. Its completely separate existence from those whom it employs means that its public pronouncements and political activities need not at all reflect their views—indeed, its employees, during their time at work in the organization each day, forego most of their own citizenship rights of free speech, press, and assembly.

On top of that, anticorporate advocates point out, its separate existence also from its owners and managers, combined with its unlimited-life charter, give the corporation a kind of immortality, whether it has outlived its original usefulness or not. Its owners' liabilities for its economic and social behavior extend no further than the value of their original direct investments in it, regardless of the extent of its transgressions. Indeed, its own legal liabilities are at present being chipped away even further with new limitations state governments are placing on what may be taken in lawsuits against it. It is a social construction nearly on the order of the state in its bearing on social life—today there are even fully legal corporate-owned towns.[27] Industrial corporations may easily sink large, thriving cities into deep economic depression with "capital strikes" (plant shutdowns and relocations) that are, unlike labor strikes, completely immune from public oversight or regulation. The largest global corporations wield assets greater than the GDP's of most of the world's nations, and can literally make or break entire societies with their investment decisions.

These are considerable charges and not really much disputable: The corporation is indeed a kind of monster out of control. One may argue about what particular things need to be or can be done about it, but behind the smoke screen of corporate self-serving propaganda, the corporation may easily be seen as the most problematic structure of social power in the capitalist world today. To the extent that state power is thought to be out of hand in the democratic nations, it is arguably the *effect* of the overgrown influence that the private corporation has upon the state.

Yet while this book is greatly in sympathy overall with the anticorporate movement and the reforms it advocates, the present chapter raises some misgivings about the focus on the corporation as the "root of all evil." First, the picture drawn in this chapter of networks and the role of financial institutions suggests that the structures of power effective in capitalism are more extensive than even the largest of its corporations. Networks combine corporations into even larger entities that coordinate to one degree or another their members' policies in common. Financial institutions sit at the heads of their corporate networks and, like nonfinancial firms in producer-hub networks, exert true directing power in them. These institutions constitute a structure as least as critical as that of the single corporation itself. Of course, reforming the corporation itself presumably could have great effect on the deleterious power wielded by financial institutions and corporate networks—indeed, the right kinds of reforms could perhaps eliminate it. Nonetheless, the analysis of this chapter hints at the need to go beyond the legal institution of the corporation in order to address the insidious power structures of capitalism.

For, in principle, the fact that the legal corporation is a power structure does not necessarily mean that the corporate structure is the source of the power manifest in it. In general, reforming any power structure may well require also reforming other, separate and distinct power structures that bolster it—thus reforming capitalist corporate power could well necessitate going far beyond the institutions defining the corporation itself. The remaining chapters of this book will show how this is so, and readers will find, I hope, that while the corporation is certainly part of the problem of social power today, the problem itself is the capitalist market system within which the corporation functions.

Notes

1. This is an example of what is known as a "repeated prisoners' dilemma" game in a context of oligopoly. Robert Axelrod, *The Evolution of Cooperation*, shows how, in such games, cooperative rather than conflictual behavior is the most successful individual player's welfare-maximizing strategy.

2. Such vertical integration in the auto industry has been much studied; see Wilson B. Brown, "Firm-Like Behavior in Markets" and Christos Pitelis, *Market and Non-Market Hierarchies*, p. 23.

3. A flagship article on this is Benjamin Klein, Robert Crawford, and Armen Alchian, "Vertical Integration, Appropriable Rents, and the Competitive Process." For critical views on the theory of the role of agency power in vertical acquisition see Frederick C.V. N. Fourie, "In the Beginning There Were Markets?" pp. 50–52; Keith Cowling and Roger Sugden, "Control, Markets and Firms"; and Charles Perrow, "Economic Theories of Organization."

4. On agency problems and legal vertical integration, see the references cited in note 3, above. Note that much vertical *disintegration*, especially in these times, seems to be occurring importantly for purposes of avoiding labor unions and otherwise high labor costs (unions are less easily organized among independent firms than among subsidiaries of a single firm). Bennet Harrison, *Lean and Mean*, pp. 38–41 and chapter 9; David M. Gordon, *Fat and Mean*, chapter 8.

5. Another possible source of the power to do this would be "short-side" power (to be discussed below).

6. On much of the following discussion on the advantages of conglomeration, see Lynn Pepall, Daniel J. Richards, and George Norman, *Industrial Organization*, pp. 447–453; and John M. Blair, *Economic Concentration*, chapter 3.

7. Edward S. Herman, *Corporate Control, Corporate Power*, extensively describes and documents this and other historical trends in market structure.

8. In fact, in a world of perfect markets there would be no need for financial intermediaries in the first place! Note that initial issues in the stock market and other direct security issues constitute only a fraction of total corporate borrowing, a fraction that may increase in good times, of course—the rest of corporate finance comes from banks. Doug Henwood, *Wall Street*, pp. 72–76, gives some recent numbers.

9. See also Table 3.1 in the preceding chapter. Concentration here is calculated from the quarterly report by the Federal Reserve Board, "Large Commercial Banks."

10. Stephen A. Rhoades, "Retail Commercial Banking," p. 182. These numbers are based on banks' deposits rather than assets or sales.

11. The term "equilibrium" then must be reinterpreted for cases of sustained short-side power, of course: Unlike in the usual terminology, a market may be in equilibrium without ever being cleared. See Samuel Bowles and Herbert Gintis, "Contested Exchange," on short-side power in general and in financial markets.

12. Doug Henwood, *Wall Street*, pp. 172 and 193, notes that Keynes believed credit rationing was the rule. See Bruce Greenwald and Joseph E. Stiglitz, "Imperfect Information, Credit Markets and Unemployment"; Corrado Benassi, "Asymmetric Information and Equilibrium Credit Rationing"; and Samuel Bowles and Herbert Gintis, "Contested Exchange," pp. 302–306.

13. This insight is most often associated with Hyman Minsky's theory on businesses' propensity to overborrow and overexpand—see, for example, Sheila C. Dow, "The Post-Keynesian School," pp. 189–200.

14. Major media attention was brought to this issue recently by a Federal Reserve study showing racial discrimination in lending: Alicia H. Munnell, Geoffrey M.B. Tootell, Lynn E. Browne, and James McEneaney, "Mortgage Lending in Boston: Interpreting HMDA Data."

15. Beth Mintz and Michael Schwartz, "Corporate Interlocks, Financial Hegemony, and Intercorporate Coordination"; and their *The Power Structure of American Business*; Linda Brewster Stearns "Capital Market Effects on External Control of Corporations."

16. An excellent introduction to business networks is Bennett Harrison, *Lean and Mean*, chapters 6–8. Harrison argues that some of the increase in informal integration has arisen merely as a replacement for *formal* integration: firms are finding it profitable because it reduces labor costs due to the elimination of unions (ibid., pp. 38–41). More broadly, business networks are a creature of the need for flexibility. Benjamin Gomes-Casseres, *The Alliance Revolution*, presents some additional excellent case studies of networks. See William Lazonick, *Business Organization and the Myth of the Market Economy*, for critical perspectives. Historian Fernand Braudel, *Civilization and Capitalism, 15th-18th Century*, chapter 3, suggests that networks are essential to historical capitalism from its beginning.

17. Benjamin Gomes-Casseres, *The Alliance Revolution*, gives several case studies of hardware and software manufacturers integration in networks, and Bennett Harrison, *Lean and Mean*, chapter 6, describes one as well.

18. Beth Mintz and Michael Schwartz, "Sources of Intercorporate Unity" and "Corporate Interlocks, Financial Hegemony and Intercorporate Coordination," as well as their *The Power Structure of American Business*, chapter 6, give theoretical perspectives. Bennett Harrison, *Lean and Mean*, pp. 150–162, critically summarizes some of the research on the Japanese *keiretsu*, networks held together importantly by fairly small mutual stockholdings.

19. Controlling interest in the stock of a firm may be merely a small portion of its

total outstanding stock, if ownership of the latter is widely dispersed—as little as 2–3 percent or even less may suffice for full control, in principle, if the holder is the largest stockholder and there are no possibilities of rival coalitions among other smaller holders. The Securities Exchange Commission's rule that stockholders with 5 percent or more of the outstanding stock must report their holdings suggests one estimate of the minimum required. See Edward S. Herman, *Corporate Control, Corporate Power*, chapters 1, 2, and chapter 6, and John Munkirs, *The Transformation of America Capitalism*, for extensive discussion of other forms of ties between firms. One firm may thus hold control of another without formally integrating the two into one legal entity. Such cases are illegal under the antitrust law when the two firms are horizontally competing and comprise together a sizable portion of their total market. Some cases in which the firms are vertically related would be illegal also, but most would not. And cases in which the firms produce unrelated or only distantly related products are not at all prohibited.

20. Such one-directional stockholding, in combination with banks' much greater number of directorship interlocks, make a case for the "bank control" hypothesis (David M. Kotz, *Bank Control of Large Corporations in the United States*). Beth Mintz and Michael Schwartz, *The Power Structure of American Business*, chapter 4, gives a critical review; John Munkirs, *The Transformation of American Capitalism*, pp. 60–80, discusses the role of stock-voting rules in this issue. While direct board interlocks between horizontally competing firms may be prohibited by antitrust law, indirect interlocks with banks and other financial (and nonfinancial) institutions are not, and are quite widespread.

21. On what follows, what I will call planners' power, see Beth Mintz and Michael Schwartz, *The Power Structure of American Business*, chapter 5, and "Sources of Intercorporate Unity," pp. 21–22.

22. There is a large literature on power in urban and regional development in which the concept of business and business-government networks is widely appreciated. Keith Dowding, *Power*, pp. 76–88, gives a review, and several of the references cited elsewhere in this book deal at some length with the subject, for example, Beth Mintz and Michael Schwartz, *The Power Structure of American Business*, chapter 8; and G. William Donhoff, *Who Rules America?* chapter 2. Other references include C. Stone, *Regime Politics*, and J. Logan and H. Molotch, *Urban Fortunes*.

23. This two-sector model both imitates and complements that of John Kenneth Galbraith, *Economics and the Public Purpose* and *The New Industrial State*. Galbraith's two sectors were a "planning" sector of oligopolistic firms with market and other power, and an "atomistic" sector of basically competitive firms behaving in the usual textbook manner.

24. Beth Mintz and Michael Schwartz, *The Power Structure of American Business*; and "Corporate Interlocks, Financial Hegemony, and Intercorporate Coordination."

25. John R. Munkirs, *The Transformation of American Capitalism*.

26. David C. Korten, *When Corporations Rule the World*, makes an excellent argument.

27. The town Celebration, near Disney World in Orlando, Florida, is effectively "owned" by the Disney company. See Joshua Wolf Shenk, "Hidden Kingdom: Disney's Political Blueprint."

5

Employer Power

The vast majority of working-age people in modern societies depend for their subsistence on income they receive as employees—from the sale of their labor to businesses, governments, or other institutions. In typical wage-employment contracts (which may be formally written out or merely implicit), what employees actually sell to employers, in exchange for wages or salaries, is their *time*. The employee agrees to do whatever work he is assigned during a workday of specified length, for a specified number of days per week and weeks per year, the rest of the time outside of these specified workdays being the employee's own to do with as he pleases. He sells his time to the employer in the sense that in exchange for a wage or salary he forgoes his own use of his time to his employer, who then does with it what he wishes, subject to whatever legal and moral constraints pertain.

Having agreed to the wage-employment contract and begun their association, either the employer or the employee may terminate the contract and their association at any point. In that sense, both parties are equally free to associate, and wage-labor is thus thought of, in stark contrast to other historic forms, as a kind of "free" labor. Yet there remains a fundamental asymmetry in the wage-employment contract. Forgoing his time to the employer, the employee gives the latter direct *command* over it, just as the seller of any other commodity forgoes command over it to the buyer. The employer, of course, does not forgo any such command to the employee, but merely pays the latter a wage. Giving command over one's time to someone else is equivalent to forgoing command over *oneself* for that time.[1] The heart of the wage-employment contract then is the submission by one party to the command of the other.

Thought of in this way, the wage-employment contract would seem to reflect some sort of underlying power relationship. After all, it is one thing to forgo command over some item that one owns to another person, but why would one forgo command over one's very self unless compelled to? Granted, it is done only for a limited time, and is done in exchange for an "acceptable" wage or salary, but there must be some kind of constraint involved as well: Were alternative opportunities available for people to earn equivalent incomes while working either for themselves or in arrangements that do not involve submission to command, most people would certainly take them. It is their lack of access to any such alternative arrangements for securing labor income that, in effect, compels people to work under others' command. The vast majority of citizens of modern societies would probably agree, on little reflection, that as wage-employees they are subject to their employers' power.[2]

Some would deny that, however—including most mainstream economists, even many who specialize in labor economics, the field in which such matters might be considered. While power relationships necessarily involve command of some sort, the converse logically need not necessarily hold. Thus, mainstream economists conceive the command relationship of wage-employment as one involving true equals, without domination by the side that gives commands. Looking at the employer-employee relationship in this way, with neither side consistently dominating, suggests that the traditional capitalist enterprise of the real world may be understood not as an institution for the exercise of owners' or managers' power over labor, but as one in which workers, managers, and owners meet and contract as equals in a kind of "cooperative association."

Command and the Firm

Thus it may be supposed that the hierarchical organization of command found in firms actually represents a structure that is fully agreeable to all the contractually cooperating parties for purposes of coordinating and administering their income-maximizing collective enterprise. Each individual's specific position in the structure of decision making and command in the firm is determined by how he fits best in the coordinated production processes of the firm, and is decided in a manner fully agreed upon to the mutual satisfaction of the individual himself and all the rest of those associated in the firm. "Best fit" is be judged, on the side of the enterprise, by the criterion of enterprise-income maximization, that being not only the prime indicator of firms' success in competitive markets but also, as noted in the last chapter, the prime source of the funds needed for dynamic competitive investment. On the employee's side, the individual's personal income (or utility) is maximized by, among other things, making his best contribution toward maximizing the enterprise's income.[3] If hierarchical command, rather than some alternative structure for making and executing decisions, predominates in enterprises in market systems, then in this view it must be because such a structure has been mutually agreed upon among all participating parties as most effective for pursuing their goals of income-maximization in such circumstances.[4]

Yet this gratifying picture of capitalist hierarchical command as a fully agreeable and benign form of cooperative administration among equals is difficult to sustain. To begin with, in no essential way does the accountability of those who command labor in capitalist firms resemble that found in organizations that are *consciously* structured to assure democratic decision making and administration. In the latter type of organization, as I will elaborate below, managers are directly elected by and accountable to either constituents over whom they have command or else duly elected representatives of those constituents. Structures of decision making and management selection and accountability are based on well-understood principles of universal suffrage, one-person-one-vote, free speech and assembly, open information, and so forth, the most important intent of which is to assure equal input into decision making and administration for all members of the enterprise. In capitalist firms, on the other hand, employees have no role whatsoever either in processes of decision making or in the selection and accountability of those making decisions and exercising command over them—those things are the exclusive domain of the firm's owners (or, where stockholders lack control, the top management).

Moreover, the idea of the capitalist firm as a collective of equals, with no significant asymmetric power relationships among participants, would seem to belie the actual experience of working people. At no point in the history of the overwhelming majority of capitalist firms have employees ever been asked their preferences regarding the decision-making and administrative structures of their firms—only those few included in top management are ever given any voice in such matters. It is true that members of democratically structured firms may well decide to "go capitalist," but once they do so, at no point thereafter need they, the new firms' wage-employees, be given any similar voice in the decision on whether to remain capitalist or not. And of course, only a minuscule number of existing capitalist firms are historical products of any such "originally democratic" organizations anyway.

There has been in recent decades a much-ballyhooed trend toward greater employee "participation" in decision making in capitalist firms—it has even been widely acknowledged generally to improve labor productivity. Yet the domain in which employees have some voice in decision making in virtually all such schemes is disappointingly small: While it sometimes may include the entirety of the day-to-day operation of the workplace itself—all lower-level decisions—it virtually never includes such decisions as those involving wage and benefit scales, promotions, the selection of production technology and materials, product and product price, and investment (i.e., the higher-level decisions). Participation schemes found in traditional capitalist firms are invariably initiated by management, moreover, and what management gives, management can, and sooner or later usually does, take away.[5] Employee stock ownership plans (ESOPs), for example, while perhaps providing a promising legal and financial framework for democratic enterprises in principle, have been in practice mostly the creatures of managers seeking novel ways of raising capital for their firms.[6]

Finally, not only is there no direct evidence that wage-employees' preferences on the matter have ever been taken significantly into account, the best of the indirect evidence that capitalist firms are nonetheless power-free structures of contractually cooperating, equal individuals is highly suspect as well. Mainstream economists take it as evident that in competitive markets, firms structured along lines of the capitalist command hierarchy have been the most successful, and presumably must represent therefore, among other things, the kind of decision making and administrative structures most preferred by employees: Presumably even if employees' preferences have never been explicitly expressed, their preferences are nonetheless revealed in their individual decisions about which firms to take employment with. Other things being equal, those firms that best fulfill employees' preferences regarding their employers' decision-making and administrative structures ought to be most successful in market competition—they are able to elicit better work from their employees and at cheaper wages than firms less amenable to workers' preferences.

But that argument is critically flawed in its presumption that the most successful firms in market competition are those that best fulfill their employees' preferences regarding structure. Clearly enough, competitive success generally goes to those firms with the most profitability, but it is no more than mere presumption to equate maximal profit with the maximal fulfillment of employees' preferences about anything at all. In fact, a commonsense view of the firm as a power hierarchy would begin by presuming precisely the opposite: That profit is best secured precisely by *denying* the maximal satisfaction of employees' preferences, at least those regarding their wages and the intensity of their work. On such a presumption, the actual evidence of employees' "revealed preferences" about decision making and administrative structures in their firms begs the critical question of why they have had no other alternatives but capitalist firms in which to choose to work.

The Association of Equals

Indeed, there are excellent grounds for supposing that the extreme scarcity of democratic firms in market systems exists despite widespread preferences in favor of working in such firms. This is a most critical point, and worth dwelling upon also to see what firms look like and how they operate when they are actually formed as associations of equals. By no means is this a purely speculative exercise: Along with a tiny but viable sector of democratic small businesses in the United States, there have also been many large and well-documented instances, and a quite substantial theoretical and empirical literature, going back at least to the nineteenth century, is available on the subject. Most notable today are the famous Mondragon network of cooperatives in Spain, the Israeli kibbutzim, and the cooperatives in the U.S. Northwest that, at one point in recent decades, produced fully one-quarter of all the plywood consumed in this country. Even more significant is the example of the postwar Yugoslav economy, a free market system throughout the entire history of which, prior to the unfortunate breakup of that country that began in the late 1980s, democratic "workers' self-management" was required for all enterprises by constitutional law. These examples provide an ample concrete basis for the considerable knowledge that exists about the general principles of democratic enterprise.[7]

The basic rules and principles of democratic association in general are widely understood, of course, and working people who associate as equals would be expected to avail themselves of such principles in the constitution of their firms.[8] In a small democratic firm, both lower-level decision making on day-to-day operation and higher-level decision making on larger issues like investment projects or pay scales could easily take place in periodic meetings of the entire workforce of the firm. A meeting facilitator may perhaps be selected by consensus or vote, and decisions would be made on a consensus or majority vote basis. In a larger firm, periodic meetings of the workforce may still be necessary, but there would also be "managers" for making decisions about and executing day-to-day operations. Managers would either be elected and recallable directly by their constituencies, or else appointed by duly elected and recallable representatives of the latter (the firm's board of directors). They would be subject to continual direct or indirect oversight by their constituencies. Representation may be structured along lines of the usual sorts of divisions within the firm. Procedural rules for decision making and execution would establish the principle of one-person, one-vote, and such critical individual rights as free speech and association among enterprise members would be established as well.[9]

Enterprise members would *join* the firm, with full and equal rights to participate in decision making, rather than being hired as wage-employees or contractors. To sustain such a structure, ownership of the firm must be appropriately constituted. Obviously the usual corporate common stock distribution with voting rights determined by shares owned will not suffice, unless it can somehow be arranged that each owner has equal shares and that the shares are nontradeable. For otherwise some individuals within or outside of the firm may accumulate shares and, correspondingly, voting rights from others (who may sell their shares, for example, for cash needed for momentary personal debt problems). This is one reason why most employee stock-ownership plans do not constitute democratic associations, although it is possible to structure them appropriately by holding worker-owners' shares in a trust managed by a worker-elected trustee. Aside from that possibility, probably the most appropriate business form currently available for democratic enterprise in U.S. law is that of the "cooperative."[10]

In general, new democratic enterprise members might be required to make an initial capital subscription (the same amount for all new members, of course), and then on leaving, for example, for retirement, would withdraw their initial subscription plus, perhaps, an accumulated portion of the firm's retained profit, which may be kept in a special retirement fund. Members would most likely decide upon an unequal compensation scale—for example, with greater pay for managers and directors, for job positions requiring extra education, for workers with dependents, and so forth—and profit shares and accumulations thus may be unequal also.

Since members collectively decide their own compensation as well as the disposal of their profit, it might be supposed that typically they would tend to forgo reinvestment of profit back into the firm, preferring instead to pay themselves more. However, in principle, this is not at all so: Compared with workers in an otherwise equivalent capitalist firm, they could pay themselves more without forgoing any profit reinvestment—simply by taking as compensation that portion of the firm's income that would otherwise go to outside owners and to those managers made unnecessary by worker self-management. Still, wouldn't the workers in a democratic firm nonetheless be motivated to pay themselves even more than that, not only reducing their firm's reinvestment of profit but perhaps seriously jeopardizing its market competitiveness?

In fact, one might expect such firms to do poorly as producers of goods in competitive markets on other grounds as well. To begin with, the difficulty of complex decision making in any enterprise of any size must be compounded when subject to democratic oversight. Thus managers in a democratic firm must have to refer back to their constituencies frequently for support on many decisions, which must considerably slow down the process. Much potentially productive work time must be eaten up in meetings and discussions about things that in a capitalist firm are simply decided upon by an appropriately empowered manager. And considerable anarchy and disorganization must often prevail, eating up additional productive work time. Second, even if workers could handle these problems of decision making effectively themselves, and even if they were well motivated to do so, they could not be expected to be very competent at it. Perhaps it is no wonder that so few such firms are to be found in actual market systems.

Yet these reservations simply do not stand up to scrutiny. First, if anything, workers in democratic firms would be expected to be far better motivated than their counterparts in capitalist firms, where nonmanagerial employees can take no responsibility for their firms since they neither participate in decision making nor share in the rewards and penalties that follow.[11] True, employees of capitalist enterprises do have the same direct and obvious stake in the continuing viability of their firm as do workers in democratic firms, to the extent that in both cases workers in a nonviable firm lose their jobs. But members of democratic firms have a major additional personal stake in the firm's net income, as well as in *all* those decisions that determine it, while obviously employees of capitalist firms do not.

To that extent, labor productivity would be expected to be greater in democratic worker-managed firms than in otherwise equivalent capitalist firms. The members of democratic firms are, in effect, themselves entrepreneurs. Moreover, because the alienated employees of capitalist firms have no particular personal attachment to the productive operations of their firms, inducing them to do the work required necessitates a whole branch of management—specifically, the management of "motivating human resources"—that in worker-managed firms is not needed. In worker-managed firms, there is no need for superiors to dole out the rewards and punishments attendant upon good or poor work: As direct participants in both decision making and profit, workers immediately experience these rewards and punishments anyway. Nor are any superiors required for monitoring their work and correcting them where necessary: Since all of them have a clear-cut stake in the firm, they will mutually monitor and correct each other. Thus those managers who are required in democratic firms need be involved in neither the monitoring of workers nor the doling out of rewards and punishments—they need only facilitate the coordination of the firm's work processes themselves.

And because the workers are closely attuned to the viability of their firm and their own individual and collective roles in assuring it, they would not be expected to expend any more of their resources than necessary in the decision-making processes required for their firm. They would economize on their meetings and discussions, delegate to their elected managers significant decision-making power, and strive for as much self-organization as possible in their work.

Granted all this, the question still remains, would workers in democratic firms be *competent* enough to manage their association as a viable enterprise in competitive markets? Empirical evidence supports the expectation that they would: Labor productivity in democratic worker-managed firms, that is, firm output per unit of nonmanagerial plus managerial labor employed in the firm, apparently generally exceeds that in equivalent capitalist firms.[12] But if working people are competent enough to run their own firms, and would prefer doing so as well, and if democratic firms are more efficient anyway, why then are the overwhelming majority of actually operating firms capitalist? With their greater labor productivity, everything else equal, shouldn't democratic firms be more competitive than their capitalist counterparts, both in producing and selling goods and in attracting workers?

Yet productivity and the preferences of workers do not directly translate into profitability. First, it should be clear that democratic firms are not structured to generate net income for *outsiders*, but only for their member-workers. Beyond the interest on their debt, land rent, and so forth, they yield nothing to any outside owners and cannot therefore attract outside equity capital. They can, of course, always borrow for investment expenditures, but no more than can an equivalent capitalist firm. Indeed, their ongoing creditability is probably less, in fact, since they offer no cushion of net income potentially available for outsiders, of which lenders generally require proof in order to help cover the risk of default, and since their owners, being workers, have less personal wealth to offer as collateral as well.

More importantly, start-up capital is especially difficult to put together when workers must use their own scant savings. The workers in a democratic firm are in effect committing large portions of their savings to a single investment, and accordingly must be either considerably less risk-averse than most people, or else correspondingly better compensated out of the firm's net income, in order to be induced into the enterprise. And while they may well be better compensated on account of the greater productivity of the firm and the workers' access to income that would otherwise go to outside owners, there is no guarantee that the extra income available will be enough to compensate for this greater risk. Thus, especially for a firm that to any significant extent employs capital intensive production, the restricted availability of finance capital, either for start up or for continuing operation later on, is critical. A viable sector of democratic firms in an otherwise capitalist economy would require a different mode of allocating investable capital from that employed by capitalist firms—most certainly some sort of public role in the capital investment process in such a sector would be necessary.[13]

Another factor working against democratic firms in a capitalist economy is the relative unfamiliarity with such firms on the part of all parties concerned, in an environment in which such firms are so rarely encountered. Lenders offer even less finance to such firms than otherwise on account of their relative unfamiliarity with them. Input suppliers are less likely to wish to do business with them when they are not certain of their solvency. Workers, the vast majority of whom are employees of capitalist firms, are profoundly lacking in any background experience in the social and organizational skills required to successfully participate in and run a democratic firm. Thus a sector of democratic firms must reach a kind of threshold in size, relative to that of the larger environment of capitalist firms in which they must operate, in order for there to be a broad enough familiarity among people for them to begin to flourish. In effect, this very tall hurdle must first be jumped *before* a sector of democratic firms can thrive.

Finally, there simply are no supporting institutions of the kind routinely available to capitalist firms. No major business schools teach the science of democratic firm management, clearly a very different kind of management from that of capitalist firms. No government subsidy programs exist to stimulate their growth (the ESOP program, as noted above, is not really aimed at democratizing firms). And no extensive legal system exists to adjudicate the individual and collective rights and responsibilities required in democratic firms—our legal system is solely devoted to the rights and responsibilities pertaining to the traditional capitalist firm. Finally, with owners and managers of capitalist firms having disproportionate influence in business schools, the government, and law, it is unlikely that these institutions would much respond to any but the most resounding popular demand for their support—another considerable hurdle!

Thus democratic firms are relatively rare in market systems not because people prefer the top-down hierarchy of capitalist firms, nor because democratic firms are less efficient than capitalist ones, but because capitalist structures militate against them. There is simply no good evidence then that the hierarchical, top-down command organization of the capitalist firm within which the vast majority of people actually spend their workdays represents anything other than what common sense suggests it is: A power structure to which people submit essentially because most have no alternative. The point may be made most clearly perhaps by considering in detail the *opposing powers of the two sides* of the employer-employee relationship in the traditional capitalist firm.

Employers' and Employees' Powers

To begin with, the employer or her representative (the employee's direct supervisor or the firm's personnel officer) may fire the employee—terminate the firm's contract with the employee and command him to leave the premises. The employee may equally summarily terminate his contract with the firm, of course, but cannot fire the employer or her representative in the sense of ordering her to part from her firm. Thus the employer may part the employee from the means by which he can produce goods or services to sell to support his livelihood, but he cannot do so to the employer.

By firing the employee, the employer may impose great costs upon him, a matter we will consider in detail below. On the other hand, by quitting his job the employee may impose costs upon the employer as well. Besides forgoing for a while whatever revenue or profit is usually associated with the employee's contribution to the firm's production, the employer also must seek and perhaps train a replacement for the lost worker. Of the two sides, however, the employer's would appear the more capable of bearing the costs of having their contract terminated: Again, the employer does not lose access to the means of producing goods or services to sustain her livelihood, while the employee does. Of course, using her firm for production requires workers, but there is typically a much larger pool of replacement workers awaiting jobs, from which the employer may hire, than the pool of job openings available for the former employee (an important matter that I will consider in detail below). And searching among the unemployed for a replacement is generally far easier for the employer—it may be done more efficiently and with more satisfactory outcome—than is the former employee's task of searching for a new job. This is so because (1) the employer may far more easily take advantage of both economies of scale and "learning by doing" in search activities; (2) most of the physical transportation costs of the employer's and employee's search for each other are borne by the worker;[14] and (3) the invariably greater wealth of the employer enables her to more easily absorb the temporary costs in lost revenues from doing without the worker than can the latter weather the costs of doing without the income from a job.

The generally much greater wealth of the employer moreover gives her many other advantages that she may exploit in her relationship with her employee. She is usually better educated and has better access to information on matters of business, finance, and markets, hence is aware of a broader set of available options and can better anticipate relevant events. She is better connected with other potentially helpful individuals and institutions—lawyers and police, government agencies and politicians, and so forth. She may even effectively influence her employee's understanding and preferences about things more easily than can the worker reciprocally influence hers—by influencing the kind of training and education the employee gets both in the workplace and elsewhere, and by influencing the social setting and culture of the workplace and the larger society (as I will discuss in the next chapter).

Thus the commonsense conclusion that it is virtually always the employer who dominates the employee, and not vice versa, is pretty difficult to avoid. Yet workers do have certain powers that sometimes may put them in an at least coequal if not superior position. First is the power of *knowledge or expertise*. The employee has specific and detailed, practical knowledge of the work involved in his position in the firm, knowledge that may be difficult or costly for the employer to obtain for herself. To the extent that the employee is therefore delegated to make decisions about details of the firm's production process, the employer-employee contract involves a principal-agent relationship. The employee then may exploit the same kind of agency power over his employer as that of the doctor or lawyer over his client, as discussed earlier. Thus employees may shirk on the job, or create alternative informal work rules of their own in place of management's, or informally decide for themselves on such matters as product quality or even who their actual supervisors are. On that basis they may extract from their employers a wage or salary premium that amounts to a kind of "payment for honesty"— and otherwise they may still get a better wage by reducing their actual workload. It is even possible, at least in principle, that the employees of a legally constituted, traditional capitalist firm may be its de facto "owners," making and executing or delegating all significant decisions of the firm while the legal owners merely collect dividends on its stock.[15]

Yet this power is generally quite limited. It hinges critically upon the employee having knowledge or expertise that is difficult or costly to obtain, and upon the employer's being unable to adequately monitor the employee's work. Both of these conditions have been greatly undermined in the course of capitalist history. First, contrary to a widespread misconception, while technological development has increased the required skill levels of some workers, for many more others it has *deskilled* their work. Second, where significant work skills remain necessary, managerial science has developed methods of appropriating for managers the knowledge possessed by workers, and of using it to extract even more efficient work from the latter by rearranging work tasks. Third, the development of both technology and managerial science has permitted vastly improved methods of monitoring employees and of assuring in other ways their compliance with managers' commands.[16]

Even where employees lack agency power over their employers, however, they may nonetheless have, second, what may be called the *power of numbers*. That is, if they can act with sufficient solidarity or cooperation they may force employers to bear the major business losses attendant upon a strike or other labor union action (I will describe one recent such event in some detail below). Not only are business owners then threatened with losses of profit and possibly their firm's assets, managers are threatened with job loss (for not being able to manage their workers well enough), creditors with losses of interest income and perhaps asset values, and customers with loss of access to the firm's product. Based on such broad threats workers may coerce from management and owners better compensation or work environments, or even some autonomy in the workplace or influence in the firm's top-level policy decisions. Sufficiently broad solidarity among the employees of many firms in an industry or region may serve to secure such benefits more broadly, and by taking even broader political action employees may, in principle, even alter the terms of the entire society's wage-labor "contract." Such things as the workday and compensation, work environment, and relations with management for the country's whole workforce may be so affected, as well as the particularly crucial policies embodied in "welfare state" benefits for low-income and unemployed workers (to be discussed further below).

It must be emphasized that their ability to accomplish such things rests critically upon employees' solidarity, the primary source of the strength of their organization. The employers' power that workers confront is essentially the power of organization—in employers' firms, in their political and social associations, and in the state—and workers cannot hope to exercise anything like an equivalent countervailing power without at least equally strong organization of their own. But workers' organizations hold together mainly by the autonomous commitment of individuals to their union, a commitment that is easily undermined by the considerable powers employers have over workers as individuals. Those powers give employers considerable capacity to divide and rule workers, that is, to prevent their acting in concerted pursuit of their collective goals, thereby eliminating or at least minimizing the losses with which workers as a group may threaten employers.

Divided, workers may not be able to threaten a successful plant closure, for example, and broader gains or political actions are out of the question if workers cannot sustain coalitions of common interest. The history of labor conflict is filled with instances of the effectiveness of the divide-and-conquer strategy of employers against labor union actions.[17] And employers have found it perhaps even more effective for preventing workers' solidarity at the very outset in the day-to-day operation of their firms, by structuring the latter in ways that minimize the likelihood of workers ever "getting together" in the first place. Thus the finely detailed specialization and bureaucratization of tasks, the elaborate stratification of command giving and status, and the minute specification of pay scales and benefits found in today's corporation derive at least as much from the advantages of having a divided workforce as from any inherent organizational or technological necessity. Indeed the major part of the modern "science of personnel management" consists, whether consciously or not, in the development of a variety of means to attaining those advantages.[18]

Thus even on consideration of the significant powers workers may, under certain circumstances, have over employers, the latter nonetheless generally and decisively dominate. In all of this, the most critical of the various elements constituting employers' domination over workers is clearly their ability to wield against individual employees the threat of firing. That threat is credible only as long as job loss is evidently and significantly costly for employees. That it is quite costly indeed, and some of the ramifications of that fact, are the subject of the next two sections of this chapter.

The Costs of Job Loss

Employees do generally take the commands of their employers dutifully, performing diligently the myriad tasks assigned them in transforming material inputs into final goods and services for their employers to sell, and do so despite having ownership or control of neither the inputs nor the products. They do so most importantly because the costs of not doing so are quite considerable. The most immediate threatened consequence of a failure to perform is demotion or a pay cut, of course, but neither of these might in itself be so upsetting for the typical employee were it not for the additional possibility of ultimately being fired from one's job: For most employees, even near the very top of the job ladder, it is the threat of job termination that most matters.

But what exactly is forgone when one is fired? In an economy of "nearly full employment" cannot most people find other more-or-less equivalent jobs relatively painlessly? If they could, then most of what has been said up to this point in this chapter—and all its implications—would be simply wrong. Employers in that case could not be argued to have any real power over workers. The command hierarchy of firms really would have to be understood, contrary to appearances and common sense, as a form of administration fully and unambiguously agreeable to both workers and their bosses. But, in fact, the costs of being fired are considerable for most employees, and the process of trying to move from one job to another job is not at all painless or a mere insignificant change in the sale of one's wares from one buyer to another.

To begin with, the time one must spend without a job is not negligible—even when the economy is at nearly full employment, the average duration of unemployment is nearly three months, and the actual duration is much more than that for many of the unemployed (Figure 5.1).

Figure 5.1 **Average Duration of Unemployment**

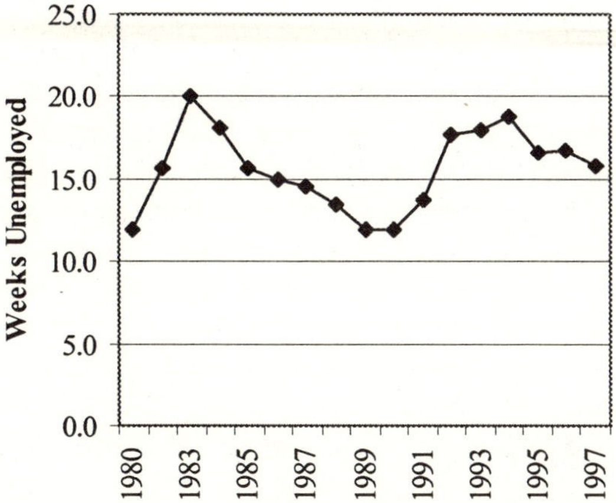

Source: U.S. Census Bureau, *Statistical Abstract of the United States 1998*, Table 677.

During that time, the former employee typically goes completely without a wage or salary (unless she has a second job), along with whatever benefits she had been receiving at work, such as, her employer's contribution to a pension, health and dental care, possibly child care, and so forth. If lucky, she may not need health or child care services during her unemployment. (And if her pension has been vested, she will at least be able to keep her former employer's contributions to it.)

Some people refuse to "lower themselves" to the point of applying for unemployment insurance and other sometimes available benefits (e.g., food stamps), but in an extended such situation, probably most do apply sooner or later. Still, in the United States these days, only about 40 percent of the un-employed typically are eligible for unemployment insurance. The amount of those benefits varies across states, but on average they only replace about 35 percent of the former employee's labor income forgone.[19] Thus while the income immediately forgone by being fired is that much less than the job income itself that is lost, the net of the income forgone even by those eligible for unemployment compensation is obviously no small matter.

Yet that is just the beginning of the total losses the fired employee takes. To the directly forgone income must be added, first, the former employee's direct costs of searching for and moving to a new job, including whatever reduction in income she must take from her former job to her new job. (Moving costs are sizable even if they merely involve a move across town; and with average real wages falling until very recently, the typical new job paid something less than the old.) Second, costs associated with the former employee's "human capital" should also be added in: She may need retraining before she can find another job at all, much less one at an income level commensurate with her previous job, especially if her previously acquired skills are obsolete in the current labor market. Thus she must either pay for the necessary retraining, or else forgo some *future* income.

In some countries a significant portion of the costs of relocation and retraining for new jobs is borne by the state, and in such countries typically unemployment insurance and associated welfare-type benefits are high as well. Other things equal, the costs of job loss are smaller in such countries than they would be otherwise, and the significance to workers of the threat of job loss is accordingly diminished. The social provision for unemployment and job search is therefore an issue of great concern for both employers and employees, and their respective organizations invariably line up in opposition over it. Not surprisingly, the countries where these provisions are greatest are those with the strongest labor unions.[20]

If the prospect of bearing the above direct costs of job loss is not enough to deter an employee from failing to perform at work, she may consider, third, the fact that typically her current employer will be a reference on the resume she must present to prospective new employers: Even if she does not list him explicitly, his testimony may nonetheless be sought or may otherwise affect her reputation. Thus her current employer may be able specifically and even arbitrarily to reduce her future earning potential.

Fourth are the effects on the former employee's nonhuman capital or wealth. If she has accumulated financial savings, she will likely have to spend them down in order to bear relocation and retraining costs, and in order to keep up payments on her debts while paying current living expenses as well. If she does not have any financial accumulation and cannot keep up payments on her debts, then she will lose in a short time whatever equity she has accumulated in the collateral assets (e.g., her title to car and house).[21] Finally, having suffered an income cut, her credit rating is already reduced, and it will be even more seriously diminished by her losing collateral assets for failure to make payments on her debts.

Lastly, the somewhat less tangible psychic costs of job loss should be emphasized. People suffer great insecurity over merely contemplating the direct and indirect monetary costs of job loss already delineated above, and the actual bearing of those costs can be truly traumatic. Even were those costs relatively insignificant, however, the fired employee may lose some of her sense of self-worth, having been told, in effect, that she is worthless to her employer—especially so if she also has trouble finding a new employer. Perhaps the most important of her social relations, moreover—those with her fellow employees, with whom she has spent the greatest part of her waking hours for some time—have suddenly been terminated. If she has to move elsewhere to a new job, her social relations in her larger community have been terminated as well. And others in her family must suffer most of the same things—children may have to be pulled from their schools and friends and may have to forgo college as well, the spouse may have to seek a new job too, and all suffer the trauma of being made to accept drastic and unwanted change in their lives.

Intangible as such costs may be, their effects are tangible and even measurable in terms of such things as health and social behavior. Social statistics on physical and mental illness (e.g., infant mortality, disease and death rates, and hospital and mental institution admissions) are measurably worsened by unemployment and income insecurity. So too is the incidence of both crimes against property and crimes reflecting family stress.[22]

It should be pointed out that for each of these less tangible costs noted here, third parties are also affected. For example, friends' and neighbors' social relations with the former employee and her family have been terminated. Moreover, many of the costs in terms of health and criminality are borne by the larger society as well: They too are clearly external costs. Employers do not, of course, bear any of the intangible external costs—any more than they contribute greatly to their fired employees' bearing the direct costs of job termination. Nor do they bear the specific external costs in terms of health and crime for which they are responsible upon firing an employee, but only their share of that fraction of these costs that is paid through general taxes and government spending on health care and law enforcement. There is rationale on these grounds for requiring something like a "job termination disincentive tax" upon employers when they fire workers.

After all this, the question might nonetheless remain, is employers' power all that serious a concern in most working people's lives? That is, granted the direct costs of job loss to employees are quite considerable, is the threat of job termination so great that many need suffer it very often? Or can most people proceed with their lives reasonably comfortable in the knowledge that their jobs are relatively secure?

First, even if the vast majority feel secure in their jobs, that would not negate the conclusion being drawn here: They may still be quite subject to employers' power, and may feel relatively secure in their jobs merely because they are "performing well" or because "times are good" in their occupation or industry or in the economy as a whole. Second, the likelihood of being unemployed for some significant time during one's career appears to be significant for employees at all levels of income and education (Figure 5.2).

Many economists consider unemployment a relatively insignificant phenomenon in market systems: As we have discussed at several points in this book, they believe that unless there are major interferences in the normal

Figure 5.2 **Unemployment, Occupation, and Education, 1995**

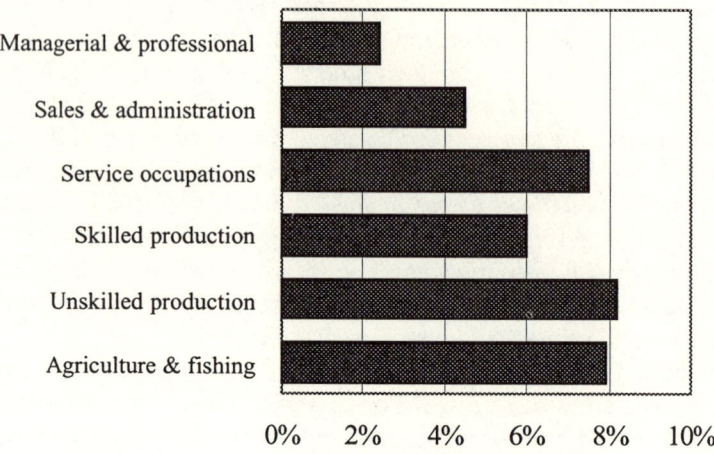

**Percent Unemployed
by Occupation**

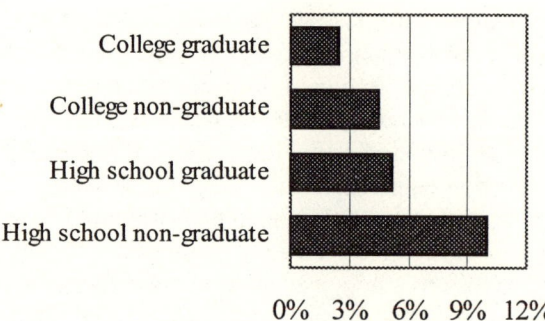

**Percent Unemployed
by Education**

Source: U.S. Census Bureau, *Statistical Abstract of the United States 1998*, Table 680.

operation of markets, there ought not to be serious "disequilibria" such as the excess supply of labor represented by the presence of unemployment. In these terms, the argument made in this chapter then rests upon a *significant rate of unemployment* being more or less perennial in the economy. One may quibble over just how "significant" unemployment actually is, of course, but judging from the statistics it would certainly seem a serious and apparently permanent problem for market systems (Figures 5.3 and 5.4). A full understanding of employers' power requires some account of why this is so.

Unemployment

Neoclassical economists argue that despite appearances there is really little or no systemic unemployment in free labor markets: Unemployment statistics are always significantly positive, but they indicate mostly the people who are voluntarily engaged in a process of searching for appropriate jobs, gradually reevaluating their wage demands in the course of their experience in the labor market until they settle upon an optimal wage-and-job combination.[23] Yet voluntary searching is not equivalent to voluntary unemployment, as the discussion of the previous section should have made clear. Only a small portion of the unemployed are those who have voluntarily quit their last jobs, presumably in search of better ones. Given that one has been fired from her last job, how else would she search for another job than "voluntarily"? Briefly, search theory may well explain the choices unemployed people make as they seek new work, but it does not help much at all in explaining how or why they have been subjected to unemployment itself: The vast majority of the unemployed seem clearly enough to be in that position involuntarily (Figure 5.5).

As students of macroeconomics should know, there is a long-standing and many-faceted debate on the causes of unemployment in capitalist market systems in which theorists from the whole gamut of schools of thought have participated. Within that debate, from the viewpoint of this book two major explanations for systemic unemployment stand out in that they fundamentally involve the concept of power. The first is based on the logic of market dynamics. *Technological change* causes the unemployment of those workers associated with old technologies—and while new jobs are created in association with rising new technologies, there is reason to suppose that, in the absence of an enlightened state policy, fewer new jobs are so created typically than those lost.

If technical change is labor saving (and most economists assume that more or less invariably it is) then unless workers' aggregate purchasing power is rising sufficiently quickly to absorb the increasing output created by a given labor force, some kind of reduction in aggregate employment must occur. Either unemployment per se must rise or else, for example, a decline must occur in the average work week or a lengthening of average vacation time per year, or a shortening of the average employee's work-life by earlier retirement or longer schooling before entering work. And workers' aggregate

Figure 5.3 **Unemployment in the United States, 1890–1999**

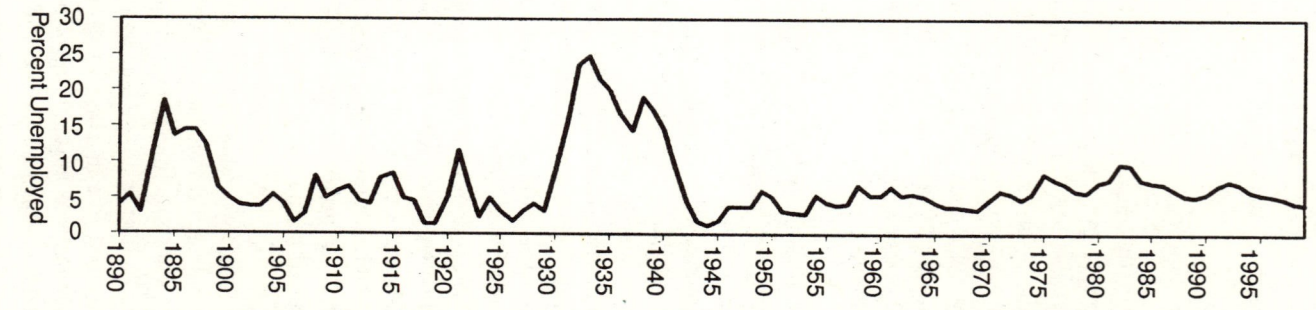

Sources: U.S. Census Bureau, *Historical Statistics of the United States*, *Colonial Times to 1970*, *Bicentennial Edition on CD_ROM*, edited by Susan B. Carter, et al. Cambridge University Press, 1997: Series D 85–86. Bureau of Labor Statistics, "Selected Unemployment Indicators, Seasonally Adjusted," in *Labor Force Statistics from the Current Population Survey*, Table A-5. Web site: http://stats.bls.gov/webapps/legacy/cpsatab5.htm, December 4, 2000.

Figure 5.4 **Unemployment in Industrialized Nations**

Highest, Average, and Lowest Annual Unemployment Rate for the Period 1970–1997

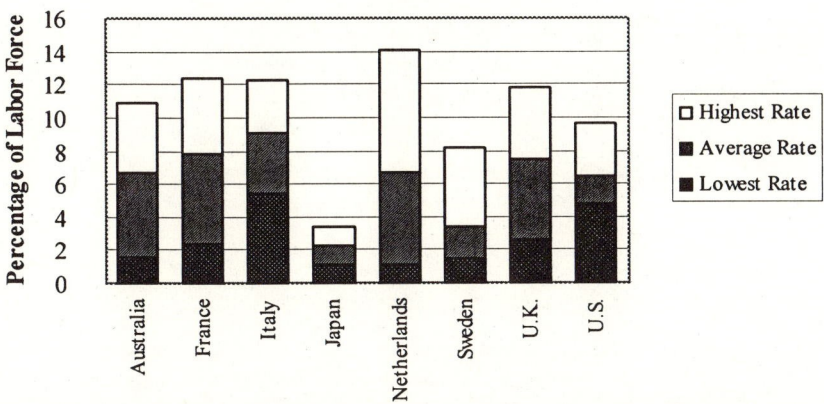

Source: International Labor Organization, Bureau of Statistics, LABORSTA Table 3A, 2000. Web site: http://www.ilo.org/public/english/support/lib/dblist.htm (August 2000).

The top of a bar segment indicates the corresponding unemployment rate, for example, the lowest unemployment for Japan was about 1 percent, its average rate was about 2.5 percent, and its highest was over 3 percent.

purchasing power does not consistently tend to improve in the process of technical change. Indeed, the general tendency may be precisely the opposite: It may tend to fall, in the absence of appropriate state policy, as new technologies generally create lower-skill jobs paying lower real wages.[24]

Moreover, supposing that for some reason the process of technical change did not generate unemployment in this fashion, the dynamics of the business cycle would ensure the requisite amount of unemployment for the sustenance of employers' command over labor. If for whatever reason unemployment were absent or negligible in the economy for some significant length of time, employers' power over labor would be eroded, and unionism and other forms of labor solidarity would expand, workers' compensation would increase, and workers would increasingly take slack time on the job. They would begin to gain some decision-making influence in their firms, and increasingly they would succeed in pushing pro-labor state legislation into effect as their unions gained in strength. The upshot would be diminished profit rates on capitalist investments, and a consequent decline in aggregate investment spending, with immediately increasing unemployment. Logically, the latter increase should continue until employers' power over workers is sufficiently reestablished that adequate profit rates and investment spending may be resumed. Briefly, the level of unemployment on average must be

Figure 5.5 **Reasons for Unemployment**

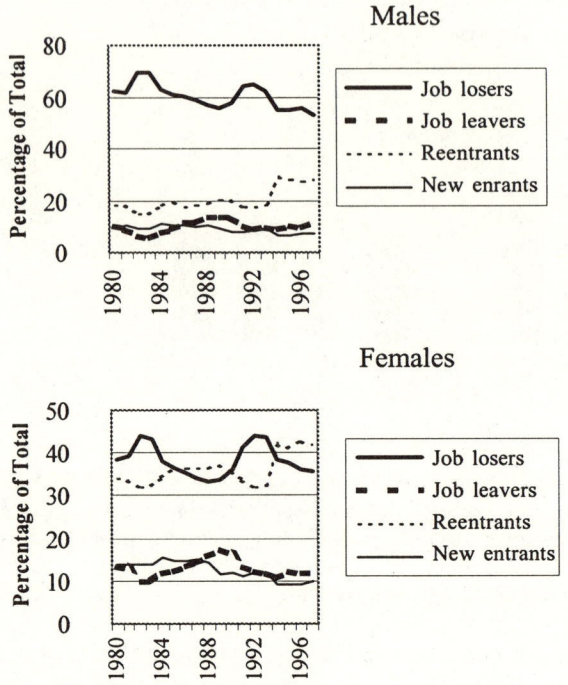

Source: U.S. Census Bureau, *Statistical Abstract of the United States 1998*, Table 682.

roughly whatever is necessary to sustain employers' power in the typical firm sufficiently for an adequate profit rate on capitalist investment.

The second of the two explanations of systemic unemployment that fundamentally involve the concept of power derives from what is known as the *efficiency-wage theory*. In that theory, profit-maximizing firms are seen as using a broad variety of different managerial tools to gain the most labor productivity from their workforces, including their wage and salary scales. Wages are understood to be determined not in accord with a level of labor productivity that is technologically given, but instead to *elicit* the level of labor productivity the firm's managers decide upon. Consequently, wages may be increased above what they would otherwise be, as long as the increase brings sufficiently better quality work from employees (e.g., more careful, diligent, and regular work) that profit is improved by doing so. Workers' pay then is directly related to labor productivity, but as cause rather than as effect. And while there is therefore a direct relationship between wages and labor productivity, workers' pay does not correlate solely with their productivity (e.g., diligence, care, and reliability at work), for it also depends upon what other tools are available to managers in the firm for improving labor productivity. For example, if the costs of monitoring the quality of employees' work in the firm are low, then the firm may simply use better monitoring rather than wage incentives to improve labor productivity.[25]

In the efficiency-wage theory as just outlined, employers' power is not usually referred to explicitly—yet it is implicitly necessary, insofar as firm managers are presumed able to set wages. In their own very different elaboration of this theory—in what they call the contested exchange model—Samuel Bowles and Herbert Gintis emphasize employers' power directly as a fundamental part of the story of efficiency wages: Singular among the several distinct incentive effects of efficiency wages on workers' productivity is the definite threat of a loss of economic welfare for a worker in the event he is terminated from the job.[26]

To see this, it is necessary first to note that the labor market clearing wage is equivalent to what may be called the sign-on wage. The latter is that which elicits a number of people willing to sign on to the *specifiable* terms of the wage-labor contract offered by employers that is just equal to the number wanted by those employers. Because the terms of the wage-labor contract cannot specify in advance the particular quality or efficiency of employees' work—only the basic requisites of their showing up and offering to take whatever commands managers give them—the sign-on wage is that which, in effect, elicits merely the number of workers that managers wish to show up at the front door. But of course, managers want workers to do more than merely show up: They want work and diligence, quality, and so forth, and are willing pay a premium for it. The actual wage paid by employers therefore includes an efficiency premium above the sign-on wage—hence exceeds the market-clearing wage. Unemployment necessarily follows, of course, and with it the manifest threat of job termination and consequently employers' power. Thus do employers get diligence from their workers by creating (presumably unconsciously) a situation in which the latter are subject to a credible threat of loss if they do not provide it.

But is there not some customary notion of an acceptable level of work efficiency on the job? If so, then that notion would be implicit in the standard wage-labor contract, and since workers would then be offering for sale a promise to work at a customarily acceptable level of efficiency, an efficiency premium above the sign-on wage would be unnecessary: The efficiency wage would be the same as the labor market-clearing wage. There may well be some such socially acceptable level of efficiency, but the actual level of efficiency with which a worker performs her particular job remains nonetheless inherently unspecifiable both prior to and during her work. This is so because workers' actual efficiency on the job is contested: Employers and employees have contending interests in how diligently the latter work. Each side of the exchange will act against the other's interest with regard to the quality of the employee's actual work, and the quality of the work done is the outcome of the two parties' continuing contest in the course of production. Without a continuing managerial effort to extract good work from employees, the latter then will invariably make only the barest minimum effort at production—hence no more than that minimal effort can be implicitly offered in the wage-labor contract. The market-clearing wage then, that which brings forth just the number of workers that employers want to contract to work, is a zero-effort wage, but management wants effort, and pays some premium to get it.

The efficiency-wage/contested-exchange explanation of systemic unemployment is complementary with the technology/business-cycle explanation, and taken together the two theories provide a most convincing story about how the labor market works in real-world capitalism. The empirical evidence that labor markets are perennially in glut is straightforward enough, as discussed earlier: Significant unemployment—a greater number of people seeking to sell their labor to buyers than the latter wish to employ at going wages—apparently always exists. With unemployment so visible, those who are employed are threatened with the possibility that they too might suffer more or less major losses of economic well-being. In their position as the owners or managers of firms' assets, employers thus have real power over workers on this basis, workers being generally unable to reciprocate any similar threat. Thus are employers able to command their employees, and to extract benefits from them in the form of profits for their firms. The issuing of orders by employers to workers in capitalism is, to that extent, therefore no different from that found in the cruder structures of labor command of earlier times: it manifests a clear-cut, nonreciprocal, threat-based power structure. And profit, whose amount therefore consists at least partly of benefits extracted in a relationship of domination by employers over workers, is to that extent essentially akin to the benefits extracted in any other domination relationship: It is at least partly the fruit of *exploitation* as defined earlier in this book.

Employers' Power on the Rise

This perspective sheds light on important recent economic developments at the national and international levels. In effect, an enhancement of employers' power over labor is occurring, with momentous consequence for working people and for the functioning of the economy. The decades following World War II were exceptionally good times for working people in the United States, but the widespread affluence to which they then became accustomed has begun to appear increasingly tenuous in recent years. The primary source of this erosion in working people's circumstances may be said to lie in "globalization," the latest chapter in the centuries-long expansion of the capitalist market system's envelopment of the world economy.

As discussed earlier, technological changes have, especially in the post–World War II world economy, served to knit more closely together than ever before productive activities of all countries. International transportation and communication costs have fallen enormously, permitting not only the competition of a greater number of producers in any given product or regional market, but also changes in production processes that have increased the degree of international specialization in the production of many major goods. Not only are there more automobile companies, for example, but the production of a typical automobile model today is accomplished by hundreds of independent enterprises or corporate subsidiaries all over the world. For the new technologies afford greater intensive and extensive control over production, that is, increasing control not only over production activities within each enterprise or subsidiary but also over related but distant production units in business networks. Finally, on account of these changes, both physical and financial investment capital have become far more mobile than in earlier times, and production accordingly may be relocated across borders with much greater speed and cheapness.

From the end of World War II through the Vietnam War, both unionized and nonunionized labor had experienced a rapidly rising standard of living based on a strongly growing, nearly full-employment economy. The latter was fueled by Keynesian policies of high military spending for the Cold War, relatively strong fiscal commitments to redistribution and welfare, a durable "accord" between organized labor and big industry, and stable and strong international economic relations among the Western countries.[27] By the beginning of the 1960s, however, business' profitability had become increasingly difficult to sustain at levels to which they had become accustomed: A serious "profit squeeze" had begun on average profit rates on production and investment. Increasing competition in international markets from producers in the reestablished economies of Western Europe and Japan, and the consequent collapse of the post–World War II "Bretton Woods" system of international exchange—followed by the further stressing of international relations with the rise of the Organization of Petroleum Exporting Countries (OPEC) oil cartel—were prime factors. Competition between firms had been heightened, and firms found themselves not only facing more international rivals but also needing to attend more closely to their own decisions on the international location of their various operations.

The other side of the squeeze was an increasing pressure on unit labor costs of production due to the sustained period of full employment, especially during the Vietnam War, and the strengthening of the welfare "safety net" and related benefits. These had the effect of lessening the likelihood of job termination by employers, as well as the cost of job loss for employees, thus undermining employers' ability to extract the quantity and quality of work they expected from their labor forces. Thus not only was business profitability squeezed on the revenue side by increasing international competition, it was also affected on the cost side by increasing unit labor costs as wages and benefits rose while labor's productivity at work lagged behind.

The upshot of this squeeze on profit was a reaction that led to a twofold retrenchment from the relative liberalism of the postwar period toward a kind of pre–Great Depression economic conservatism. In the public sphere, first, the Federal Reserve began a stringent "monetarist" policy of tight money and credit that eventuated in a major recession in the early 1980s, with high unemployment continuing for most of the rest of the decade. At the same time, the federal government, under Presidents Reagan and Bush, began a period of rollbacks of welfare-state fiscal policies and attacks on organized labor. (Reagan's famous firing of the Professional Air Traffic Controllers Organization (PATCO) strikers and hiring of permanent replacements was one of the first momentous acts taken in his administration.)[28] Together these reactions in the public sector had the direct effect of increasing the cost of job loss for employees, as well as their perceived likelihood of being fired, strengthening employers' power over workers while undermining unions' ability to resist it at the same time.

In the private sector, second, businesses' efforts had similar effect. With the support of the federal government, they began to take a more aggressive stand in their relations with unionized labor, more boldly going on the offensive in ways both legal and illegal. They relocated to the more antiunion South, where American labor was cheaper. They took advantage of developing investment opportunities in the mostly nonunionized "service sector," where labor was similarly cheap. They turned increasingly to the use of "contingent" labor, for example, part-timers or temporary employees whose wages and benefits were less than full-timers,' or else competitive, nonunionized subcontractors, whose employees were similarly lower paid. And, of course, subject to increasing international competition in a more globalized economy, they also searched farther and wider for foreign cheap labor than ever before.

The upshot of all this was a substantial improvement in business profits but, of course, at the expense of workers, who increasingly found themselves in competition with other cheaper prospective employees not only at home but in distant countries. For when firms are subject to greater competition from imports, the likelihood of their employees' job loss is accordingly increased; when firms are also more ready to relocate either at home or abroad, that increases even further the likelihood of layoffs. Both unionized and non-unionized workers were increasingly asked, in effect, to renegotiate their compensation in light of either their employers' diminished ability to pay it or their employers' improved access to cheaper labor elsewhere. The threat of losing their jobs was all the more powerful, of course, in circumstances of higher unemployment and a weaker safety net. And the shift to the service sector and the increased use of contingent labor further increased the cost of job loss by undermining the wages workers could expect to get in the new jobs they got after being laid off. "Concession bargaining" of their compensation then became the norm, not only in unionized firms but for nonunionized workers as well.

Most recently, through the 1990s, some of this decline in the position of workers vis-à-vis their employers has been ameliorated, at least in the United States, since here unemployment has been declining. Yet even with the corresponding declines in the threat of job loss—as of this writing, the national unemployment rate is at a thirty-year low—average workers' real pay and benefits have failed to recoup the losses they took after the mid-1970s. Even mainstream economists now conjecture that the "natural unemployment rate" has declined, since inflationary pressures seem simply nonexistent even at very low unemployment.[29] If such a decline has occurred, it is likely the consequence of the enduring increase in employers' power that has developed over the last two decades. Even with low unemployment, workers still perceive a relatively high threat of job loss, for they are subject more than ever to competition with cheaper labor at home and abroad in a world of hypermobile capital—partly the result of supposedly pro-labor government policies of President Clinton's administration (e.g., the North American Free-Trade Agreement [NAFTA]). And they lack bargaining power due to both a high cost of job loss and a lack of organized support in labor unions: The welfare-state safety net remains significantly weaker than in earlier decades—also partly the result of the Clinton administration's policy (i.e., in welfare reform). Perhaps most worrisome of all, unions are now substantially weaker than at any point in this century in the United States: Less than one in ten private-sector employees in the United States today belong to unions.[30]

A Strike

While the decline of labor union membership may, of course, be looked at as one of the causes of the deteriorating position of workers vis-à-vis their employers, it is equally importantly a *consequence* of the same underlying set of developments. Layoffs and concession bargaining among unionized employees eviscerate labor unions, as they not only lose existing members but lose their attractiveness to potential new members. And government anti-union policies have their intended effect. Unions' capacity to pose a threat to employers thereby diminishes accordingly—both in those firms who employ their members and in other firms employing nonunionized labor but potentially subject to unionization—which of course further exacerbates the decline of unions' reputation as an effective organization in the eyes of working people. Both unionized and nonunionized working people thus lose with the decline of unions.[31] When a large, effective, and successful nationwide strike occurs in a major industry under such circumstances therefore, it is an occasion for considering whether perhaps some reversal of this downward spiral may be in the works. Such was the case in the two-week strike by the Teamsters Union against United Parcel Service (UPS) in 1997.[32]

UPS was in some ways immune to the difficulties businesses began experiencing in the late 1960s described above: As a delivery system with great economies of scale it enjoyed some of the elements of a natural monopoly. Yet it did have some competition in its domestic market (from Federal Express and some smaller deliverers, as well as the U.S. Postal Service) and in its foreign markets as well. It was never threatened with going under, but with this competition and the increase in fuel costs after 1973, and given the pressure on unit labor costs in the late Vietnam War era and the relative labor intensiveness of UPS operations, it too increasingly explored opportunities for labor cost cutting.

The company was unable to directly "bust" the union to which most of its employees belonged, the Teamsters, with bargaining for union concessions, nor would other tactics (e.g., union decertification elections or firing union leaders among its employees) have been expected to work very well as they had in other types of industries. For one thing, the Teamsters remains a most formidable union in the strength of its members' allegiance to the union, this despite decades of media coverage of the union as an organization permanently tainted by the corruption scandals among its leaders in the 1960s and 1970s. Its members' strong commitment to the union derives from a more fundamental source of strength relating to the particular occupations in which they work. As employees of transportation systems, the threat of striking that they can exert is often considerably greater than that of employees in other industries, since a broad diversity of unrelated producers and consumers may be hurt by a lack of transport, hence far greater pressure can be brought to bear on the management of their firms. Equally critically, their employers cannot use the threat of relocating operations to cheaper sources of labor, as can producers in other industries whose locations are not in themselves essential to their production (e.g., automobiles). Thus the union's "strike card" can be significantly more threatening to employers, the union is accordingly more effective in pressing their interests, and Teamsters members consequently have been among the most loyally pro-union in the country.

Yet the Teamsters corruption scandals of the 1960s and 1970s had been a major setback for its members' interests, and their solidarity was significantly less than it could have been. Not only did the media harp on the affair continually, but the affair was itself indicative of a leadership not totally committed to members' welfare. To some extent, the decline in membership that the Teamsters Union experienced during the 1980s was, like that in other unions, on account of disaffection with a bureaucratic unionism that was not only less effective in pushing members' interests, but also perhaps vulnerable to corruption. A movement had arisen from within the union—the Teamsters for a Democratic Union—aimed at pressing organizational and leadership changes that would make the union more actively responsive to members. As unions in general were increasingly threatened by the developments of the 1980s, this movement gained clout among the Teamsters, and its activist attitude on rejuvenating unionism broadened within the entire AFL-CIO. Ron Carey, one of the activists and a former UPS driver, was elected Teamsters president in 1991 in the first secret ballot election in that union's history, and immediately undertook a major cleanup of the union's national and local leadership. John Sweeney, another from the activist camp, was elected president of the AFL-CIO in 1995.

Narrowly reelected in 1996 against James Hoffa, whose father had been at the center of the Teamsters scandals, Carey led the union in the strike against UPS. The strike had extremely strong support from the membership, and was backed as well by the AFL-CIO's much needed $10-million contribution to the Teamsters' strike fund: At $55 a week for each of its 180,000 strikers, the union's $17-million available assets fell considerably short. (The company, on the other hand, was financially very strong, with a $4.5-billion credit line.) UPS had instituted a number of "speed-up" changes since the 1970s, and had one of the worst occupational safety records of any firm in the country. It was, moreover, gradually increasing its employment of nonunionized contingent workers—up to 60 percent of its workforce in 1997 were part-time or temporary (quite a few part-timers were actually working full-time or more as well). It was also increasingly turning to nonunionized subcontractors for routine deliveries. This was, of course, primarily to save on labor costs, but also has the added benefit of "dividing and conquering" workers and the labor union—for contingent workers and subcontractors may well be looked at much the same as union members look at "scabs," that is, as outsiders unwilling to participate in union solidarity (but willing to accept the benefits of better compensation achieved by the union) and competing as well for the same jobs as the full-time, permanent workers in the union.

The company's offer in the strike negotiations demanded a number of union concessions, but being virtually shut down in its operations during the strike, it apparently was forced to back down from most of them. At one point during the strike the company was considering hiring permanent replacement workers for the strikers—a move that would have greatly escalated the conflict in this case as elsewhere. The company's final concession to the union on contingent workers—that it would stop subcontracting except in peak seasons and create 10,000 new full-time jobs into which it would move part-time employees—seems a small capitulation given the extent of its contingent workforce. Significant, however, is the fact that the union apparently deliberately bargained for the nonunionized part-time workers: In addition to securing full-time jobs for some of them, it also got them far greater pay increases, more on a par with those of the full-time workers, than the company was offering, as well as an increase in the minimum guaranteed hours of work per week. While falling well short of eliminating the problem of contingent labor at UPS (obviously a problem for both contingent and full-time workers!), this represents a progressive stand that the older union would never have taken and recognition of the intertwined and common interests that full-time and unionized workers share with contingent and non-union workers.

Since then the Teamsters have continued their momentum: They successfully took a complaint to the National Labor Relations Board (NLRB) against Anheuser-Busch on that company's use of contingent labor. They organized toward Teamsters' Union representation for Federal Express Company workers. And they successfully pressed without a strike for compensation improvements for drivers of automobile-hauling companies (a segment of the trucking industry that is strongly unionized—many other truckers are nonunion, especially the large sector of "independents"), and prevented those companies from subcontracting with Mexican-owned and -operated trucking companies. They successfully stifled a UPS-attempted worker participation scheme, arguing in a suit before the NLRB that its purpose was to undermine workers' bargaining strength. All this has occurred under the leadership of James Hoffa, who won the union presidency after federal authorities ruled Ron Carey's win in 1996 invalid on the basis of financial irregularities (of which Carey himself seems to have probably been innocent—incidentally, Hoffa's campaign finances have also been under investigation). Will Hoffa's leadership, under pressure for greater responsiveness to the membership, keep up the momentum? Will the union continue branching out to more organizing drives among nonunionized workers? Will the AFL-CIO and its other affiliates continue their more activist direction?

It is possible that if the lower unemployment prevailing at this moment continues, the tide of labor unions' fortunes may turn, as workers both organized and unorganized find themselves in a stronger bargaining position. Yet these are different times from the post–World War II decades, and while some improvement in bargaining position would certainly follow on continuing strong employment, with its greater mobility and its apparently better access to government and the media, business may still keep the upper hand. A hard core of unions will almost certainly remain, even if all the rest disappear at some point in the future, and these lucky ones will likely succeed in protecting their members' fortunes. Perhaps the critical question will be whether organized labor will then be able and willing to lend much help toward the larger political efforts that will be necessary to reverse the present broader course of things.

Notes

1. Thus wage-labor differs formally from indentured servitude only in the specification of the time period during which the "buyer" has command over the "seller."

2. Studs Terkel, *Working*, is filled with working people's expressions of this observation.

3. This account of individual behavior in such an enterprise is consistent with the neoclassical explanation of personal income inequality as the consequence of differences in the "value" of individuals' (marginal) contributions, the latter being determined in the combined processes of market competition and individual-firm contracting described here.

4. Armen A. Alchian and Harold Demsetz, "Production, Information Cost, and Economic Organization" is the flagship academic article on this view of the firm as a team. This and related views are well criticized by Charles Perrow, "Economic Theories of Organization."

5. The collection of works in Jon D. Wisman, *Worker Empowerment*, covers many of the alternative variations on worker participation from a sympathetic viewpoint. Also Paula Voos, "Employee Involvement and Representation" is a good introduction. Samuel Bowles, Herbert Gintis, and Bo Gustafson, *Markets and Democracy*, is an excellent theoretical treatment.

6. David Ellerman, *The Democratic Worker-Owned Firm*.

7. A good introduction to ESOPs and cooperatives in the United States is Ramon Vela Cordova, "Why Economists Are Wrong about Coops"; and Corey Rosen and Chitra Somayaji, "Economy in Numbers" In addition to those references cited in note 4 of chapter 1, see also John Wisman, *Worker Empowerment*, and David Ellerman, *The Democratic Worker-Owned Firm*.

8. See Robert A. Dahl, *On Democracy*.

9. Some sort of allowance would also be specified for fission of the firm into smaller units (which would then behave as independent firms, probably contracting

with each other) if the members decide. Note that the one-person, one-vote rule is obviously required for *democratic* structure, but not necessarily for *participatory* structure: In principle, votes could alternatively be allocated by income level or even by shares of ownership, although in the latter case if workers own little or no stock, the firm is actually capitalist, of course. Many of these sorts of basic distinctions are summarized by Charles Rock, "Workplace Democracy in the United States."

10. The main shortcoming of ESOPs with regard to democratic representation of workers is that the trusts are managed by and responsible to appointees of the firm's management, not representatives of the workers.

11. In fact, in accordance with traditional "Taylorist" management principles, workers typically do not even participate in decision making about how to do their own work! Harry Braverman, *Labor and Monopoly Capital*.

12. Most studies indicate higher labor productivity with worker participation, and especially with worker management. See David Schweickart, *Against Capitalism*, pp. 99–103 for discussion of the issues and literature, and Malcolm C. Sawyer, *The Challenge of Radical Political Economy*, pp. 65–75, for broader perspectives.

13. In Yugoslavia, of course, investment capital was obtained from the state; in Mondragon, it is pooled from the entire network of cooperatives and parceled out to those individual cooperatives needing it.

14. Scale economies and economies due to learning-by-doing in these search activities are considerable for firms of any size, but for workers may be somewhat significant only for those who have very frequently had to change jobs. Note also that it is probably easier for an employer to survey and certify the relevant attributes of a prospective employee than it is for an employee to similarly ascertain the relevant information about a prospective employer.

15. See Charles Perrow, "Economic Theories of Organization" for summary and critique of the view that this "agency" power of workers is very significant. Also Michael Burawoy, *The Politics of Production*, for an argument that workers in fact widely use such power.

16. For example, in computer- and telephone-using jobs. Note that production technology and managerial science would likely not have developed along such lines historically had wage-workers been in the dominant position in the first place—see Stephen Marglin, "What Do Bosses Do?"; Harry Braverman, *Labor and Monopoly Capital*; and Richard Edwards, *Contested Terrain*.

17. Jeremy Brecher, *Strike!* is a very nice history, with plenty of accounts of the divide-and-conquer strategy, from a viewpoint strongly sympathetic with labor.

18. Richard Edwards, *Contested Terrain*. Other divisions of the workforce such as those along lines of race and sex also fit very well this model.

19. U.S. Census Bureau, *Statistical Abstract of the United States 1998*, Tables 618, 619, 683, and 766. See Juliet B. Schor, "Class Struggle and the Macroeconomy" for an estimate of the total cost of job loss in terms of forgone income.

20. Because obviously economywide supply-side benefits accrue to a more generous provision of these things—in the form of a more mobile and better trained labor force—the reasons why they are not better provided should be sought in their adverse effects on employers' power. See the collection of essays in Richard B. Freeman, *Working Under Different Rules*, for discussion of several dimensions of these differences between the U.S. and European labor environments.

21. Note that those most frequently suffering job termination have little or no savings with which to help bear all of this. That is one of the primary reasons for the racial wealth gap in the United States being greatly out of proportion with the income gap: Blacks are unemployed so much more often than whites that their wealth gets spent down before it can accumulate. Family income for blacks is, on average, 54 percent that of whites, while the net worth of the average black family is only 12 percent that of the average white family. Edward N. Wolff, *Recent Trends in Wealth Ownership*, Table 6.

22. See, for example, John W. Lynch, George A. Kaplan, and Sarah J. Shema, "Cumulative Impact of Sustained Economic Hardship on Physical, Cognitive, Psychological, and Social Functioning"; also, International Health Program, "Health and Income Equity."

23. Job search theory is a basic element of mainstream economics today. See Steven A. Lippman and John J. McCall, "The Economics of Job Search: A Survey," and Theresa J. Devine and Nicholas M. Kiefer, *Empirical Labor Economics: The Search Approach*. Note also that the official unemployment statistics significantly understate the true extent of unemployment by excluding both "discouraged" jobseekers no longer actively looking for work and part-time employees seeking full-time work—these are now estimated and reported by the Bureau of Labor Statistics, but not greatly publicized. See Bureau of Labor Statistics, "Range of Alternative Measures."

24. If workers' income is not rising sufficiently, then an increase in investment as a share in aggregate spending must occur in order to prevent rising unemployment. In the short run such an increase may be feasible—via debt expansion, etc.—but in the long run it must be limited to the extent that consumption demand as a portion of aggregate income is limited by workers' income, since that is the primary source of the demand for the products to be produced by the new capital stock (factories, offices, etc.) upon which investment spending is made. The post–World War II experience of real wages rising in tandem with labor productivity—hence bolstering aggregate consumption demand and the economy as a whole—in this view, would be seen as an exceptional phase in capitalist history, as I will explain further below. See for example, Malcolm C. Sawyer, *The Challenge of Radical Political Economy*, chapter 11, and Howard J. Sherman, *The Business Cycle*.

25. George Akerlof and Janet Yellen, *Efficiency Wage Models of the Labor Market*.

26. Samuel Bowles and Herbert Gintis, "Contested Exchange: New Microfoundations"; see also the other articles in that special issue of *Politics and Society* devoted to a discussion of Bowles and Gintis's theory. See James Rebitzer, "Radical Political Economy and the Economics of Labor Markets" for some earlier background on their work.

27. Some references for the following discussion on the post–World War II growth regime and its decline include the collection of essays in Michael A. Bernstein and David E. Adler, *Understanding American Economic Decline*; Michel Aglietta, *A Theory of Capitalist Regulation*; Alain Lipietz, *Towards a New Economic Order*, chapters 1–6; Malcolm C. Sawyer, *The Challenge of Radical Political Economy*, chapters 11 and 12; David M. Gordon; Thomas E. Weisskopf and Samuel Bowles, "Power, Accumulation, and Crisis"; and Howard J. Sherman, *The Business Cycle*.

28. Jeremy Brecher, *Strike!* chapter 9; Patricia Cayo Sexton, *The War on Labor and the Left*.

29. Jeff Faux, "The Fed's Unnecessary Assault on Wages"; Lawrence Mishel, Jared Bernstein, and John Schmitt, "Finally, Real Wage Gains."

30. U.S. Census Bureau, *Statistical Abstract of the United States 1998*, Table 712.

31. The positive spillover effect of unions on nonunionized workers is widely understood: Nonunionized firms pay higher wages in unionized environments, partly to attract labor from higher paying jobs elsewhere, partly to "bribe" employees to eschew unionization. Howard M. Wachtel, *Labor and the Economy*, pp. 142–144.

32. On the UPS strike, see Jeremy Brecher, *Strike!*, pp. 358–362.

6

Purchasing Power

Recall the three distinct meanings of power considered in earlier chapters: Accomplishment or the power to do things, influence or the power to affect people, and domination or power over people. In those terms, most would agree that purchasing power is the primary constituent in people's powers of accomplishment in market societies. Indeed, in such societies, virtually all aspects of an individual's personal and social accomplishment depend crucially upon the particular kind of power that is conferred by having access to money in the form of income, wealth, or credit. The material goods and services people require for the pursuit of their goals and activities are mostly available only by means of purchase in markets—what few goods and services remain not yet completely commoditized are, in the most advanced capitalist societies, left for provision by what is, in these times, an increasingly tenuous public sector that provides only the most essential minimum of education, health care, transport, insurance, and some forms of recreation.

Thus, judging from the actual distributions of personal income and wealth, there is in capitalist market societies an enormous inequality in people's abilities to fulfill their material and other needs, to develop and pursue their personal faculties and aspirations, and to sustain whatever relationships with others are necessary for their existence as social beings. Yet while economic inequality manifests a great disparity in people's powers to do things, it may not follow directly that it represents also any major disparity in people's abilities to attain and exercise positions of power in the critical sense of the term with which this book is most concerned, domination power. Most mainstream economists would agree that economic inequality is equivalent to inequality in people's powers to accomplish things, and perhaps to influence others, but would stop well short of accepting that it therefore constitutes also a form of power *over* others.

But purchasing power is an essential element in structures of domination in market systems, and to see what is wrong with the viewpoint of mainstream economics on this, we need to consider first the related and even more erroneous view of what I call the "perfect equality model" of market systems. This model represents a way of thinking about purchasing power that is often apparent in popular discourse on free markets, both in the mass media and in daily conversation. Among economists, those inclined toward an extreme advocacy of laissez-faire market systems—Austrian and new classical school economists and other libertarians, even some neoclassical economists—venture quite close to the thinking represented in this model, though few would go so far as to attempt to support it explicitly. The model states that contrary to most people's intuitions about the appearance of significant economic inequality, the reality is that market systems accord great equality to people's powers of accomplishment. Alternatively, other things equal (i.e., inborn personal characteristics and abilities), in market systems people with vastly different purchasing power may nonetheless accomplish similar goals: Purchasing power inequality itself is not equivalent to inequality in the power to do things.

The Perfect Equality Model

This is so, it is said, because while purchasing power itself is obviously greatly unequal, *access* to it in a free market system is roughly equal among all market participants—or at least, with only very little enlightened public interference in markets, can be made so easily enough that it is not an issue. Assuming a minimal such public policy, in a market system people can, with nearly equal ease, obtain whatever amounts of purchasing power they may wish, within limits imposed only by their inherent talents or aptitudes, regardless of their prior material circumstances.[1] The objective sources of purchasing power are equally available to all who have any innate aptitude for it: (1) all are equally free to choose occupations from which they may earn *labor income*; (2) for those who wish, wealth is equally easily amassed, and *property income* therefore is equally easily available as well; and (3) *credit* for whatever amounts of purchasing power people may wish beyond what they possess at any particular moment, is equally available too. On this line of thinking, the rich person's seeming privilege of great purchasing power compared with the poor person's is only apparent, for the latter can, if she chooses, through normal processes of market transaction, attain similar riches herself. People's real powers to accomplish things in market systems are therefore roughly equal, even though their purchasing powers may differ greatly: Simple purchasing power, as measured by one's real income, wealth, and access to credit at a point in time, is not equivalent to one's power to "do things" in a market system.

The defects of this unfortunate notion should be scrutinized in some detail. To begin with, in order to have equal opportunities to earn labor income in freely chosen occupations, obviously people must have equal access to whatever education and training may be required in those occupations. Certainly people are differently endowed with inborn talent—but more importantly, they are also differently endowed with property inheritances and work and social skills acquired from their homes and environments. For those with lesser such acquired endowments, an education and training system specifically aimed at compensating their disadvantage is necessary in order to assure equality of access to the variety of occupations available for all with equivalent inborn aptitudes. Ideally, such a system must enable people to choose their occupations in light of their own inherent preferences and talents, after significant exposure to information about alternative occupations and the associated training costs and expected incomes—and most importantly, it must enable them to do so regardless of their own and their parents' ability to pay schooling and training costs.

But even an exemplary such system of public education and training could not by itself assure equality of access to labor income. First, many important occupational skills are acquired at home and on the job rather than in formal schooling or training. Differences in these skills reflect differences in peoples' acculturation, social connections, and job histories, and probably cannot be anywhere near fully compensated by any amount of formal schooling and training. Second, as long as people have access also to private schooling and training (i.e., that which is purchased in markets), those with greater purchasing power from whatever sources—labor income, wealth, or credit—will be able to obtain more and better quality education for themselves and their children. Finally, even with an exclusively public system, that is, without private schooling and training being also available, unequal wealth accumulations imply major differences in people's abilities to subsist while forgoing labor income during whatever time may be necessary for their education.

These are merely the most basic of the disparities that exist in people's ability to acquire what economists call human capital or socially acquired marketable skills (other disparities will be noted in the section following). Clearly they would be difficult at best to correct by a public policy effort to equalize access to labor income from freely chosen wage employment in capitalist market systems. Most of these disparities might perhaps be negated were there equal access to the other form of capital, "nonhuman capital" or wealth: With equal access to personal wealth and the property income that accompanies it, people could, with equal ease, not only buy private education and training but also forgo labor income during the process if necessary. In capitalist market systems, however, there are fundamental disparities in people's abilities to acquire nonhuman capital.

Wealth may be acquired (legally) by normal accumulation from savings out of labor or property income, from inheritances or gifts, and from good fortune or perspicacity in financial or business investments. Of course, simply *having* wealth, for example, from an inheritance, is helpful in accumulating more, in that the more wealth one has, the greater is the investible surplus one has in the form of purchasing power above and beyond whatever expenses one requires to live. That is, different prior endowments of wealth constitute for their owners different abilities to accumulate additional wealth, and equality of access to purchasing power in the form of wealth is thus impossible as long as wealth earns income and is a priori greatly unequally distributed. Needless to say, this means there cannot be equal access to *property income* either—helpful as that kind of income is for the further accumulation of wealth, since it comes free of the necessity of laboring for it. Inherent disparities exist then in the accumulation of nonhuman capital, just as they do in the accumulation of human capital.

On the other hand, perfect capital or credit markets could serve to equalize opportunities to acquire human and nonhuman capital. If there were equal access to borrowed funds for purposes of investing in the accumulation of either occupational skills and/or personal wealth, that would fully compensate for differences in people's prior endowments of these. Unfortunately, credit markets, as discussed in an earlier chapter, are greatly imperfect. Uncertain of borrowers' creditworthiness, lenders insist that borrowers have an assured excess income cushion, or better yet some collateral, roughly in proportion to the amount of the loan, to cover lenders' losses in case of default. The amount of credit to which people have access is thus directly and closely correlated with their already existing income and wealth.[2]

Some very basic imperfections in the most critical markets involved therefore give rise to major disparities in people's access to purchasing power. Some of these may, in principle, be avoidable in a capitalist market system, but none are easily corrected and some may not be corrected at all without fundamentally altering the essential capitalist nature of the system. As a consequence, inequalities in access to purchasing power closely follow whatever prior inequalities exist in the distribution of property endowments, that is, in the human and nonhuman capital conferred upon individuals by their families and homes and the social environments in which they are brought up and live.

Without considerable additional government intervention—extending far beyond a mere commitment to schooling, training, and a "social safety net"—there can be no pretense of equality of access to purchasing power in a capitalist market economy. On all counts it is clearly true, as in the popular adage, that aside from the important role that pure luck also plays, "it takes money to make money." The appearance of great economic inequality therefore does reflect a substantial inequality in people's real powers of accomplishment.

The Real World of Inequality

In a world based on the perfect equality model, all individuals would have perfectly equal opportunity to get whatever purchasing power is required to pursue and fulfill their own aspirations in life. In reality, opportunities to get the requisite purchasing power are greatly unequal, being directly determined, first and foremost, by people's prior endowments of human capital and wealth conferred upon them by their families and social backgrounds. A number of other important sources of unequal opportunity or access to purchasing power ought to be noted as well, since their effect is to reinforce that economic inequality that is due to disparities in people's personal backgrounds.

First, formal education per se (and to a similar extent occupational training) is not merely a system for providing people with basic competencies plus whatever additional "human capital" they may choose to derive from it. Formal education also functions as a structure for sorting people into "appropriate" social positions and occupations, and does so, to a significant extent, in accordance with their already given backgrounds. First, public school students are sorted among schools the qualities of which depend significantly upon the tax bases of their neighborhoods and school districts—students thus get public spending on their educations that varies with the neighborhoods in which their parents can afford to live. Second, within a school, sorting is similarly correlated with prior background. For example, verbal skill or creativity and uninhibitedness are competencies that alert teachers and counselors to direct a public school student who has them toward a particular set of possible occupations. But such competencies are likely to have been acquired in the first place in households where parents work in similar such occupations. Education is not merely an institution in which people make occupational choices and acquire some of the requisites of pursuing them; it is also, equally importantly, part of the social structure that further constrains people's opportunities in accord with their already acquired propensities and skills. To that extent the system of education reinforces, rather than counteracts, the role of social background in determining people's opportunities.

It is easily argued therefore that the sorting processes involved in education actually constitute a kind of discrimination among students by social class.[3] There are also, of course, processes of discrimination by race and sex, another major source of unequal opportunity or disparity in access to purchasing power about which volumes have been written. Race and sex discrimination are found throughout society and translate into major deficiencies of access to many occupations and to positions of social status for nonwhites and women. The role of discrimination in education and the workplace has obvious direct effects on people's economic prospects. And discrimination in lending institutions and the housing sector continue to be important factors in the racial segregation of schools and neighborhoods.[4]

Third, occupational associations often construct barriers to entry into the education or training required, as well as into the occupations themselves, that make it difficult for any but those who are already advantaged to be admitted. Restricting access yields higher incomes to those admitted into the occupation, of course, but also raises the price of the education or training involved (by increasing the demand for admission to these while reducing the number of students in the education or training supplied), hence restricts access disproportionately for those with lower incomes. Health care, law, and other professional occupations, as already discussed in an earlier chapter, are well-known examples of this sort of exclusion.

"Institutionalist" theories of labor markets shed light on some other systematic disparities of opportunity that exist for various groups. In internal job markets, firms look to workers they already employ, rather than to outside job applicants, to fill job openings elsewhere in the firm. This tends to be practiced by very capital-intensive firms using skilled labor that also requires much on-the-job training, especially where production would be easily disrupted by poor labor morale (e.g., on assemby lines): the firm then finds it profitable to boost labor productivity by providing its workers job security and regular advancement. To the extent this is done, however, actual labor markets mainly allocate labor only to entry-level jobs, and access to more advanced jobs is restricted to those already admitted to the right such entry-level jobs. Workers whose early job experience is in firms in which internal job markets are not used—secondary sector firms—are less likely to have access to jobs in primary sector firms (i.e., those using internal job markets), than are workers already admitted entry to the latter. To the extent that labor mobility is thus restricted in such segmented labor markets, those with the luck of early admission to jobs in the primary sector obviously have greater opportunities for advancement than do secondary sector workers. Sorting processes in schools, as well as race and sex discrimination, tend to reinforce this division of the workforce in directing new workers to entry-level jobs.[5]

All of these additional disparities in opportunity mainly compound, rather than offset, the more basic disparities discussed earlier: Those whose family and social backgrounds put them at a prior disadvantage are all the less likely to succeed in their aspirations on account of these additional factors. After all of this, one may wish to emphasize nonetheless the degree of freedom people have in choosing their occupations in capitalist market systems, but one simply cannot argue that the choices available are anywhere near equal for all.

To reiterate: Economic inequality reflects real inequalities in people's opportunities to acquire purchasing power, not just differences in, for example, their preferences about "labor and income vs. leisure." Consequently economic inequality manifests substantial disparity in people's actual abilities to pursue their aspirations and personal development. Just how much economic inequality is there in capitalist systems today?

Income and wealth disparities by race and sex are sometimes discussed in the media, and these disparities are quite astonishing: Family income for blacks is, on average, 54 percent that of whites, while the net worth of the average black family is 12 percent that of the average white family. Women with full-time jobs still earn only 73 percent of what men earn, even after the significant economic progress made in the last few decades. Of course, even were there economic equality between the races and sexes, a great deal of inequality would still remain—there would still be "the rich, the poor, and the rest." In the typical large U.S. corporation today, the chief executive officer receives annual compensation that is several hundreds of times what the average production employee earns. And the net worth of the least wealthy member of the Forbes 400 is several thousand times that of the average family in the United States. On the other hand, about one in eight people in the United States live in households whose incomes make them officially "poor"—based on a standard set in 1960!—about one in four children live in poor households. CEOs and the superrich are merely extreme cases and only a minuscule portion of the population overall, and the poor are, after all, a small minority too—and these disparities therefore cannot by themselves really convey the degree of inequality existing in this society as a whole. To get a clearer picture of that requires looking at measures and illustrations of the distribution of income and wealth such as those in Figure 6.1.[6]

Judging from the facts shown there, great disparities do indeed exist in the powers of accomplishment socially conferred upon people generally in capitalist market societies. Moreover, unequal as people's purchasing powers are, recent decades have witnessed substantial increases in the extent of economic inequality in most market societies, increases that may be expected to continue into the future. The distributions of income and wealth remained virtually unchanged during the post–World War II decades of high economic

Figure 6.1 **Shares of Aggregate Income, Net Worth, and Financial Wealth for Income or Wealth Classes, 1998**

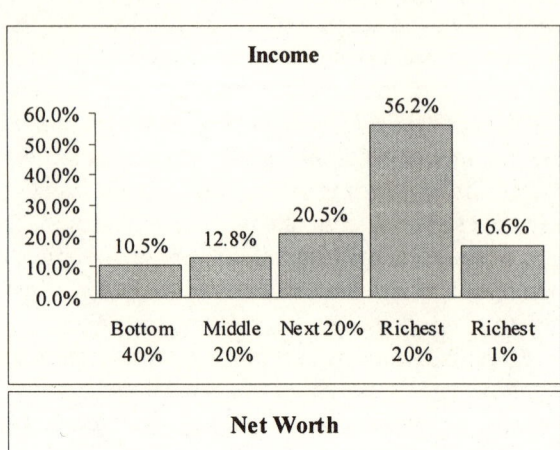

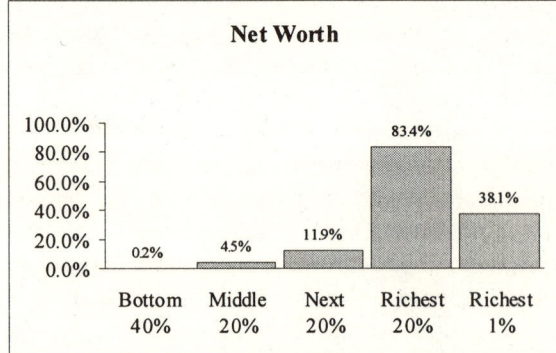

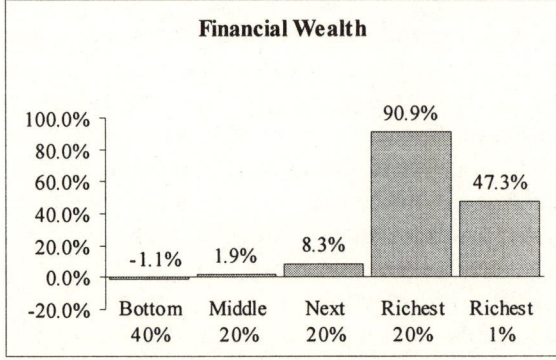

Source: Edward N. Wolff, "Recent Trends," Table 2.
Note: Income is money income of households; net worth is households' total assets minus debts; financial wealth is households' total financial assets minus total debts.

growth, but from the late 1970s to the present, changes in these distributions have significantly expanded the disparities among people. Why this has happened and what is portended for the future are matters I will take up later, after considering more closely the connections between economic inequality and social power.

Economic Inequality and Power

As great an issue as is the disparity among people's powers of accomplishment due to purchasing power inequality, the connections between the latter and power in the critical sense of domination are not necessarily obvious. Do such disparities in people's powers of accomplishment on account of economic inequality necessarily implicate relationships of power *over* people? Neoclassical economists generally would answer that question in the negative: Power as domination, and power as merely the capacity to accomplish things, are two distinct phenomena, and there is nothing about the latter that necessarily implies the former. Yet while that seems logical enough, our intuition may say otherwise, for virtually anything we may accomplish constitutes an opportunity for exercising power over someone. How can it be maintained that economic inequality does *not* implicate domination relationships? Before we can get to the heart of the structure of power in market societies, we need to examine that most critical question.

To begin with, it may be argued that economic inequality in and of itself constitutes a form of domination or power over people, albeit diffuse and anonymous in its effect. Purchasing power inequality means that people have unequal influence, or "cast unequal votes" as purchasers of goods and services, in their society's decisions about the allocation of resources. But the economy's resources consist of nothing else than the collection of its members' labor capacities and properties. Influencing the allocation of resources is therefore equivalent, in principle, to influencing one's fellow members of society. In their market transactions then, people with unequal spending power unequally influence each other. Thus the power to accomplish things that is represented by purchasing power is the same as the power to affect other people, and when people may affect each other unequally, power in the critical sense seems implied. If individual A may influence individual B more than the latter may influence him, then A surely may be said to have power over B in some important sense.

Of course, the asymmetric mutual influences that people exert upon each other in the process of purchasing things in markets are extremely diffuse and slight, but that does not essentially alter the case. However, neoclassical economists would ask, precisely how can money expenditures objectively measure such influences? If one person is able to spend twice what another may spend in markets, in what sense can he be said thereby to exert twice as much influence upon the other as the latter does upon him?[7]

The classical economists' *labor theory of value* had a resolution of sorts for this problem of measuring people's mutual influence on each other as purchasers in markets. According to that theory, market prices tend to be such that goods exchange in accordance with the labor required to produce them.[8] It then follows that an individual's purchasing power measures the amount of other people's labor that she may "command" in the course of purchasing goods in markets. By comparing the amount of labor so commanded with the amount of labor an individual must perform in order to obtain her purchasing power, a relationship of unequal mutual influence may be delineated between two groups of people: Some individuals' incomes allow them to command more labor in their market purchases than what they themselves perform in obtaining their incomes—while other people, of course, must labor more for their incomes than what their incomes may command of others' labor. In effect, those in the latter group *work for* those in the former group, and may be construed to be subject to them in the sense that they are able to command less labor from them than what they must accede to them.

The traditional Marxist analysis focused on wage-employees as the most conspicuous and important group among those who must make such adverse unequal labor exchanges in market systems.[9] According to this analysis, if employers (i.e., owners of firms) are to earn positive profit from their employees' labor, then employees' wages must necessarily command less than the total value of the goods they produce. But if employees must produce a product embodying a greater value than that of their wages, then the labor theory of value implies that in return for their wages, employees must perform more labor themselves than what they can command of other people's labor by means of purchases from those wages. The "extra" labor employees perform then—above and beyond what they can command by means of purchases out of their wages—is work performed for their employers, and is the very source of employers' profit income. Capitalist firm owners thus exploit workers, get the latter to devote some of their activity to owners' benefit and not their own, and are therefore, merely by virtue of this unequal labor exchange, in a position of power over workers.

Yet neoclassicals would point out correctly that, in the simple logic of unequal labor exchanges, those subject to adverse exchanges do not necessarily suffer as a consequence. Indeed, unless market imperfections are present, voluntary market exchanges must be presumed to be mutually beneficial. For example, if one exchanges something embodying three hours of one's own labor for something else embodying only one hour of other people's labor, one has not necessarily thereby been adversely affected in any way by the exchange. If the exchange occurs in a well-functioning market without major imperfections, then it must be presumed that one has given "full consent" with "full knowledge of the alternatives," and so forth, and that one merely values the product of one's own labor relative to that of others accordingly. If anything, in such circumstances products exchanged that involve unequal labor are actually valued by transactors more or less equally. Thus, in particular, the exchange between worker and employer cannot be shown to constitute a power relationship merely on account of its involving an apparently unequal labor exchange. Of course, the preceding chapter showed that a power relationship does exist between employer and worker, and an unequal labor exchange is therefore implied—but the latter may not be taken by itself as *proof* of a power relationship.[10]

Thus while purchasing power inequality may represent people having unequal influence upon each other in some sense, it cannot be argued to constitute in and of itself a power relationship in the critical sense used here: In a market society, the rich do not, merely insofar as they are rich, *thereby* have power over the rest. What then exactly is the connection between economic inequality and domination power?

Sam Bowles and Herbert Gintis's work on power in labor markets, discussed in the last chapter, gives perhaps the best answer to this question, without reference to the heuristic convenience of "unequal labor exchanges" or the classical labor theory of value. Given that the relationship between boss and worker is one involving power—the boss has dominating power over the worker in the critical sense developed in the last chapter—the important question remaining is, what determines who is a worker and who is a boss? Bowles and Gintis's answer is, purchasing power.

Why do people become employees? Lacking sufficient income, wealth, and access to borrowed capital to create an independent business or acquire other income-earning property compels one to be a seller in the labor market in order to subsist, and thereby to subject oneself to an employers' power. On the other hand, of course, having sufficiently great purchasing power, especially in the form of wealth and the crucial labor-free form of income that comes with it, enables one to be on the buyers' side of the labor market (i.e., in command over workers). Of course, since one's purchasing power is primarily a function of one's prior endowments of human capital and wealth, one's position in the power relationship between employers and workers is primarily determined by these prior endowments also.

In fact, employers' power over workers cannot even be clearly elucidated without reference to economic inequality: Were there equality of access to

purchasing power (or equivalently, equality of purchasing power itself)—
that is, were the real world like that of the "perfect equality model"—
workers would not be concerned about the threat of unemployment and
income loss upon which employers' power rests. For they would have the
same access to whatever funds are required to invest in a business or other
income-earning asset—in the form of income, wealth, and credit—as do their
employers, and losing their jobs would not represent a serious matter. Employers' power therefore rests not merely upon the threat of unemployment,
but just as importantly upon the economic inequality that compels some people
to sell their labor services for purchasing power in the first place.

Thus while purchasing power is not, in and of itself, a form of domination, purchasing power inequality is a fundamental constituent in at least
one instance of domination, namely, employers' power. On reflection, it is
equally essential in other major instances of power discussed so far in this
book as well, for example, the power of financial institutions. As should be
evident, one's ability to attain and exercise a position with lender's power—
that is, to be a creditor rather than a debtor—derives crucially from one's
access to purchasing power. In a world of equality of access to purchasing
power, those who would otherwise be subject to lender's power could, by
their access to purchasing power, just as easily be in a dominant lender's
position instead, and therefore would not really be "subject" at all.

Much of the same logic of economic inequality pertains to a great variety of other positions of power in market systems as well. Indeed, arguably
this logic may be extended to *all* power relationships in such systems. That
is, since having purchasing power conveys access to superior positions in
power relationships, lacking it is at least part of what determines the
subordinacy of the subjects in all such relationships. Consider the power
position of the in-between class of *managers*, who do not own firms but do
command workers: With sufficient purchasing power (again, a function of
family and social background, etc.), one may obtain the human capital required for a managerial position; otherwise one is compelled to sell one's
labor for nonmanagerial work (i.e., in a subordinate job). Similarly, who
has the power of monopoly or monopsony, and who cannot afford to find
alternatives or to escape being subject to it, are determined by the distribution of purchasing power—that is, by who has it and who does not. Obviously the power of men over women has been and continues to be at least
partly a function of their greater purchasing power. Even the power of
parents, in market societies, is importantly bolstered by the legal exclusion
of the young from property, contract rights, jobs, and most importantly,
money. Economic inequality thus lies at the very heart of all the major
power structures of market systems.

The Roots of Power in Capitalist Systems: The State

Again, purchasing power is not in itself a kind of domination power, but the fact that it confers on its possessors the ability to obtain and exercise positions of such power, and that those who lack it are unable to avoid positions of subordinacy, makes purchasing power *inequality* an essential constituent of every such power relationship. On the other hand, it can be argued that great economic inequality such as exists in modern market systems implicates a social structure of power as well, that is, that such economic inequality could not exist without a structure of power that both gives rise to and undergirds it. This is so insofar as economic inequality is constituted in a system of unequal private ownership of income-earning property that functions to apportion the work of market economies without the full consent of those who labor.

To see this, consider that it is those who are on the short end of the distribution of income and wealth who must labor in modern market systems, since, lacking income-earning property, they cannot obtain subsistence otherwise than by work.[11] Those at the other end of the distribution can avoid the necessity of working in order to subsist, merely by living off the income on their property. Thus, in market systems, the fact that some must work for their subsistence while others need not is due to the system of unequal ownership of income-earning property.[12] But those who have been freed from labor by their ownership of property live at least partly upon the labor of those who have not, for their property income yields them a share of the total product of those who labor. To that extent, those who do not own property *work for* those who do, and while this does not in itself imply exploitation in the relationship between the haves and the have-nots, as discussed earlier, it certainly begs the question of whether the system of unequal property ownership represents a structure of dominating power.

The argument that it does indeed represent a system of domination is straightforward: Income-earning property owners are enabled to live off the labor of nonowners by virtue of a prior distribution of *socially conferred* endowments of property. That is, the prior endowments of human and nonhuman capital, which enable the haves to accumulate sufficient property to live off its income, while compelling the have-nots to labor for their livelihoods, are bestowed upon both groups by their social environments, not naturally or genetically. But those on the short end of the distribution of income and wealth, in any fair and democratic social decision on the question of what an appropriate prior distribution of human and nonhuman capital should be, arguably would not consent to such a disparity. Thus those who, by virtue of lacking income-earning property must work to subsist, logically must be subject to domination of some kind.[13]

To reiterate: Working people act (labor) partly for property-income earn-ers and not for themselves because of their position in a prior distribution to which, in a democratic decision on the matter, they would not consent. Obvi-ously this logic itself does not show the *nature* of the dominating power to which they are therefore subject (i.e., the specific relationships and struc-tures by means of which they are dominated) but merely that they must be subject to some such power. In order to make the argument unequivocally, it must still be proved that in a fair and democratic social decision on the mat-ter, working people indeed would not give their full consent to the existing prior distribution.

Real "proof" would be difficult, to say the least, but radical critics of capitalism since the dawn of this system have pointed to an extensive array of relationships and institutions embodying social power that apparently serve to develop and maintain a mostly uncontested hegemony of the system of unequal property ownership, while stifling any significant dissent from it by working people.[14] These include, first and foremost, the *state*, which repre-sents, in the view of radical critics, not primarily an arena within which di-verse interests contend, but instead the most important instrument of rule by the propertied.

To begin with, the system of unequal private property rests upon the use of direct, physical threat-based power by the state to enforce property rights and to punish their infringements. Obviously a public power is required to enforce any system of rights and prohibitions that is to be at all impartial. In a system of unequal property ownership, that power must have some basis in physical threat against those who violate it (i.e., with punishment at least by incarceration) in order to be fully effective upon those at the bottom of the distribution of property who clearly cannot be much threatened with mere property loss. (In such systems, one would moreover expect, and there is excellent evidence to show, that the severity of enforcement of property rights against those who violate them is not actually impartial but biased in favor of the propertied.)[15]

State power also plays a critical role in the processes by which property rights are created and defined in the first place, as I noted in an earlier chap-ter. For example, in the transformation of feudal land rights into modern land ownership rights in Europe, the rights of tenants had to be delineated and those of owners expanded, in order for the latter to claim rents on threat of eviction. The requisite enclosure of the commons and expulsion of countless serfs from their feudally granted dwelling rights was accomplished with the ongoing complicity of monarchs and the Church. Similarly, the acquisition of land and resources from the native dwellers of the America's was done from the very beginning with the force of state edict (a process that continues to this day, as is evident in the unceasing contraction of reservation land while nonnatives' rights of use in reservation land is expanded).

Of course, states cannot be understood to operate as outsiders or aliens in their own societies. First, in order to exercise its powers over citizens, a state must directly and specifically command other citizens to act in the requisite ways—that is, it must have power over its own personnel. Aside from having direct, physical threat-based power to command some of its personnel (e.g., in the police and armed services), in market societies states also make use of their own employer power and purchasing power, wielded by virtue of the same market mechanisms as do private individuals wield such powers as described earlier. Also critical in the constitution of states' command over their own personnel (as well as over nonstate employed citizens, as I will elaborate below) is the power of belief or allegiance, or what is called patriotism.

Second, power in the private sector is also wielded conversely *upon the state*. In democratic states, individual citizens exert influence by their participation in voting, political discourse, and various advocacy activities of public decision making. But this influence is greatly unequal among individuals, being strongly correlated, like other kinds of power discussed here, with individuals' purchasing powers (i.e., with their ownership of property): Those who must work to subsist have less time and energy for politically oriented activities of all sorts, including even simple voting, than do those who may subsist at least partly from their income-earning property. The funding and staffing of politically oriented activities and organizations by people with surplus purchasing power—with contributions to advocacy organizations, parties, and candidates—buys further government attention to their needs. The disproportionate funding of government itself via taxes yields those with substantial purchasing power an additional influence over the activities of the state. And the capacity of the propertied to wield also the threat of "capital flight" in case of any broad-reaching and serious impingement of the given rights of property is also effective. Purchasing power inequality then underlies substantial political inequality, and the activities of the state consequently favor property to that extent.

Thus in advanced market societies, the direct, physical threat-based power of the state is rightly considered by radical critics to be an extension of the powers of business and the wealthy—and the state, even the "democratic" state, is indeed "the right hand of the capitalist class." In particular, in contexts of public decisions that affect the distribution of purchasing power or the prior distribution of nonhuman and human capital endowments, the voice of those on the shorter end of the distribution arguably counts for disproportionately little.

Value Power and Corporate Power

However, in the vast and enormously complex coordination of subordinate working people's activities in modern societies, something more than mere compliance with the commands of superiors and the state-enforced requisites of the property system is also needed: Working people's active *consent* and even *allegiance*, at least that of many of them, are required as well. Certainly an active allegiance on the part of most of those state personnel who enforce the property rights system—from judges and police to tax office clerks and jail guards—is required at the very least. And a great majority must give at least sufficient consent to the system to abide by an honest observance of property rights in their daily lives, or else the enforcement of property rights and the simple conduct of trade and pledging of contracts will be prohibitively expensive (indeed perhaps impossible).[16]

Thus the question is, if in a fair and democratic social decision a very large minority or even a great majority of people would not consent to this system, how can it be that in reality the majority apparently does consent to it, at least in the sufficient sense? The best answer is probably some combination of two distinct possibilities. First, people may "consent" to their own subjection because they are deceived about what feasible alternatives to their situation may be available. Particularly important as the means by which such deception may be accomplished are the mass media.

Good arguments may be made—see the works of Noam Chomsky, Edward Herman, and Robert McChesney, in particular—that overall, the media from which people get the vast portion of their information on the available alternatives to the status quo are essentially a system of propaganda.[17] Media institutions in capitalist market systems are themselves mostly private property, owned, like most other private property, mainly by those who, at the top end of the wealth distribution, have most benefited from the system, and who thus in principle have both material interest in and influence upon the entertainment and public affairs content of the media. Media personnel, while presumably as honest as any other group of people, are also as subject to the command of their firms' owners and top managers as any other group of wage employees. As discussed in an earlier chapter, the mass media as an industry is moreover increasingly concentrated, and space exists within the range of media alternatives for fewer and fewer real competitors to the largest media firms, which themselves increasingly encompass all media content. Because the predominant source of the revenues of these firms is the sale of advertising space, the noncommercial content of the media serves essentially as "packaging" for advertisements and commercials. Both the media firms and those firms to whom they sell advertising space thus have a great interest in making sure that the packaging is appropriate to the product, that is, that the nonadvertising content does not incline its audience toward too critical an attitude about advertising or about the larger commercial, capitalist system of which it is a part. Not surprisingly then, analyses of the content of the media show some pretty clear-cut biases against dissenting views on the system and advocacies of alternative systems, both in public affairs and in entertainment content.

The other possible explanation of the apparent widespread consent to the system is that because people's preferences or *values* are formed importantly by their environments, their values may be such that they actually do consent (more or less fully) even to a situation from which they would strongly demur were they offered a choice in more congenial circumstances. Securing consent of this kind involves the exercise of what Randall Bartlett called "value power," that which, when used, alters people's preferences, values, or attitudes from what they would be otherwise.[18]

While sometimes overlooked, especially by mainstream economists, value power is as fully consequential a form of power in its own right as any other, being present both in interpersonal relations (e.g., between parent and child or between a charismatic person and his followers) and in larger social contexts. Such power may also serve to bolster other kinds of power, of course, and from the viewpoint of powerful people, the costs of exercising it may well be far outweighed by its benefits in reducing the difficulties of securing the compliance of subjects by other means (threats and sanctions and deception). Thus a regime with the allegiance of its subjects is literally more "efficient" than one without. Moreover, the benefits of securing something at least close to the full consent of subordinate working people can be especially great in modern social contexts, where a highly developed specialization and consequent high degree of interdependence among production processes means that noncompliance by even small groups may impose large costs upon the powerful.

Economists have mainly left for others the study of the nature of people's preferences or values, confining themselves to the barest minimum of what may be relevant for economic theorizing (e.g., the "law of diminishing marginal utility"). They have sometimes considered the implications of minor variations on their basic model of the values of a narrowly self-centered individual, having found altruistic individual preferences, for example, to be of some interest. But they have virtually never allowed for changing individual values, much less for any discussion of why and how people's values may change. Yet unless one insists on a purely genetic account of human behavior—with people's preferences formed at conception and immutable thereafter—some consideration of these things would seem critical in all the social sciences.[19] The question of the formation of people's preferences requires an analysis of, in William Dugger's words, the "organized pattern[s] of roles, often enforced with positive and negative sanctions . . . [and] the patterned habits of thought learned by individuals performing those roles."[20] Alternatively, it requires a study of institutions, hence has been of keen interest among economists mainly only in the traditional "institutionalist" school of economic thought.

Institutionalist economists and radical critics of capitalism have considered in some detail the influence that business and the wealthy have in shaping their society's values as they exercise their purchasing power, employer power, and other influence in and upon cultural institutions (i.e., the media, universities and schools, churches, government, and other organizations). In modern market societies, these large institutions are the conveyors of the most critical informational and affective content of their cultures, deeply affecting people's attitudes about all things. To the extent that they are either the property of the wealthy or otherwise disproportionately beholden to the wealthy (for investment capital, financial contributions, taxes, advertising revenues, etc.), none of these institutions can be expected to convey a stream of information and attitudes that does not largely support the system of subordinate wage-labor and unequal private property.

Moreover, a "corporate hegemony," as William Dugger shows in his book by the same title,[21] has arisen in such societies in a variety of more subtle processes by which the other institutions of the society have mostly come to adopt the same values as those that direct the modern capitalist *corporation.* First, individuals emulate other individuals who stand out as powerful or successful in competition (as Thorstein Veblen so well described in his *Theory of the Leisure Class*). This occurs throughout all levels of all hierarchical institutions, and insofar as corporate personnel already imbued with corporate values participate in other institutions, even noncorporate people in the latter tend to adopt some of their values.

Second, other institutions are also similarly contaminated by corporate values as they find it convenient to conduct their affairs in businesslike ways— even churches adopt a competitive marketing approach to gathering their memberships, for example. Third, the subordination of other institutions to the needs of the corporation also brings the values they promote more closely in line with those of the corporation. This is perhaps most obvious as it applies to the media, whose revenues, as noted above, derive directly from sales to private corporations. But none of the other cultural institutions are immune: To the extent that schools and universities, for example, in order to be viable institutions in a corporate economy, must graduate students prepared to enter positions in corporations, they must subordinate certain of the values they would otherwise follow to this necessity. And churches are most beholden to their wealthiest contributors. Finally, by processes of "mystification" people both within and outside of all these other institutions come to find the traditional symbols expressing their values manipulated and usurped for the advancement of corporate values instead, confusing and misleading people to support things that are in fact quite counter to their actual interests. For example, "if workers value the right to earn a living, mystification can get them to value the *right to work*."[22]

Thus do the cultural institutions of the modern capitalist market society promote various myths supportive of that system—for example, the myth of sole personal responsibility for individual success or failure, the myth of equality of opportunity and freedom of enterprise. Thus do they highlight the individual benefits of acquiring personal property—in the form of status, respect, and admiration—but not the costs, for example, alienation. Thus do they cast forms of behavior required by the system in a favorable light—individualism, materialism, aggressiveness, competitiveness, careerism—while disfavoring others. Thus do they discredit alternatives to the system or minimize balanced discussion of them. And so forth.

Of course, the values which cultural institutions promulgate are not necessarily unambiguous and simple: There is diversity, contradiction, and change in their "values content." For example, the individualism that is requisite for sustaining allegiance to the private property system may conflict with the conformism that is required for success in the corporate form of business now pervasive in such systems. Similarly, the strong work ethic that appears to be necessary to keep people working with commitment and diligence in a system in which they labor as subjects of power may conflict with the consumerism that is necessary to keep them buying the enormous output of their productivity. In universities, an unabashed propagandizing of the capitalist market system may conflict with a commitment to the objective pursuit of truth that is an important legitimization of their activity. At all levels of education, inculcation of the values of "free citizenship" conflicts directly with the need to impart the values of an undemocratic workplace and a larger system of economic inequality. And of course, there is continual tension between the values of traditional religion and those which its institutions adopt from the capitalist environment by processes of emulation, contamination, and subordination.

Thus contradictions abound, and the analysis of these and other values-forming institutions and sites (e.g., families, workplaces) is complex indeed, constituting a major portion of the subject of sociology, at least, if not economics. But complex though the matter may be, that in itself does not negate the implication of the analysis given here: The values-formation process is engendered by structures of power; and in market societies value power, or the power to affect people's values or influence the social values-formation process, is closely correlated with purchasing power. Briefly then, the values most widely promulgated in the system of unequal private property are those most effective in attaining consent from a population who presumably would, in more equitable social decision-making circumstances, with free choice and full cognizance, dissent from that system.

Increasing Economic Inequality

The subject of the connections between economic inequality and structures of social power should not be left before looking briefly at the current troubling trend toward increasing inequality. As I noted earlier, the degree of economic inequality reflected in the distributions of income and wealth has increased significantly in the past couple of decades. The proximate cause is, of course, that higher income families and households have experienced greater real-income growth, while lower income people have experienced less growth or even decline.

All measures of inequality in family or household income in the United States show increasing inequality—Figure 6.2 shows graphically what has been happening. While in the 1980s there was some dispute about whether the data actually indicated a trend, by now there can be no doubt. Moreover, it is also pretty clear that rising inequality overall has been the result of increasing inequality both in labor income and in the distribution of total income between labor and property (i.e., in the "functional" distribution of income). At the same time that aggregate wages and salaries have risen (even though individuals' wage-rates have stagnated or fallen, as explained in the last chapter), (a) all measures of wage and salary inequality have risen, and (b) there has been an increase in the ratio of aggregate-property income to labor income (that is, the share of total personal income that the largest portion of the population receives is declining, while that of the much smaller portion that receives most of the property income is rising).[23]

Inequality in the distribution of personal wealth, already much greater than that in the distribution of income, is increasing also.[24] To some extent the increase in wealth inequality is due to differences in the rates of appreciation of corporate stock and private housing: The former, which is owned mainly by people in the highest wealth classes, has risen in value far more than has housing, the most important form of wealth of the rest of the population. This accounts for only a portion of the increases in wealth inequality, however, and according to the extensive and exceptional studies of Edward Wolff, rising wealth inequality should be seen as closely correlated with rising income inequality.

Figure 6.2 **Increasing Income and Wealth Inequality, 1983–1998**

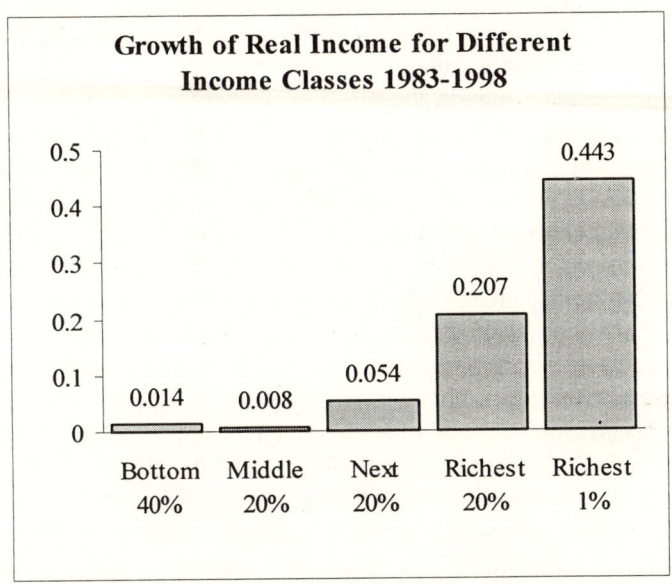

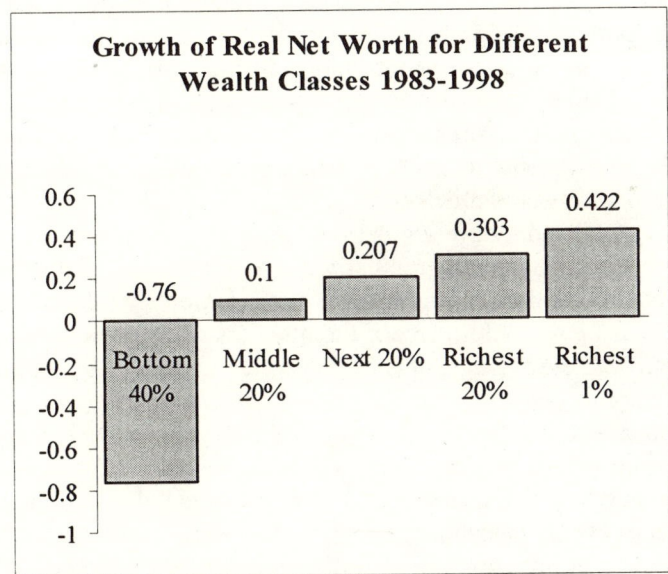

Source: Edward N. Wolff, "Recent Trends," Table 3.
Note: Growth in real income (in 1998 dollars) for households, and in real net worth (total assets minus debt in 1998 dollars) for households.

Moreover, even that portion of increasing wealth inequality that is due to the stock and housing markets should not be looked at as unrelated to the trend of rising income inequality. First, since housing predominates in the wealth portfolios of the nonrich population while stock is mostly in the hands of the rich, differing growth rates in the incomes of these two groups will lead to differing growth rates in their respective demands for housing and corporate stock as assets into which to place their savings. Thus the demand for stock would be expected to rise more quickly since the incomes of the rich are rising more quickly than those of the rest. Second, the shift in the functional distribution of income from labor to property most importantly reflects labor cost reductions that have yielded business profit increases, as I will elaborate below. The latter accrue to stockholders, of course, as both increased dividends and stock-value appreciation. Thus rising wealth inequality is, in fact, at least in part merely another aspect of the rise in income inequality.

Some observers of the trend in income inequality who are inclined toward the perfect equality model described above have bravely proposed that recent changes in the labor-market demand for different levels of skill have affected incomes differentially according to the inherent and inborn aptitudes people have to offer in labor markets.[25] In light of the analysis of the sources of economic inequality given in this chapter, such explanations of rising inequality cannot carry much weight: Rather than being determined by inborn aptitudes, people's incomes relative to others' are in large part determined by the objective opportunities available to them, and the latter are in turn shaped by the economic backgrounds of their families and communities. That labor markets are changing is perfectly clear, but that people's genetically given talents to any significant extent determine the effects on their livelihoods is not at all clear.

Other commentators have argued that increasing inequality has resulted from demographic changes, particularly the recent increases in the participation of women, youth, and immigrants in the nation's workforce. In principle, such changes would increase the numbers of workers earning lower wages relative to the average, thus adding weight to the bottom of the distribution of labor income and stretching out the overall distribution. (Note that while women entering the workforce would itself tend to increase inequality, the disparity between men's and women's average wages has fallen, as women's wages have risen while men's have stagnated—that, of course, would tend to reduce overall inequality.) Yet the extent of these effects of new labor-force entrants does not appear to be sufficient to account for more than a fraction of the total increase in labor-income inequality at best. The evidence suggests that inequality is increasing in labor incomes *within all groups* regardless of sex, race, or age—for example, among men only and among women only—and is increasing as well in occupations and areas of the country in which labor forces have been only little if at all affected by immigration.[26]

Moreover, any adequate explanation of rising economic inequality must explain not only the increasing disparity within all groups of workers' earnings but also that between workers overall and property owners (i.e., in the "functional" distribution of income). The discussion of this chapter suggests that an explanation for all of this should be sought in the interplay between the momentous economic changes taking place in these times and the structures of social power that most importantly underlie the distributions of income and wealth. Let me first reiterate briefly some relevant points made in earlier chapters.

To begin with, following on technological advances in transportation and communication, the increasing mobility of capital and the consequent globalization of markets has had the effect of expanding the competition between the workforces of different countries, thus reducing labor compensation toward the "lowest common denominator" among countries. As explained in the last chapter, not only do workers increasingly compete with their more cheaply paid cohorts elsewhere, but national governments increasingly compete for capital investment location by, among other things, promoting antilabor public policies such as antiunion laws, welfare spending cuts, and "monetarist" macroeconomic policies that further reduce labor compensation.

As a number of labor economists have noted, there is a fairly clear empirical relationship between labor unionism and labor-income equality: A large decline in unionism such as has been experienced recently (as discussed in the last chapter) would be expected to give rise to a greater disparity in labor incomes.[27] And overall reductions in labor incomes resulting from the whole set of changes in the balance of class power are not isolated effects: Wherever they occur there are corresponding increases in property incomes. That this is so regarding business profit is straightforward: The firm that relocates a plant to a country with cheaper labor thereby improves its profits; and antiunion policies, welfare spending cuts, and "monetarist" unemployment that lower workers' wages and tighten discipline in the workplace have the effect of raising employers' profitability similarly. Interest and rent income increases occur also, as finance, real estate, and development firms' profits are similarly improved, as monetarist higher interest rates are imposed, and as improved industrial profitability increases the incomes of creditors and renters doing business with industrial firms. Thus clearly the shift of income shares from labor to property in recent decades is at least partly a case of the dynamics of social class in market systems today.[28]

Indeed, that the dynamics of class lie at the very heart of the matter may be seen in other dimensions of the trend of rising inequality as well. For one thing, as I pointed out in discussing business organization changes that have occurred in recent times, much of the globalization of markets that has been permitted by technological advances in communication has occurred because of the closer organizational control permitted by those technologies (as opposed to the facilitation of market exchange that has also resulted from them). Organizational control has improved by means of better monitoring of subordinates in more widely placed locations, better access to relevant information by superiors, and greater rationalization of bureaucratic control structures by improved information processing. In itself, greater control translates directly into both increased labor productivity and reduced labor compensation. It permits more effective means of "dividing and conquering" labor in the workplace, as the increased bureaucratization of business stratifies more greatly the incomes of employees in a firm, with workers being placed in positions on a lengthening "ladder" and competing more closely with their peers in the internal job market. And the differences in employees' incomes between the primary sector (big business) and the secondary sector (small, more competitive firms) also spreads, as the latter firms are increasingly subordinated to the big firms with which they do business and accordingly are forced to squeeze their employees all the harder to cut costs. Clearly, not only does increasing inequality in labor incomes follow all of this, but so too does an increasing disparity between labor and property income, as these changes yield increases in business profit and the other forms of property income (at least in the primary, big business sector) at the expense of labor income.

Technological changes also affect the distribution of income by their impact on the level and mix of the job skills required for production. It is usually presumed that especially the sort of technological changes occurring in the late twentieth century have had the effect of increasing the average necessary skill level of labor: New technologies are invariably more complex, hence require greater intellectual facility in those who use them. Insofar as it is usually presumed that wages are correlated with skill levels, the consequence should be a rising average level of labor income.[29] In fact, however, the impact of technical changes on job skills, and the effects of changes in the latter on the distribution of income, are more complicated.

Clearly, increasingly complex technologies require stronger intellectual facility in those who must comprehend them—their inventors, those who must manage the equipment and organizations built around them, and those who must maintain and repair the facilities embodying them—but that conclusion does not at all necessarily extend to those who must actually use the equipment at work. Indeed, the more typical case would seem to be a *deskilling* of the actual production jobs employing equipment and processes that embody new technologies: Firms seeking to lower labor costs will, other things equal, prefer new technologies that require lower-skilled labor, since the necessary educational background and on-the-job-training, not to mention the wage-bargaining power, of such workers is less than for other workers. Thus the overall effect on the required skill level may be merely to increase the *spread* between the high- and the low-skilled jobs in the sectors affected, the presumed direct consequence being an increasing inequality in labor incomes. That this is a significant aspect of what is now happening is lent credence by the increasing disparity of labor incomes both between younger and older workers and between those less educated and those more educated.[30]

All of this has bearing on the functional distribution of income as well. Since an increasing spread in skill levels would be expected to aggravate the stratification and division of the workforce, it must aggravate the deterioration in labor's bargaining position with employers, hence further diminishing labor's share in aggregate income relative to property's share. Apparently this and the other effects on the functional distribution that I referred to above have been great enough to have completely stifled any real-wage increases since the mid-1970s (at least until most recently).[31] If labor productivity increases that result from technological changes occur without corresponding real-wage increases, then the functional distribution of income shifts further in favor of property. Moreover, as I noted in the last chapter, an increasing tendency toward unemployment follows upon such a change in the functional distribution as well, because the consumption demand of a given labor force must tend to stagnate in such circumstances relative to the output it produces. This further favors property's share in total income, as labor's wage-bargaining power is cut by the increased likelihood of job loss. Only in the unprecedented boom of the last few years have the relatively high rates of unemployment in the United States since the 1970s abated (while elsewhere in the world unemployment has currently climbed quite high indeed)—it remains to be seen whether the current good times will last long enough to offset some of these changes.

Thus have the momentous technological and economic changes of these times had the effect of altering the power relations that underlie the distribution of income and wealth in market systems today. The advantage has shifted in favor of employers' power over workers in labor markets and the workplace, in favor of employees in ranking positions over those in subordinate positions, and in favor of property-income recipients over wage and salary earners—and these power shifts have directly translated into increased income disparities. Besides the increasing inequity thus manifest in a society in which the most critical determinant of individual opportunity is personal income, what is most alarming about these changes is the prospect of their building upon or reinforcing themselves in a vicious circle of increasing social stratification, culminating perhaps in some sort of "new capitalist feudalism."

For these increases in income and wealth disparity must have the effect of strengthening the economic, political, and cultural forces that maintain and promote further such disparity: Power leads to economic disparity, and the latter leads to more power. In terms of the analysis given earlier in this chapter, increasing economic inequality places those on the short end of the income distribution, whose lack of income denies them access to whatever alternatives may exist, all the more firmly in positions of subordination, while the affluent are all the more secure in their positions of dominance, for example, as employers, managers, or lender/investors.[32] And access to participation in political processes and in processes of cultural "values formation" becomes increasingly unequal too insofar as these are functions of personal income and wealth. As economic inequality grows, political decisions are thus increasingly biased in favor of the haves, and in favor of political, legal, and regulatory system changes that further bolster their already strengthened positions. The tone of the cultural discourse of the mass media as well as in all other spheres of life becomes increasingly conservative and, in particular, increasingly complacent about rising social stratification and affirmative of system changes that contribute further to it.

Notes

1. Lars Osberg, *Economic Inequality in the U.S.*, chapter 8, gives an excellent summary of the argument that competitive free markets lead to a kind of "perfect equality" of what may be called "psychic income" among market transactors. What follows is based on that argument. What I call the perfect equality model may alternatively be called a model of free market equal opportunity.

2. In the post-Keynesian economic theory, the most critical financial market imperfection is the uncertainty inherent in credit market transactions. In effect, that very same uncertainty also lies at the heart of the inequality of access to investment finance referred to here.

3. See Samuel Bowles and Herbert Gintis, *Schooling in Capitalist America*, for a most convincing argument that this is so.

4. An excellent introduction to both neoclassical economics and political economy theories of race and sex discrimination is Randy Albelda, Robert Drago, and Steven Shulman, *Unlevel Playing Fields*, chapters 5 and 8. Also, Edward N. Wolff, *Economics of Poverty, Inequality and Discrimination*, chapters 12–14. A fine short collection of academic articles on the subject is Frank Ackerman et al., *The Political Economy of Inequality*, Part 8.

5. The theory of segmented labor markets is mainly one of political economy, not mainstream economics. Howard Wachtel, *Labor and the Economy*, chapter 11, however, an excellent text on both schools in labor economics, gives it coverage. See especially Richard Edwards, *Contested Terrain*, chapters 9 and 10.

6. The facts quoted here may be found in the following sources: On racial income and wealth differences, Edward N. Wolff, *Recent Trends in Wealth Ownership*, Table 6. On income differences between men and women, U.S. Census Bureau, *Money Income in the United States*, Table B. On CEO pay, Frank Ackerman et al., *The Political Economy of Inequality*, pp. 61–77. On the Forbes 400, for those not willing to obtain a copy of the relevant annual issue of *Forbes Magazine*, see http://www.forbes.com/400richest/. On the extent of officially defined poverty, see United States Census Bureau, *Poverty in the United States 1998*.

7. The problem here is essentially what neoclassicals call the impossibility of making "interpersonal utility comparisons": Market purchases by two individuals that are equivalent in money terms cannot be assumed to affect either the buyers' or other people's utility equally.

8. While all of the classical economists—including Smith, Ricardo, Mill, and Marx—adhered to the labor theory of value, today it is held, at least in the United States, mainly among Marxist economists. A very nice, short—if somewhat contentious—summary of the theory and some of the work done on it is Fernando Vianello, "Labor Theory of Value."

9. John E. Roemer, *Free to Lose*, chapters 7 and 9, gives an extensive analysis of such unequal labor exchanges, including other kinds deriving from, for example, creditor-debtor relationships.

10. The issue here, just as in the discussion of chapter 2 on how power may be present in market exchanges, revolves around the necessary voluntariness of exchanges in "perfect" markets: If markets are perfect, then the exchange involved in the employee working for someone else is necessarily voluntarily.

11. And welfare and the social safety net in modern capitalist market systems are invariably stingy enough to assure that strong incentives remain, even in the most affluent societies in human history, for those on the short end of the distribution to do the required labor.

12. It is for this reason that economic inequality would remain a critical issue even in (hypothetically) benign market systems, regardless of the system of labor—be it wage-labor, self-employed artisanship, or partnership or cooperative employment—for example, in "market socialism." See Roemer, *Free to Lose*, chapters 7 and 9.

13. Again, this too would pertain even in the absence of overt, threat-based domination by employers—that is, in the absence of wage-labor, for example, in a worker-owned enterprise market system—as long as there is greatly unequal income-earning private-property ownership (Roemer, *Free to Lose*, chapters 7 and 9; also Eric Schutz, "Social Power in Neo-Marxist Analyses"). Note that the intermediate case of managers as a special, privileged class of employees is easily added in this model of social power and inequality.

14. Sharon Zukin and Paul DiMaggio, *Structures of Capital*, is a nice collection on this. Michael Parenti, *Democracy for the Few*, is a classic introduction. Also, G. William Domhoff, *Who Rules America?*

15. Michael Parenti, *Democracy for the Few*, chapter 9.

16. See Randall Bartlett, *Economics and Power*, pp. 180–186, on how important a component of "efficiency" is the voluntary observance of property rights.

17. Robert W. McChesney, *Rich Media, Poor Democracy*; Edward S. Herman and Noam Chomsky, *Manufacturing Consent*.

18. This wording reflects Bartlett's own usage. More in conformity with the concept of power used in this book would be the following definition of value power: "That which, when used, alters people's preferences, values, or attitudes from what they would be in free, equitable and democratic circumstances."

19. Randal Bartlett, *Economics and Power*, chapter 9.

20. William M. Dugger, "Power: An Institutional Framework of Analysis," p. 898.

21. William M. Dugger, *Corporate Hegemony*.

22. Ibid., p. 46, my emphasis.

23. A number of excellent books have appeared on the subject of the economics of increasing inequality by now, including Frank Levy, *The New Dollars and Dreams*; Frank Ackerman et al., *The Political Economy of Inequality*; Paul Ryscavage, *Income Inequality in America*; Ray Marshall, *Back to Shared Prosperity*; Sheldon Danziger and Peter Gottschalk, *America Unequal*; James K. Galbraith, *Created Unequal*; and Lawrence Mishel, Jared Bernstein, and John Schmitt, *The State of Working America 1998–99*.

24. See Edward N. Wolff, "Recent Trends in Wealth Ownership," and Chuck Collins et al., *Shifting Fortunes*.

25. Claude S. Fischer et al., *Inequality by Design*, is an outstanding source on this controversy.

26. Paul Ryscavage, *Income Inequality in America*, gives a good overview of this and other mainstream theories of the recently increasing inequality.

27. Sheldon Danziger and Peter Gottschalk, *America Unequal*, pp. 130–132.

28. John Smithin, *Macroeconomic Policy and the Future of Capitalism*, considers this from the viewpoint of macroeconomics.

29. There are two basic economic models of a direct relationship between skills and wages. In the neoclassical *human-capital* model, skill is directly related to both the training required for and the productivity of jobs in an occupation. Wages are higher for jobs requiring greater skill therefore, both to compensate for the greater training costs borne by workers, and to equate with the higher marginal product of labor in those occupations. In the *bargaining* model used in many heterodox economic theories, the greater skill required of some jobs leads to greater bargaining power for those workers: Such jobs require more formal and on-the-job training, hence are costlier for employers to replace workers; they likely involve more "agency" power; they are more likely to be unionized; and so forth. Their greater bargaining power yields them higher wages. See, for example, Howard Wachtel, *Labor and the Economy*.

30. Sheldon Danziger and Peter Gottschalk, *America Unequal*, chapter 7.

31. On real-wages stagnating while productivity continues growing, see Lawrence Mishel et al., *The State of Working America 1998–99*, Introduction, Figure A.

32. That is, increasing inequality, with a given degree of vertical income mobility, has the effect of making it harder to move vertically sufficiently to escape being placed in positions of subordinacy. Only if mobility is also increasing will it offset this effect, but what little good evidence there is indicates mobility is declining. Lawrence Mishel et al., *The State of Working America 1998–99*, chapter 1.

7

Conclusion

The broad picture of modern market systems that has been given in this book is far from what is conveyed in mainstream neoclassical economics. There, the market system is viewed as a kind of congenial anarchy, a harmonious competition among equals. Market participants enter their relations with each other without differential advantages of any kind, regardless of whatever inequalities may hold among them in other spheres of life—nor do their relations as buyers and sellers create any differential advantages among them either. The larger directions of their exchanges and their economy's development are shaped only by their own wants and preferences, the given constraints of their own physical makeup and that of the natural world, and the otherwise anarchic interplay of their exchanges and productive activities. No individuals or institutions stand out among them as singular in their influence on the shape of things, none have any significant effect on the constraints to which others, as market transactors, are subject—certainly none may be said in any sense to be able to dominate any others.

In the account given in this book, however, market transactors do not appear at all to be equals: The differential advantages that hold among them in other spheres of life may matter deeply for the nature of their market transactions, and those transactions create and re-create further advantages and disadvantages among them. In no sense is the market system an interplay of equals—there are singular individuals and institutions with significantly disproportionate influence on the shape of the constraints to which the rest are subject. There are even "movers and shakers" in this account, who actually constitute, in effect, the planners of the market economy, the development of which is therefore better understood as guided, not anarchic.

These very definitely dominate the rest, not only in the sense of decisively shaping the directions of their economy's development but also in the sense of exploiting the rest, or subordinating the rest for their own advantage. Let me reiterate briefly what has been covered in the preceding chapters.

Recapitulation: Power and the Capitalist Market Economy

As just elaborated in the last chapter, even in a hypothetical world of something close to "perfect" capitalist markets, there would be inequalities in people's property endowments, and thus market participants would be unequally subject to the need to work for the income necessary to obtain their subsistence in markets: Some would have to work, while others would have sufficient income-earning property to sustain themselves at subsistence or better without having to work. The latter group would dominate those who have to work, in the sense that they would live off the product of the labor of those who work, while the working class, unless they have had the opportunity of full participation in a fair and democratic social decision about this particular economic setup, cannot be said to consent to it.

Thus it must be inferred that even if working people were not subject to the direct power of the dominant wealthy class as employees of the latter— that is, even if, hypothetically, all working people labor in self-owned private businesses—there must be some sort of power structure present, some sort of institution(s) by means of which this domination is accomplished, or else working people would not go along with an arrangement to which they do not consent. The power structure required for such a hypothetical perfect capitalist market system is none other than that which undergirds the institution of private property itself: It rests upon the coercive power of the state and the value power that is effective in the society's cultural institutions. Even in the best possible case of the textbook capitalist market system, then, power in the invidious sense used in this book is a fundamental and necessary fact.

Of course, the real world is not one of perfect capitalist markets. That is, reality has features that make it such that the textbook model of the ideal system cannot be conceived as something that could ever be incorporated into the actual world in which we live. Without dwelling on them, these imperfections include the well-known facts that all knowledge and prediction are uncertain, that all material resources and inputs are to varying degrees immobile, that indivisibilities and scale economies exist, that major external costs and benefits are unavoidable, and that intelligent and self-concerned humans may be opportunistic and employ strategic behavior.[1] From the viewpoint of mainstream neoclassical economics, these may be said to be the underlying realities by virtue of which various *additional* sorts of power structures—aside from those which necessarily underlie the private property system itself—also exist in market systems. Readers of this book should have seen that the power structures thereby arising in market systems are by no means minor and mostly correctable, they are not merely unfortunate by-products of an otherwise congenial system. Instead, besides being utterly unavoidable, they are fundamental to such systems and major in consequence. The congeniality of the system in which they arise is therefore even further subject to question.

Consider these additional power structures. To begin with, "business" in market systems is not merely a hodgepodge collection of small, independent firms interacting anarchically in the course of producing and selling goods and buying inputs from each other. First, power structures based on market monopoly and monopsony—arising from a variety of "imperfections"—are more widespread than even the available information on market concentration would suggest. There are plenty of obvious instances of monopoly, oligopoly, and dominant firm power among large corporations, as well as the corresponding variations of buyer-side power—and the data on market concentration suggest plenty of less obvious cases too. Informal horizontal, vertical, and conglomerate network connections among firms are also extensive throughout the economy. Thus market power, in the textbook sense of the term, is widespread.

Second, in conjunction with monopoly and monopsony power, network connections, especially those involving the financial sector, imply a business hierarchy in which a decision-making and -execution process occurs that is clearly akin to what economists have traditionally called centralized planning, that is, the allocation of production inputs by direction from the apex of a hierarchy. If planning in this business hierarchy proceeds more effectively than it did in the old Soviet-style bureaucracies, it is because the market system within which it is imbedded rations resources and products so much more effectively, that is, without the kinds of obvious incentives problems or disruptions of excess supply or demand that were extant in the Soviet Union. The business hierarchy also parallels the Soviet-type system, as Western economists understand the latter, in its essential detachment from "popular sovereignty" in those decision-making processes that determine the broad directions of economic development.

Just as there is a command hierarchy organizing relations among firms, there is also one organizing the relations among people within each firm where, of course, market allocation processes do not take place. People who lack property income are compelled to work in one way or another for their subsistence, and to be thereby exploited by those with sufficient property income to avoid work. But working people are also specifically subject to more direct domination by business owners and managers in firms because of the perennially short-sided labor market: Labor market "imperfections" cause unemployment, which manifests for wage-employees the always present threat of job loss. Firms are thus structured as hierarchies in which managers exercise actual command over workers, rather than as democratically constituted enterprises in which managers merely facilitate and administer. Under certain circumstances individual wage-employees may have power of their own to counter their employers' power—as agents of their employers, with knowledge and skills that the latter cannot acquire—but these circumstances are relatively rare. Of course, with sufficient solidarity among their members, labor unions can effectively counter employers' power, but their strength can often be countered, in turn, by employers' divide and conquer strategies of various kinds, as well as by government policy. Ultimately unions' ability to counter employers' power is a close function of labor's relative influence on the political sphere, especially in determining labor relations law and policy and the social safety net, and this influence too derives most critically from labor solidarity.

Finally, while purchasing power does not in itself constitute a form of power "over" people, inequality in the distribution of purchasing power plays a critical indirect role in all structures of power in capitalist market systems. Lacking purchasing power, people lack access to alternatives to their subjection in direct power relationships of all sorts, while possessing it enables people to take the dominant positions in those relationships. Thus, who must work and who need not, who must borrow and who may lend, who must purchase from firms with monopoly power and who has other options, and who may exert value power or influence in cultural institutions and who may not—all are determined by who lacks and who has sufficient purchasing power. Inequality in the distribution of purchasing power is then an essential element common to all of these (and other) social power structures. Of course, while purchasing power inequality is a determinant of power structures in capitalist market economies, it also arises from the ongoing functioning of those power structures, each of which yields benefits to those in dominant positions in the form of purchasing power that is, in effect, taken from subordinates—for example, business profit and personal wealth derived as a benefit of exercising employers' power over labor. Thus are power and economic inequality of the same coin.

In principle then, capitalist market systems constitute societies that are just as hierarchical as those based on other economic systems, for example, Soviet-style central planning, feudalism, and ancient slave-based systems. How can this incontrovertible fact be reconciled with the congenial picture of capitalist systems conveyed in mainstream economics? In fact, these two opposing perspectives on the nature of market systems are not necessarily inconsistent.

Power, Freedom, and Economics

For what the "pro-market" viewpoint of mainstream economics emphasizes most importantly of all is the individual freedom that the citizens of a market-based society have. That freedom, when considered in terms of the analysis of power developed in this book, is not inconsistent with the kind of command hierarchical society described here. Freedom, in the pro-market view, is essentially the freedom to choose one's economic relations with other people, entering into and withdrawing from any such relations that one pleases when one pleases. Yet choice is never without limits—there are always constraints of one kind or another—and the freedom to choose must be understood as the equivalent of having choices within the limits of those constraints. Having freedom to choose then is not inconsistent with being subject to power, for power consists in the ability to alter the constraints to which a person is subject in her decisions. Even very great freedom—over an extremely wide range of alternatives within the given set of constraints to which one is subject—does not in itself mean that one is necessarily free from another person's capacity to alter those constraints. Freedom to choose is not freedom from subjection to power.

"Freedom," alternatively, refers to the scope of autonomous action that individuals have, that is, the range of possible activities they may undertake without experiencing interference or impingement by others. "Power," on the other hand, refers to the capacity of a person to alter the scope or range of autonomous action of an individual, or to change the boundaries or parameters of the individual's freedom. If we grant that market systems allow their members an extended scope of autonomous action—obviously a critically important thing in people's ability to fulfill their aspirations and direct their own destinies—that still does not at all preclude that in such systems people are subject to power, nor does it imply that they are necessarily any less subject to power than in other kinds of economic systems or that the power to which they are subject is any less insidious.

And whether capitalist market systems actually do allow people greater freedom to choose is a critical question that is still subject to debate, despite the fact that many, especially mainstream economists, would take it as unquestionable truth. Two very basic, critical points are notable in this regard. First, there are some quite important kinds of things that capitalist market systems are especially poor at providing opportunities for people to choose: Opportunities to consume collective or public consumption goods, as many authors have elaborated, tend to be sorely underprovided in market systems; so too are opportunities to engage in collectively organized production activities, that is, democratically structured workplaces (as I elaborated in an earlier chapter).[2] If capitalist market systems provide an enormous scope of choice of other kinds of things, but do not provide as much scope of choice of these as do other systems, then it cannot be clear that market systems allow unambiguously greater freedom of choice.

Second, there is the problem of distribution: If capitalist systems are, as seems apparent, conducive of greater material inequality than are other systems, then while better-off people may have greater freedom in such systems than in others, those worse off may have less freedom than they would in others. Logically, capitalist market systems cannot then be said to allow unambiguously greater freedom to their subjects: Unless it can be shown conclusively that the general level of affluence such systems create necessarily "trickles down" all the way to those at the bottom of the distribution, those least well-off in capitalism may be worse off—and have accordingly less freedom of choice—than their counterparts in other less affluent economic systems.

Again, however, even if such questions could somehow be resolved definitively in favor of capitalist market systems, concluding that such systems do indeed extend people's freedoms by no means allows us to suppose that they therefore provide a world in which there is necessarily less power impinging upon people than in other systems: We could then only conclude that the power relations to which people in market systems are subject impinge upon them, in some sense, more remotely, or in ways more removed from direct and immediate experience.

Nor can it be concluded that whatever power does impinge upon people in capitalism is necessarily any less injurious. That is, again supposing that capitalist systems do unambiguously extend "freedoms" so understood, that still does not make them somehow better, when major structures of domination are as critical in such systems as in other kinds of economies. For the nature of power is such that those subject to it, were they able to effectively choose under more congenial circumstances, would elect not to be subject to it. To put it differently, it could be that, had people a choice in the matter under more congenial circumstances, they might offer to give up some of the expanded freedoms allowed in the capitalist market system, in order to be free of the power structures that are also necessarily associated with it.

That is mainly speculation, of course, at best merely intimating an objective critical evaluation of capitalist market systems. Yet while theorists in the other social sciences routinely take up these and related questions about capitalist societies, mainstream economists, whose field more than any other consists in the study of markets, do not generally venture anywhere near this far. That is the result of their studious avoidance of issues of power: Mainstream economics has contributed next to nothing toward a general understanding of the articulation of capitalist market systems in terms of the power structures intrinsic to them, much less toward a comprehension of the moral and other implications of those structures. So thorough has that avoidance been among economists that it is almost as if a decision had been made somewhere along the line to define the field as devoted to the study of things not involving power, and not to be concerned with any critical perspectives employing that concept. One suspects that a decision to avoid such consequential matters in so august a field may be ideologically rather than scientifically motivated.

For the argument that dominating power is intrinsic in capitalist systems can be adequately addressed, logically, in only two ways, neither of which is even attempted in mainstream economics. First, one may try to demonstrate that in reality people in capitalist market systems have roughly equal power over each other, or at least that the logic of power structures in markets, as laid out in this book and elsewhere, is descriptively inaccurate or significantly incomplete as an accounting of people's actual powers. Of course, avoiding the concept of power completely prohibits making any such demonstration. On the other hand, there is a strong and often observed bias in mainstream economics toward every possible theoretical fancy that would lend weight to such a demonstration were it ever attempted—from the recent use of "contestable markets theory" to counter evidence of the seriousness of monopoly and monopsony power, to the defunct but routinely unearthed claim that unemployment is mostly voluntary, as in "search theory"; from "efficient capital markets" theory to the theory of "rational expectations"; from neoclassical "balanced growth" to new classical theories of "real business-cycles." The propensity of the mainstream of the field is to refuse admission to critical arguments that major power structures are intrinsic in capitalist market systems, while indulging every novel potential counterargument, almost regardless of how strained and far-fetched it may be. Notably, mainstream economics is accepting of analyses of power only when they concern "extra-market" power structures that impinge upon the normal (i.e., supposedly power-free) functioning of markets, that is, when they involve government and labor union interference with markets.

The other possible approach logically to the issue of power in markets is to deny validity to the larger social-theoretic discourse of which the concept of power is an integral part, that is, to deny the idea of individual free human agency. Since it is impossible to conceive of anyone who lacks free agency as having power of any kind, the concept of social power cannot play a role in such theories as genetic determinism or extreme variations of structural determinism. In strict genetic determinism, for example, no individual can be supposed to exercise real choice, so no one could ever exercise any power over others, not even in objective circumstances that would permit someone with free choice to do so.[3] Of course, individual free agency has been a critically important underlying assumption in mainstream economics—the term "agency" itself has even achieved an established status in the field. Whatever its other faults, neoclassical welfare economics, the foundation of everything prescriptive or normative in the mainstream of the field, is simply unsustainable without the supposition that market participants are free humans who make their own choices. Denying the discourse of free human agency is not an option for mainstream economics.

The field does, however, ignore one major facet of human free agency, thereby avoiding a whole set of critical issues concerning power. By consistently making the supposedly harmless assumption that people's "tastes and preferences are given"—by adopting, in other words, for purposes of analysis a genetic determinist account of human wants and needs, albeit not of human behavior per se—mainstream economics avoids some of the more critical issues having to do with human learning and self-consciousness. With tastes and preferences given, people may learn or discover at most only what their individual preferences actually are and how best to fulfill them in their activities in the larger world—they cannot learn in the sense of discovering or coming to adopt for themselves others' values. Thus, they may be dominated by deception, being misled about how best to fulfill their own preferences or about what their preferences actually are in the first place, but they may not be dominated in the sense of the concept of value power, the exercise of which actually shapes or alters their values or preferences. The whole set of issues arising in consideration of the culture of capitalist market systems—its nature and impact on people in various circumstances, the question of who most influences or shapes it, the processes by which they do so, and the implications for the progress of human welfare—cannot even be expressed in the vocabulary of mainstream economics, where people's values are presumed given.[4]

Thus mainstream economics, the field whose study is most importantly capitalist market systems, has utterly failed to be of help in fostering a balanced and objective understanding of them. It has promoted a one-dimensional picture of the reality that is the object of its study, thereby impeding any real comprehension of that reality. Students seeking a broad and in-depth understanding of capitalism must turn to the other social sciences. Perhaps most importantly, the effect of the avoidance of the subject of power in mainstream economics has been to impede the development of means of countering the oppressive exercise of power in capitalist systems today: on that too, those concerned must turn mainly to the other social sciences for insight.

Power and Progressive Social Change

Critics of capitalist market systems are often accused of lacking "constructive alternatives." That accusation is simply ill informed (thanks in part to mainstream economics), for alternatives and potential changes have abounded, both in modern history and in the voluminous writings of those very critics. What sorts of things could be done to check or negate the oppressive consequences of the power structures I have described in this book?

The primary guiding principle for thinking about progressive changes and alternatives must be, of course, *democracy*, the antithesis of power as I have described it. Over the past two centuries, the worldwide democratic movement made great inroads into the political sphere of social life, as well as into relations between the races and between the sexes. The most critical challenge now for further progress in these and probably all other facets of our lives may be to democratize the economy, the one major sphere of life in capitalist market societies that remains to this day in most of the world relatively untouched by the democratic movement.

The various distinct power structures in social life undergird or reinforce each other by serving to deny people alternative spaces in which to conduct their life activities free of domination: A person's subjection in one power structure, or the threat thereof, is part of what maintains her subjection in another, it is part of the larger set of constraints that constitutes her having to submit in one power structure as well as others. Thus power structures in economic life reinforce those power structures in politics and in racial and sexual relations that still remain after these centuries of democratic progress. In principle, at some point in the progress of democratization of the polity, the family or any other social sphere, it becomes critical that economic democracy be furthered also.

Once, we had kings and nobles—now we have elected and recallable presidents and legislative representatives. Once, only propertied men could vote—now all adults of all races may. Once, only the supremely wealthy had access to written knowledge and basic skills of political discourse—now virtually all have at least some access. Given our experience with the process of democratization over the last two centuries, what is required to similarly democratize economic life is not difficult to conceive. What is difficult is actually accomplishing the required changes. For the decisive question that arises in thinking about social power structures is, how can social changes be accomplished that counter the dominance of those in positions of power, when those who are dominated, by definition, lack the power to accomplish such changes? In fact, such changes cannot be accomplished unless the circumstances engendering the power structures themselves change the balance of power: Progressive changes cannot occur "until the times are right."

Activists working for progressive change, however, take heart from two facts repeatedly observed in the history of the democratic movement. First, the circumstances engendering power structures are changing continually and, apparently, fairly rapidly in modern times—the capitalist market system itself being perhaps the most potent source of change ever in human history. Of course, the whole point of this book has been to show that that system is likely to continue to engender major power structures. But other dynamics than those described in this book are at work in human history, and the dynamic of markets profoundly affects all of them even as they also, in turn, affect it. Thus it seems certain that at several points in modern history, the dynamics and evolution of markets were clearly themselves responsible for major progressive changes—markets evolved in such a way that, in effect, they undermined their own foundations. For example, the Great Depression was arguably the single event most directly responsible for enduring progressive changes in labor-management relations in the twentieth-century Western world.

While the direction of things today may not seem especially conducive of progressive change, there are also grounds for hope. It may be speculated, for example, that the increasing complexity of the organization of production and the high and rising level of affluence of these times together may militate against authoritarian relations at work. If that is why worker participation schemes have spread among firms, disappointing as those schemes may be in comparison with real workplace democracy, then it may be that the same changing circumstances could eventually tip the balance more in favor of the real thing.

The second fact from which activists take heart is that, because it simply cannot be known in advance whether the "circumstances" are or are not actually conducive for progressive change at a point in time, surprises sometimes occur that reward the difficult work involved. That is, we may speculate about the prospects for democratizing the workplace, for example, and will likely come to various conclusions, but only time will tell for sure, and those who have committed to working for such changes may well end up being the ones proved correct. Alternatively, we cannot know the actual state of the "circumstances"—whether they actually are conducive or not, and precisely how so—except by means of progressive activism itself, which is then as much an exploration and testing of things to see the possibilities of change, as it is the work of actually accomplishing progressive change. Thus the ultimate ground for hope is the simple fact that one cannot know until one has tried—and even then one will probably not know for sure.

Of course, activism requires a commitment to solidarity among those working for any progressive change if it is to be effective. Part of what makes the times right for progressive change is the existence of sufficient cohesion among the numbers of those working for and benefiting from the change to tilt the balance in their favor. For power must be, in effect, reciprocated by means of structures that may be used to counter the efforts of the powerful to maintain existing power structures (i.e., with threats and/or influence or value power returned in kind). Lacking this, new and enduring structures and institutions cannot be created to more permanently countervail or negate or undermine the existing power structures. Social power rests on organization and can only be countered similarly.

Solidarity in activists who are devoted to countering the power structures delineated here, furthermore, most be both local and global. Locally, solidarity is required in order to bring to bear coordinated actions to press those locally powerful with sufficient strength to gain concessions from them. Solidarity is just as critical at the state or national or international levels, however, where without it localities or regions or political groupings can be played off against each other to extract capitulations that may reverse any gains made, but where, with solidarity, local gains can be protected by broader support or broader gains can be secured.

Democratizing the Economy: Politics

To what sorts of changes must activists commit themselves in order to counter the oppressive power structures described in this book? While we have much experience in the principles of democracy in the political sphere, and more recently in the relations between the races and between the sexes, precisely what would be meant by "democratizing the economy" may not be quite as clear. Thus it would be fitting to close this book by outlining broadly the sorts of changes that would be required or helpful. I reiterate that those who have criticized market systems, both theorists and those more directly involved in activism, have written voluminously on progressive changes and alternatives: Among the suggestions that follow, little or nothing can be taken as new in that sense.[5] It should also be noted at the outset that after the *regressive* changes that have been brought about in the last two decades of conservative political dominance in the United States, a number of the suggestions offered here amount to mere repairs of what's been damaged—these changes then are not at all new but only reconstructions of already tried-and-true policies (many of which remain in use in other countries, undamaged and serving their citizens quite well).

Insofar as the progressive changes that follow require national, state, or local governmental legislation, progressive changes in *political processes* are critical for bringing them about and for maintaining them once they are achieved. The reverse is true as well, as I stated earlier: Democratizing the economy is critical for further improvements in political democracy. Progress in both the political and economic spheres must be a single commitment, while, of course, whatever individual pieces of either of the two interlocking parts may be progressively altered at any point in time should be the focus at that point. Enormous strides have been made in democratizing government over the last two centuries, but there is much remaining to do, and inadequacies of democracy in the political sphere are plainly a fundamental part of the general problem of power in capitalist market societies. Thus, while this book is about social power in the economy, some review of the progressive changes needed in our political structures and processes is called for at the outset.

Political processes are in critical need of further democratization simultaneously in three most important areas. First, the *financing of political parties and campaigns* needs to be moved toward public sources of funds rather than private donors. Recent decades seem to show that there is no completely satisfactory way of policing private political contributions, and more importantly, the sources of these funds strongly bias politics in favor of the affluent and their institutions and causes. Democratic political representation is properly considered what economists call a public good, and accordingly the basic principle of public financing for public goods is properly applied.

Second, in the United States at least, a greater *diversity of political parties* is needed. We have essentially a political oligopoly (specifically, a duopoly), and the lack of alternative voices is stifling our public discussion of political issues and severely restricting our public policy choices at all levels of government. Nonmainstream political parties need the same access to public funding as the dominant parties. They need easing of the restrictions on the access of their candidates to ballots. And perhaps most importantly, they need the sort of access to influence in the halls of public legislation that apparently can only come with "proportional representation" of the kind extant in Europe—a major change for the United States, but many believe a practical one. Some greater diversification of the political spectrum could perhaps be achieved by somehow giving greater autonomy to each of the various constituencies of the two main political parties (by democratizing, in effect, each of those parties!), but even if that were done, major constituencies would still remain that are excluded from the two dominant parties. Thus, we simply need more political parties.

Third, major changes are needed in the role of the *mass media* in political discourse and decision making. Public financing of political parties' campaign and other advertising would help in this regard, but what is needed also is either publicly subsidized or else publicly regulated media space for political and related public issue debate and discussion. The former could be accomplished in the same context as public ownership of mass media enterprises, for example, the Public Broadcasting System. If the public regulation approach is instead to be taken, then private media firms should be required, for example, to provide some major prime-time space for political parties' presentation, discussion, and debate, and on a continuing basis, not merely for presidential elections—and be open to all legitimate parties, not just the two dominant ones. (Current media coverage of public decision making, such as we already have in cable television coverage of legislatures, is certainly helpful, especially for constituencies' oversight of their elected representatives. But it is nowhere near sufficient for assuring an appropriate public airing of political debate and discussion, since less affluent people do not have cable, since this kind of coverage cannot bring focus on in-depth arguments of political advocacy, and since most of the debate that is covered is not during prime time.)

There are grounds, by the way, for extending public regulation or subsidy or ownership into not merely the broadcast media but also local daily newspapers. One possible alternative might be a legal requirement of a diversity of community representatives on a democratic board of editors of the newspaper. Dailies are monopolies in all big cities by now—and most are outsider-owned at that—hence may properly be considered, in all essential aspects, public-utility–type common carriers that ought to be subject to public oversight on their openness to diverse news sources and to access for political discussion and debate. As things stand currently, as one may easily judge from the volume of space they devote to news as opposed to advertising, daily "news" papers are actually in the business of providing media and audiences for private commercial product advertisers.

Progressive reform of the mass media should extend also to the newest and potentially most revolutionary of modern communication media, the Internet. The novelty and rapid spread of this medium in the last few years calls for some further comment. The enormous promise of the Internet for democratizing access to information and participation in the public discourse is clear by now, and its potential use as a means of organizing politically oriented popular action is becoming increasingly clear as well—witness the recent internationally organized demonstrations over globalization and the World Trade Organization. Indeed, one can easily imagine the Internet being employed as the means for a truly democratic participatory economic planning, perhaps of the sort Michael Albert and Robin Hahnel had in mind in their several books on the subject.[6] At the very least, as the already well-established Internet auction sites now available have demonstrated (e.g., ebay.com), it can be expected to facilitate a considerable democratizing of markets—that is, access to relevant information for market transactions and the means for carrying out those transactions—by cheapening these and thereby allowing a much wider population to take advantage of the benefits of exchange.

Yet this enormous potential is blocked by two major obstacles. First, access to the benefits of the Internet is, and will remain for some time, greatly unequal. Hardware and software prices may continue falling, of course (although most recently some of these prices have actually been stagnant or rising), but the educational costs of people attaining sufficient competence with computer and Internet use are significant. Not only will many people continue to lack the time for learning the necessary skills, but the latter will continue to be unequally available to students as well. As is usually the case, the less affluent and their schools receive at best the hand-me-downs from the more affluent. Moreover, not only are the best noncommercial computing equipment and Internet connections available mainly only to the very affluent and those in professional or intellectual occupations, but the most direct and visible benefits of computer and Internet use are available only to those groups as well, hence people in the working class have less apparent incentive to become competent in these things. This is partly due to the second of the major obstacles in developing the democratizing potential of the Internet: its commercialization, which has already proceeded far beyond what would be healthy for a democratic medium of communication.

Aside from its obvious benefits to business, the commercialization of the Internet offers direct economic benefits to the affluent and those in professional and intellectual occupations, most of whose livelihoods are already directly tied to commerce and whose consumption expenditures are in any case high enough to benefit from "economies of scale" in the purchase of consumer goods over the Internet. But commercialization interferes directly with other more progressive uses of the medium for artistic expression and social discourse on public affairs: It clutters people's work in such areas with irrelevant advertising, it forecloses activities that do not yield some kind of market revenue, and it biases the content of what little noncommercial Internet publication remains.

Browsing Web pages, for example, requires spending time with the advertisements sold to cover the costs of their publication, but as long as other ways of paying the costs of Web page publication, e-mail, and so forth are not available, people must turn to the selling of advertising. Exactly as in the mass media, commercial interests, and among them mainly the better endowed, tend to prevail, and access to noncommercial Internet content becomes more and more difficult as it becomes harder and harder merely to find it with the available, increasingly commercialized search facilities. Active participation too, for example, in Web page publication, mail- and news-servers, chat rooms, bulletin boards, and so forth, with other ends in mind than commercial ones becomes more difficult as well, even for those who can afford it, since the audience or the range of other participants is increasingly restricted to more commercially motivated users. Strictly noncommercial Internet use is significantly restricted to those in noncommercial institutions—universities and the government—but even there private commercialism is increasingly to be found, as advertising revenue is sought to help defray costs. Finally, as has also happened in the mass media, as commercialization proceeds and the corporate ownership of Internet media and content becomes increasingly concentrated, noncommercial Internet content is bound to be increasingly treated by the corporations in control as "packaging" for the advertisements from which they get their profit—to be selected in accordance with its appropriateness for audience receptivity to the ads with which it is presented.

All of this suggests a critical need for a major public role in the Internet, access to which should, in principle, be equally free and open to all, but with special regard to all noncommercial interests. Public subsidy of noncommercial Internet use and content production for individuals and nongovernmental organizations might be offered, for example, with substantial tax breaks. This could be combined with public-utility type regulation if necessary on the prices charged by service providers for access. A sizable sector of publicly owned nodes with free access for noncommercial users and content providers, and with as full a set of facilities as are provided by privately owned nodes, would be another approach. Without some such public role in the provision of Internet access, the latter is likely to go the same route as radio and television have in their brief histories to date: From potential resources for the real democratization of life, to actual tools for the further empowerment of those benefiting from already established structures of domination.

Turning now to changes directly concerning power structures in the economy, I will present these in the same order as they were discussed earlier in this book: First, those directly aimed at business power (i.e., monopoly power, networks, and financial hegemony); then those directly involving employer power; and finally, those having to do with purchasing power and income and wealth inequality.

Progressive Change in Business

We now have over a hundred years of experience with *antitrust policy*, and even more with *public utility regulation*, as effective and well-understood public checks on business power based on monopoly. Both of these policy approaches have been seriously eroded in recent decades, however, to the point that deregulation is now the common "wisdom" on "protecting the public interest" with regard to natural monopolies like cable TV and electric power, while huge corporate mergers take place routinely that would not even have been contemplated before the anti-antitrust era of the Reagan years.

What is needed in antitrust is merely a retrenchment of traditional progressive liberal thinking in existing administrative structures and a major strengthening of the resources those structures have available for pressing their tasks of breaking up excessive market power and preventing its rise by mergers or strategic anticompetitive practices. There is much work to do in comprehending how best to deal with the complex and rapidly changing high-tech industries and the role of globalization in both traditional and new industries as matters of concern for antitrust policy. Cutbacks on antitrust agencies' funds and personnel, and relaxation of their prosecutorial stance on market power concentrations—merely on account of supposedly "greater competition" in markets due to changing product substitutability and market turmoil—is no policy in the public interest.

Similarly, great changes in the affected industries' technologies have not in the least made obsolete the public-utility regulation approach to natural monopolies. Just because there is now a national grid connecting electric-power producers does not mean that your local supplier is competing with other suppliers across the country for your and your neighbors' business. And while cable TV companies have been competing with satellite TV and video recording and other media, as I pointed out earlier, concentration in all these industries is proceeding at dizzying rates and companies are merging all across these and other communications sectors as well: It is not a time for deregulation and lax antitrust but for a renewed and strengthened commitment to the principles of these two tried-and-true policies.

There are grounds for considering more progressive *public ownership* approaches to the problem of monopoly power as well. Especially in the energy and mass media industries, where the problem is enormously consequential for the public good—in the former because of its fundamental role in all economic and environmental development, and in the latter because of its role in all cultural development. The profits of publicly owned firms may go toward financing public goods, for example, investments in more energy-conservative and environmentally sustainable public infrastructure. Of course, public enterprises may alternatively be run to take losses—by being subsidized from public funds, as in public broadcasting, as well as in most public mass transit—in order to provide public goods where private providers would never be induced to do so. The high profitability of the energy industries as now constituted suggests that some public ownership there would return income to public treasuries, and publicly owned firms could also perform the role of rivals to existing private firms: They could offer alternative and/or higher quality products and could induce more competitive behavior from them. Subsidized publicly owned firms may accomplish the same end, as has the Public Broadcasting System to some extent probably improved the quality of the private networks' offerings. Monopoly power in both the energy sector and the media is a critically important impediment to increasingly needed social change in these times—the energy oligopolies and their associated corporate networks, for example, are clearly committed to what now appears to be an increasingly irrational expansion of fossil-fuel–based energy consumption. The existence of major publicly owned firms in these sectors could act as a lever for inducing approaches and directions in private and public investment that are alternative to those now being pursued.

We have considerable experience in public ownership, of course, in the mass media as well as in public-utility industries like electric power, water, sewage, and mass transit, but like antitrust and public-utility regulation, public ownership is currently quite unpopular. Our national public broadcasting service is being eviscerated with funding cuts and is beginning to look and sound like just another "medium for advertisers." Our public parks and recreation areas have always been under pressure to be leased or sold to private producers wanting their resources, but are now increasingly being turned over to private companies for management—as are our prisons being privatized and increasingly even our normal government administration itself (for example, in the administration of certain welfare activities).[7] Our public schools may well follow, if vouchers catch on and public schools shrink while private schools flourish. Thus far, fortunately, our publicly owned utilities have mostly escaped this movement toward privatization: As economic enterprises in the public interest they have proved by and large far too successful to be let go to the private sector.

Some privatization may actually be constructive, in principle. In practice, however, all too frequently it is motivated merely by private investors' greed for access to the profit available in public funds, and by public officials' willingness to cheapen the provision of public goods and services by avoiding public employees' labor unions or cutting back on the monitoring of the quality of the goods or services produced. What is too often purposely forgotten in the privatization movement is the essential reason for public ownership. If accountability for democratically determined purposes is desirable to one degree or another in an industry, then either public regulation of some sort or else public ownership is necessary. Other things equal, the greater is the degree of such accountability that is sought—specifically, the stronger is the need for democratic accountability in the day-to-day provision of the services of the firm—the clearer is the need for public ownership. Schools, prisons, parks and recreation, and the financing and administration of the provision of public income transfers are not good candidates for privatization, because the details of the day-to-day activity of the enterprise are precisely what must be subject to democratic accountability, and can only be adequately monitored in the public interest on a more or less close and continual basis. For example, if under private ownership, public monitors would be needed to make daily visits to the site of production, then publicly employed managers, directly responsible to public officials rather than to outside owners, may well be a better bet.

As publicly owned enterprise has smacked of "evil socialism," especially in this country in these times, so too has *public investment*, or even any significant overt public role in determining the broad directions of private investment. Of course, there is nothing even remotely democratic about the determination of the directions of economic investment when left solely to the market: Insofar as the determination is made by "dollar votes," these would not be equally distributed even in an ideal capitalist market system. And in the real world of imperfect markets in capitalist systems, the public's input into decision making on investment is limited to something far less than in the textbook account of consumer sovereignty. Business network and financial powers dominate the process, as I pointed out in an earlier chapter—with advertising, public relations, and political influence then assuring adequate consumer demand and public sector cooperation to justify whatever major private investment projects are decided upon on high. Insofar as all such projects have broad public impact—for example, again, in the energy sector—democratizing the economy requires some significant democratic public initiative in the decision-making process on investment.

In principle, this is neither difficult nor undesirable in its "distortion" of markets. Many countries have successfully used public "guidance" in directing the broad contours of national private investment, indeed it is arguably at the root of the post–World War II economic dynamism of such exemplary cases as Japan and France. It is not necessary, of course, for the public to be the sole disburser of investment funds, but government either must have some significant such funds of its own for key investments to induce additional private investment spending in whatever directions are appropriate, or else it must have influence in the disbursement of private funds. In the former case, the funds may be obtained from tax revenues or by special savings arrangements, perhaps social security or other retirement savings funds, and may then be offered on special favorable terms for private firms' investment projects in industries that have been singled out for development. Planning for projects would be aided by government, which may also make loan guarantees or provide other incentives to firms as necessary in related industries.

Loan guarantees are one way for government to influence the direction of private funds for investment. Other ways would include credit allocation at the level of the central bank—or from publicly owned banks (an especially good reason for some significant public ownership in the financial sector); public representation on the boards of directors of private banks; or special investment regulations (i.e., on banks' investment portfolios). With the exception of central bank activities, of course, all of this can be done at the national, state, or local levels of government. At each level, there are major investment opportunities that beg for public action, for example, in the development of alternative energy sources and modes of transportation, environmental recovery, and the associated urban and suburban restructuring, none of which will occur without fundamental involvement by government in the decision-making and planning processes and in directing the necessary financing.

We have, in fact, instituted some progressive public investment policies more or less permanently already. Community development corporations—the intention of which is to assure that some investment is channeled into relatively unglamorous but essential local development, under broadly represented local control, especially in lower income areas or inner cities—are merely the best known instances of progressive public policies for influencing investment.[8] The amounts employed have been cut back in post-Reagan years, however, and many similarly progressive investment portfolio regulations for banks and other financial institutions have been cut as well.

On the other hand, a significant government role in influencing private investment has in fact been the case all throughout the history of market systems—from the financing of the earliest private explorations of the New World, to the subsidization of private railroad construction; from the subsidization of the automobile by means of the highway system and the encouragement of mortgage lending for suburbanization, to the subsidization of the airlines industry by means of the construction and operation of airports; from basic research and development in state universities to space exploration. It is often noted that the long-term vibrancy of the U.S. economy since World War II is importantly a consequence of "military Keynesianism"—the still massive devotion of public expenditures to the military—as substantial an example of what can be done with public-private sector cooperation, planning, and investment as any that can be offered.

A more overt and democratically accountable role for public influence in the direction of private investment is proscribed by private sector financial and corporate power because it tends to reduce private profit (by redirecting investment in something other than a profit-maximizing way). Outright public investment (i.e., public lending), that is subject to democratic accountability is at least equally vigorously condemned by private sector power because it directly claims investment returns that could otherwise be available to private investors—probably the most important reason for business sector proscription of public enterprise in general as well. But the real question is not whether we will have a "planned economy" in the sense of a substantial role for government in the economic investment process—we have one now. Instead the important question is, who will do the planning? Will it be mainly private financial and corporate power behind close doors, motivated by the maximization of private profit, or people who are in one way or another more accountable to the broader public?

Progress for Working People

Public enterprise and public influence on investment could perhaps be used to help undermine employers' power in the private sector. However, since public enterprise and investment can only directly impact a fraction of total economic activity, and since they will probably be subject primarily to other ends as well, democratizing employer-labor relations will require a much broader set of changes. Foremost among these, given the breadth and effectiveness of the forces arrayed against labor solidarity—all the things that work to "divide and conquer" labor to the benefit of employers—is public commitment to the support of *labor unions.* To some extent this must involve merely rolling back some of the changes made since the Reagan presidency, that is, merely committing to the spirit of already existing labor law. Thus the National Labor Relations Board must be seated with people other than those representing employers' interests, and the resources available to the board for prosecuting and hearing cases must be greatly expanded. These two changes by themselves would help considerably, for example, by shortening the time spent waiting for a case to be heard, by increasing the likelihood that cases such as those against employers who fire union leaders will be decided and prosecuted appropriately, and by providing enough monitoring of compliance with existing labor laws to assure their effectiveness.

But the decline of labor unionism in these times has deeper roots than that, and reversing it will require progressive changes in established labor law itself. First, the practice of firms' hiring as permanent employees replacement workers for those temporarily on strike, instituted over the last two decades as a result of President Reagan's infamous action in the PATCO strike, needs to be disallowed in this country, as it is in most other advanced market economies. Giving striking workers the right to return to their jobs after the strike is over would, in effect, give them a minimal and completely appropriate "ownership" stake in their jobs, and would also, of course, lighten the potential costs to workers of using the strike as a tool for countering employers' power.

Second, states' so-called right-to-work laws must be repealed. These were a concession to states' rights in the Taft-Hartley Act, and while very much in the mostly antilabor spirit of that act, are not at all in the spirit of labor law as a whole, where workers' and unions' rights and responsibilities otherwise are defined for all national citizens, not merely those of some states. (Similarly lenient states' rights have not been built into much other national legislation, for example, on occupational safety and health and environmental affairs.) Right-to-work laws, in effect, disallow the unionized workers of a firm from deciding that *all* the employees of the firm who are covered in its contract with the union must be union members. In right-to-work states, employees who are not members of the local union thus receive the full benefit of the union's contract without having had to participate in helping to secure it or to pay union dues or to bear any of the risks of the employer's bias against union members. They are "free riders," whose numbers considerably reduce union power by reducing unions' membership and by serving the purpose of "dividing and conquering" firms' workforces.

Two other significant progressive changes in the law pertaining to unions would be, first, easing the process of certifying a new union in a workplace, and making more difficult the decertification process; and second, removing some of the restrictions on workers' rights to organize unions or to go on strike. Regarding the former, the process of creating an official union in a workplace, that is, one which is fully protected by applicable law, is tedious, time-consuming, and thoroughly bureaucratized in current practice, allowing employers to use all sorts of divisive tactics during the wait period to discourage potential union members, and deflating much of the energy and initiative from the organization of the union. At the same time, with the help of labor-relations consulting firms that employers may contract for the purpose of "busting" their employees' unions (or preventing their employees from forming unions in the first place, of course), employers may all too easily initiate decertification elections.

Workers do not all have the right to organize official unions—nor to go on strike even if they belong to one, thus eviscerating what real power many unions might otherwise have. Notably excluded from these rights are schoolteachers, whose unions cannot legally call strikes in many states, and agricultural workers in all but a couple of states, whose pay and work conditions are the worst of all American workers today. "National security" has sometimes been used as a rationale for exclusions from the right to organize, but it is difficult to see how it may aptly pertain to these two groups.

Perhaps the single most effective change that could be made for countering employers' power over workers would be an economic policy of *full employment*. Such a policy, were it executed with commitment, would include, of course, the usual textbook monetary and fiscal approaches, with perhaps some broadening of the latter by use of special counter-cyclical investment funds (which accumulate during business-cycle expansions and then are spent during contractions). Aside from these, government could also use its role in investment planning more generally, as described above, partly for the purpose of bringing the economy to full employment. Nor is there anything, in principle, undesirable about government employment in public works jobs, such as were used during the Great Depression—indeed, such jobs merely amount to direct government production of public goods, that is, goods that the private sector cannot be counted upon to provide in sufficient quantities and that would thus require public provision anyway. Finally, government could support workers' expenses for job training and retraining and job relocation much more than it does currently—the United States spends considerably less on such programs, which improve the "allocative functioning of labor markets," than do other advanced market societies. Full-employment programs could easily be targeted toward those groups most in need of employment; and local control in contexts of democratically responsible decision making (e.g., using federal revenue sharing and grants) could easily be used for assuring that their focus is properly on those most needy groups and on projects most beneficial for communities.

Achieving durable full employment would remove one of the most critical sources of inefficiency in market systems, of course, but there may be fundamental questions of its feasibility, precisely on account of its fundamental role in employers' power. The upshot of the analysis given in earlier chapters is that unemployment is essential for undergirding the power relations necessary for getting alienated employees to labor with sufficient diligence to generate profit for business owners, and that it is automatically created in sufficient amounts by the "natural" working of the business cycle. Permanently removing unemployment by means of the policies just delineated would indeed jeopardize the entire structure were it accomplished in a context in which no other changes were also being made.

But other features of the economy that more broadly determine the environment of work can be changed. Were employees' attitudes about work less alienated because of increased real participation in the management of their firms—obviously a desirable change in itself, and one I will discuss shortly—the "stick" of unemployment would perhaps be less important as a work incentive. Even without an expansion of direct workplace democracy, were it perceived that the division of the fruits of workers' productivity improvements over time between workers, management, and owners were fairer—in particular because workers have, by means of strong labor unions and a more sympathetic government, an appropriate influence on that division—the macroeconomic problems of full employment would be far more easily manageable than at present. This sort of circumstance held during the labor-management accord in the United States, as I noted in an earlier chapter, and continues to hold in some European countries, where it has provided a means of checking the wage-price spiral of inflation that would otherwise follow upon an extended period of full employment. Briefly, real-wage changes are kept in parity with labor productivity increases over time by firms' keeping price increases in check and workers' unions' limiting wage increases in return. Inflation then becomes a purely monetary (and/or international exchange-rate) phenomenon, manageable by means other than economic recession. The key, however, is sufficient labor strength that unions, in tandem with a pro-labor government, can compel employers to limit their price increases to no more than any cost increases they experience, and can guarantee labor compliance in return.[9]

The most direct approach to countering employers' power would be to create a gradually expanding sector of *democratic, worker-managed firms*. A full commitment to democratizing work would have as its ultimate aim the expansion of the sector of such firms to the entirety of the economy—or at least to a great enough portion of it to allow people some choice of what kind of workplace they prefer, and a real voice in all decisions affecting their work if they so choose. I described broadly the operating structure of democratic worker-managed firms in an earlier chapter. It should suffice here to reiterate that democratizing work would require a strong public commitment to encouraging such firms.

For as I showed, democratic firms are generally absent in market systems not because they are less efficient nor because people do not desire to work in them, but because the milieu of traditional capitalist enterprise militates against them. Because they fly in the face of the whole system, in order to effectively construct an economically viable sector of democratic firms, the fullest possible commitment from government would be required. Investment loan guarantees and subsidies would be necessary, of the same order of magnitude as government now extends to traditional private business. A system of new management schools or special divisions of existing management schools and research facilities devoted to democratic worker-managed firms, all subsidized with public funding at least initially, would also be necessary. So too would a system of special banks, or else special banking laws applicable to existing banks, be required to assure the continuing availability of capital to an expanding sector of such firms. A new ownership form for enterprises would have to be created: Common stock ownership, including the employee stock ownership plans currently in practice, will not suffice for economically viable democratic firms, nor will the cooperative form of existing law. A new kind of "limited liability" enterprise, with one-worker-one-vote and democratically determined shares of enterprise profit, will be required. Correspondingly, there will also need to be constructed an entire legal system devoted to litigation and adjudication of workers' rights as owners of their firms under the new form, including especially their rights as democratic participants in firms' decision making.

Of course, these changes would be quite radical and could not be successfully implemented all at once. A good deal of learning about the operation and culture of workplace democracy will be necessary in the course of a gradual expansion of a sector of democratic firms. Labor unions will have to play a role in such a process, in both the creation and the ongoing development of a viable such sector. While unions in present circumstances are understandably reluctant to advocate worker participation plans that are initiated by management and merely co-opt employees and their unions, it is likely that only labor unions will be able to give sufficient voice to people's desire for real workplace democracy. Of course, if they are themselves truly democratic, then unions will be the strongest proponents of such change. Moreover, once instituted, democratic enterprises in practice will not eliminate the need for separate and distinct democratic organs representing and advocating for workers. Were labor unions to be fully devoted exemplars of the larger aims of democracy, they could easily advocate both for democratic enterprises where those do not exist, and for workers' rights in those existing democratic enterprises that may fail the test of full democracy.

Changing Income and Wealth Inequality

In principle, were all the changes in business and labor just described to be successfully put in place, the subsequent distribution of income and wealth would be one of dramatically greater equality. Monopoly and other related sources of excess business profit would be greatly reduced; the share of profit and other property income in aggregate income overall would be cut, while labor's share would be expanded; greater equality in labor incomes would also follow; and with targeted public investment and full employment, poverty would be greatly reduced as well. Countering structures of power, in other words, counters also the economic inequalities arising from them.

On the other hand, one can also conceive this relationship in the reverse direction, for in terms of the analysis of the last chapter, dismantling economic inequality would remove a critical piece of the foundation of all power structures extant in capitalist market systems. Employers' power, in the most obvious example, would not exist without sufficient income and wealth inequality to guarantee a class of people compelled to sell their labor to subsist. And political power and cultural influence would be much dispersed were participation in politics and culture no longer curtailed by economic constraint for some people while practically unlimited for others. Thus, putting aside the structural changes in business and labor outlined above, economic egalitarianism would all by itself constitute a broad attack on the power structures of market society.

From the viewpoint of activist strategy, however, this does not mean that there is a choice between egalitarian economic redistribution and changes in the structures of business and labor such as those outlined above. In principle, a nonegalitarian might be concerned about social power and might wish that the power structures of market society could be dismantled without having to address the distribution of income itself: Merely make structural changes like those described above and let the distribution be what it will. Conversely, others might wish to redistribute income and wealth on other grounds than their relationship with social power, hence prefer that direct alteration of given structures of power not be attempted in the process. But arguably neither such approach is likely to be successful from a strategic viewpoint, for the issues are too closely interrelated. Moreover, the historical experience of the international advance of political democracy shows that mere alterations of political processes in the direction of democracy cannot begin to effect real political democracy without economic redistribution, nor can major improvements in economic equality be accomplished independently of real political democracy. Similarly, activism for economic democracy must support both structural changes and egalitarian redistribution together as parts of an overarching strategy, for accomplishments in the one are unlikely without accomplishments in the other.

In what sorts of ways might the distribution of income and wealth be more directly addressed from the perspective of a concern with social power? For one thing, because economic inequality in the United States is so greatly structured by differentials arising from race and sex discrimination, policies aimed specifically at correcting for these need to be in place. Not only are antidiscrimination policies necessary, but real "affirmative action" in hiring, in pay and promotion at work, in education and entertainment, in housing and lending, and in public spending and investment needs to be restored. Additional policies aimed at freeing women from bondage to the home— child-care subsidies, paid parental leave, and so forth—need to be established. Beyond that, three broad sets of direct changes in the distribution of income and wealth could easily be pursued on the basis of historical experience with the necessary social mechanisms involved (with or without changes in the structures of business and labor such as outlined earlier): (1) improvements in the quality of and access to public education, (2) universal social insurance, and (3) a progressive tax system.

Universal education has been treated by many political liberals as nearly a panacea for economic inequality. The preceding chapter should have made clear that it is not at all so, yet even in a world of full employment and political and workplace democracy, equalizing access to both a vocational and a liberal education that is as extensive as society can afford would remain a primary concern for the achievement of a sustainable economic democracy. To begin with, the education system at all levels should be expanded in terms of both the resources expended per student and the number of students accommodated. Public spending per student should be increased at all levels, for there are severe limits on how much the quality of education can be improved without reducing class sizes and teaching loads and paying for better teaching and facilities. The property-tax funding of public schools, in which spending per student is a direct function of the average income of families in the school district, should be supplanted by funding from state and federal revenues such that all schools are brought up to the spending levels of those in the most affluent districts. And postsecondary public education should be offered free to all those who cannot afford it, with the higher education system expanded to accommodate those students who are now denied access by their inability to pay.[10]

Equally important, in an affluent society that is on the path toward true democracy, people can be expected to seek from their educations much more than a mere preparation for personal vocations and careers and a training for passive work and acquiescent citizenship. The education system overall should embody in its curriculum and personnel a liberatory philosophy in which people are prepared not only for work but also for personal growth and for active democratic participation in the workplace and all other spheres of their community and larger society. And higher education should become something to which people may easily turn at any point in their lives for whatever goals of personal growth and social participation they may have, without jeopardizing their jobs, their health, or their places in their community.

Social insurance is a public good only grudgingly provided in the history of most market societies to date, yet social insurance systems have been perhaps the most successful of all progressive innovations of modern times. Thus, the provision of retirement security has raised fully half of the population of those who would otherwise be poor out of poverty; and while job loss remains a major trauma in people's lives, unemployment insurance, at least while it lasts (usually up to twenty-six weeks in the United States), makes job loss something less than totally catastrophic. In a world of true full employment, the need for many kinds of social insurance would be greatly reduced: Far fewer people would be in need of unemployment insurance, welfare, housing support, food stamps, and so forth. Yet some would still be in need, and adequate systems providing such support would remain necessary, just as would universal retirement security and health-care insurance systems. On various grounds, all these sources of support should be either publicly provided, or else privately provided subject to public regulation. Social insurance is, in many ways, a public good; incentives for quality private provision of it are lacking, and in an affluent society access to these forms of insurance should not be determined by ability to pay but universally guaranteed.

In real-world capitalist market societies today, poverty remains the most insidious of the consequences of economic inequality—in some countries much more than in others (by most good measures the United States has at least twice the poverty rate of other advanced capitalist societies). The threat of poverty in people's lives is the bedrock of the harshest forms of social power deriving from economic inequality—its complete elimination would be an historic first step in the direction of both a more egalitarian and a more humane society.

That in principle poverty might be completely eliminated, at least as it is officially defined, is not at all farfetched. Each year the U.S. Census Bureau publishes data on the "average poverty deficit"—the amount of additional income that would be required on average to bring the income of an individual living in poverty up to the "official poverty line" income level. The aggregate poverty deficit in 1998, the amount required to bring *all* people in poverty up to the poverty line, was $82.5 billion, an amount that represents *less than a third* of the U.S. government's military spending that year. Indeed, this amount represents merely 1.4 percent of the aggregate U.S. expenditure on personal consumption: Poverty, as officially defined, could be completely eliminated by simply transferring to the poor the revenues from a mere 1.5 percent federal sales tax! Of course, this is not to say that either a sales tax or a straight income transfer would be the right way to approach the problem of poverty—but that amount may be considered an estimate of the *maximum* cost of an effective public commitment against poverty.[11]

And experience with public policy to date is encouraging regarding the possibilities of such a commitment, as well as about exactly how it might be made. Besides full employment macroeconomic policies, targeted public investment aimed at poverty areas and groups, education funding increases and redistribution, and so forth, systems of direct public support for people in poverty could be greatly strengthened as well, that is, welfare payments and subsidies for food, housing, health care, and child care. And recent welfare "reform" could easily be reversed (removing current limitations on eligibility); more extensive public subsidization for vocational training and job search and relocation could be provided; and a serious commitment to day care for the children of lower income working parents could be made as well.

The success of social insurance policies to date in bringing people out of poverty is perhaps nowhere better shown than in our experience with Social Security and Medicare. By itself, Social Security is responsible for cutting the poverty rate in the United States by a third—that is, in comparison with the actual poverty rate of about 13 percent, our poverty rate would be about 21 percent were retirees to be cut off their Social Security (Medicare, as an "in-kind" income supplement for the health needs of retirees, reduces our poverty rate further yet). Both of these programs are now under assault in the ongoing conservative offensive of recent decades, for as highly successful programs of social insurance, they represent institutions that profoundly undermine the established structures of power in market systems by significantly reducing the ever-present threat to working people of their retiring in poverty.

Progressive taxation would be the third critical element in any successful public policy committed to a more egalitarian distribution. Instituting the structural and redistributive changes that have been discussed up to this point would likely require increasing the overall level of taxation by some amount. (Unless perhaps the necessary funding were to be obtained by cutbacks in defense spending!) Of course, in the popular culture purveyed in the mass media these days, taxes have come to symbolize all "evil government"—as if the public goods and services provided by government, unlike those sold in markets, could and should be had for free. Public provision is the only means of producing some essential kinds of goods, and these are no more cost-free than others. More importantly from the viewpoint of this book, the public sector is critical for countering power structures that arise in market systems. It is both the necessary enforcer and ultimate executor of all democratic decision making in the society, and indeed the only sphere of social action in which democratic decision making may be securely constituted in the first place. Briefly, although government is not necessarily democratic, certainly all real democracy requires government—and government requires taxes. Thus a government committed to redistributional spending for whatever reasons—for equity in people's material welfare, for sustaining aggregate consumer demand, or, as in this book, for democratizing the economy—will have no good reason for not employing progressive tax policy as part of the same commitment.

Our tax system overall today is only barely progressive, if at all: While federal personal income taxes are progressive, their effect is offset by regressivity in federal Social Security taxes, state sales taxes, and local property taxes.[12] "Flat" personal income taxes, the darling of some on the extreme right in the United States, would amount to abandoning any pretense of commitment to progressivity or even neutrality in the federal tax system, hence would make our tax system overall significantly regressive. A flat personal consumption tax would be even worse, since its effective tax rate on higher incomes would be less than on lower incomes to the extent that higher income people spend a smaller portion of their income on consumption. Regarding personal income taxes, what is needed is, first, further increases in the tax rates applied on higher income categories (and reductions in those applying to lower incomes); and second, closing the worst of the loopholes in the personal tax system, for example, the deduction for all mortgage interest, even on additional homes beyond that in which a family lives and regardless of the price of the home or the family's income level. Raising taxes on corporate income to levels such as pertained in earlier post–World War II decades—perhaps with a business value-added tax instead of the corporate income tax—would take some of the political pressure off the personal income tax system and permit it to be more progressive without so much resistance from upper-income groups. Major increases in federal revenue sharing with state and local governments would reduce the need for reliance by the latter on their regressive sales and property tax systems.

Finally, taxes on personal wealth would be needed for any serious public commitment to redistribution. Estate/inheritance taxes in the United States today, under fire from the right wing as "stifling of investment and entrepreneurial incentives," actually represent an absurdly low tax on personal wealth by international standards, and yield only a tiny federal revenue, with only the very wealthiest families paying. Major increases are needed in the effective taxes collected on sizable fortunes in the United States—perhaps by means of a simple wealth tax (using proportional or progressive rates without loopholes) on personal wealth above some upper-middle-class threshold (for example, $250,000).[13]

Utopianism?

This list of structural and redistributive reforms for democratizing the economy is by no means exhaustive—other changes, intended with the same goals in mind, could easily be added. Some of these reforms may seem "radical" to American readers, many others merely reinstitute policies already long in place in the United States but abandoned in the conservative movement of recent decades. None of the reforms I've suggested are completely new: Each has been used successfully somewhere in the world in recent times, and there is documented and extensively studied experience upon which to base their implementation here. Thus, while merely listing these reforms is not the same as specifying them in the kind of detail required to actually institute them, it is not for lack of a detailed understanding of reforms like these that most of them are not on "the agenda" in U.S. political discourse today.

It cannot be said then that these reforms are utopian, as opposed to practical or workable. They are quite realistic, in that sense, and would be beneficial to the interests of the vast majority of people as well. The reason these and similar reforms are not on the agenda is easily seen in light of the argument of this book: They violate the particular interests of those most benefiting from the power structures of the capitalist market economy. It may seem unrealistic to hope to counter that power, but if modern history teaches anything, it is that what is unrealistic at one point in time can indeed become commonplace reality at another.

Notes

1. Robert Kuttner, *Everything for Sale* is one of the more accessible references on the variety of market "imperfections" and their consequences.

2. See John Kenneth Galbraith, *Economics and the Public Purpose*, chapter 29, on the system-induced scarcity of public goods and overabundance of private goods. On the importance of meaningful work as a criterion for evaluating economic systems, see David Schweickart, *Against Capitalism*, pp. 224–236.

3. Randall Bartlett, *Economics and Power*, pp. 20–26 and 175–180, on the absurdity of assumptions of "given and fixed preferences."

4. Ibid.

5 . Some helpful references on much of the "platform" that follows include Tom Hayden, *The American Future*; Geoff Hodgson, *The Democratic Economy*; Joshua Cohen and Joel Rogers, *On Democracy*; Philip Green, *Retrieving Democracy*; Samuel Bowles and Herbert Gintis, *Democracy and Capitalism*; Christopher Gunn and Hazel Dayton Gunn, *Reclaiming Capital*; Randy Albelda, Robert Drago, and Steve Shulman, *Unlevel Playing Fields*; Bennett Harrison and Barry Bluestone, *The Great U-Turn*; Claude S. Fischer et al., *Inequality by Design*; Rebecca M. Blank, *It Takes a Nation*; Ray Marshall, *Back to Shared Prosperity*; Jon Wisman, *Worker Empowerment*; and Richard Edwards, *Rights at Work*. On what individuals can do to help accomplish all this in concrete terms, see David E. Driver, *Defending the Left*.

6. Michael Albert and Robin Hahnel, *Looking Forward* and *The Political Economy of Participatory Economics*.

7. The Lockheed-Martin, IBM, and Electronic Data Systems companies, for example, are now being contracted to administer local welfare operations. See Demetra Smith Nightingale and Nancy Pindus, "Privatization of Public Social Services."

8. Christopher Gunn and Hazel Dayton Gunn, *Reclaiming Capital*, discusses these in the context of the need for local democratically initiated and guided development.

9. On the "high (wage) road" in national labor management relations, see the collection of essays in Richard B. Freeman, *Working Under Different Rules*.

10. School vouchers are probably the biggest issue in education today. Progressives have rightly resisted the voucher movement insofar as it has been motivated by a desire ultimately to privatize education. Yet in principle, vouchers may be understood to be merely a kind of scholarship, hence may be administered in any of a number of ways and granted to students on any of a number of criteria. Thus vouchers for attendance in public schools and appropriately certified, nonreligious private schools, granted to students strictly on the basis of financial need (for example, with graduated values determined by family income) could be quite appropriate.

11. The aggregate poverty deficit may be computed from information given in U.S. Census Bureau, *Poverty in the U.S. 1998*. pp. vi and x. For military expenditures, see Council of Economic Advisers, *Economic Report of the President*, Table B-78. Aggregate personal consumption expenditures may be found in the same report, Table B-29. The aggregate poverty deficit may be considered an estimate of the maximum cost of eliminating poverty because the costs of other approaches than simple transfers, especially, for example, public provision of jobs and job training, could be at least partly offset by their returns in additional aggregate output.

12. Joseph A. Pechman, *Tax Reform, the Rich and the Poor*; Joel Slimrod, *Tax Progressivity and Income Inequality*.

13. Edward N. Wolff, *Top Heavy*, pp. 33–34.

Bibliography

Ackerman, Frank; Goodwin, Neva R.; Dougherty, Laurie; and Gallagher, Kevin, eds. *The Political Economy of Inequality.* Washington, DC: Island Press, 2000.

Aglietta, Michel. *A Theory of Capitalist Regulation: The U.S. Experience.* London and New York: Verso, 1979.

Akerlof, George, and Yellen, Janet, eds. *Efficiency Wage Models of the Labor Market.* New York: Cambridge University Press, 1986.

Albelda, Randy; Drago, Robert; and Shulman, Steven. *Unlevel Playing Fields: Understanding Wage Inequality and Discrimination.* New York: McGraw Hill, 1997.

Albert, Michael, and Hahnel, Robin. *The Political Economy of Participatory Economics.* New Jersey: Princeton University Press, 1991.

————. *Looking Forward: Participatory Economics for the Twenty-first Century.* Boston: South End Press, 1991.

Alchian, Armen A., and Demsetz, Harold. "Production, Information Cost, and Economic Organization." *American Economic Review* 62 (1972): 777–795.

Angresano, James. *Comparative Economics*, 2nd ed. Upper Saddle River, NJ: Prentice-Hall, 1996.

Axelrod, Robert. *The Evolution of Cooperation.* New York: Basic Books, 1984.

Bachrach, Peter, and Botwinick, Aryeh. *Power and Empowerment: A Radical Theory of Participatory Democracy.* Philadelphia: Temple University Press, 1992.

Bagdikian, Ben H. *The Media Monopoly*, 5th ed. Boston: Beacon Press, 1997.

Bain, Joe S. *Barriers to New Competition.* Cambridge, MA: Harvard University Press, 1956.

Bales, Kevin. *Disposable People: New Slavery in the Global Economy.* Berkeley: University of California Press, 1999.

Balzer, Wolfgang. "Game Theory and Power Theory: A Critical Comparison." In *Rethinking Power*, Tom Wartenberg, pp. 56–78. Albany, NY: SUNY Press, 1992.

Bardhan, Pranab. "On the Concept of Power in Economics." *Economics and Politics* 3 (1991): 265–277.

Bartlett, Randall. *Economics and Power: An Inquiry into Human Relations and Markets.* Cambridge, UK: Cambridge University Press, 1989.

Baumol, William J. "Contestable Markets: An Uprising in the Theory of Industry Structure." *American Economic Review* 72 (March 1982): 1–15.

Baumol, William J.; Panzar, John C.; and Robert D. Willig. *Contestable Markets and the Theory of Industrial Structure.* San Diego: Harcourt Brace Jovanovich, 1982.

Baumol, William J., and Blinder, Alan S. *Economics: Principles and Policy*, 8th ed. New York: Dryden, 1999.

Benassi, Corrado. "Asymmetric Information and Equilibrium Credit Rationing." *Rivista Internazionale di Scienze Economiche e Commerciali* 35 (1988): 993–1020.

Ben-Rafael, Eliezer. *Crisis and Transformation: The Kibbutz at Century's End.* Albany, NY: SUNY Press, 1997.

Bernstein, Michael A., and Adler, David E., eds. *Understanding American Economic Decline.* Cambridge, UK: Cambridge University Press, 1994.

Blair, John M. *Economic Concentration: Structure, Behavior and Public Policy.* New York: Harcourt Brace Jovanovich, 1972.

Blank, Rebecca M. *It Takes a Nation: A New Agenda for Fighting Poverty.* New York: Russell Sage Foundation, 1997.

Blaug, Ricardo. *Democracy Real and Ideal: Discourse Ethics and Radical Politics.* Albany, NY: SUNY Press, 1999.

Bowles, Samuel, and Edwards, Richard. *Understanding Capitalism: Competition, Command and Change in the U.S. Economy*, 2nd ed. New York: HarperCollins, 1993.

Bowles, Samuel, and Gintis, Herbert. "Contested Exchange: New Microfoundations for the Political Economy of Capitalism." *Politics and Society* 18 (1990): 165–222.

———. *Democracy and Capitalism: Property, Community, and the Contradictions of Modern Social Thought.* New York: Basic Books, 1987.

———. "Alienation and Capitalism." In *The Capitalist System*, 3rd ed. Edited by Richard C. Edwards, Michael Reich, and Thomas E. Weisskopf, pp. 141–149. Englewood Cliffs, NJ: Prentice-Hall, 1986.

———. *Schooling in Capitalist America: Educational Reform and the Contradictions of American Life.* New York: Basic Books, 1976.

Bowles, Samuel; Gintis, Herbert; and Gustafson, Bo, eds. *Markets and Democracy.* Cambridge, UK: Cambridge University Press, 1993.

Braudel, Fernand. *Civilization and Capitalism 15th-18th Century, Volume 2: The Wheels of Commerce.* New York: Harper and Row, 1986.

Braverman, Harry. *Labor and Monopoly Capital.* New York: Monthly Review Press, 1974.

Brecher, Jeremy. *Strike!* Boston: South End Press, 1997.

Brown, Wilson B. "Firm-Like Behavior in Markets: The Administered Channel." *International Journal of Industrial Organization* 2 (1984): 263–276.

Burawoy, Michael. *The Politics of Production: Factory Regimes Under Capitalism and Socialism.* London: Verso, 1985.

Bureau of Labor Statistics. "Range of Alternative Measures of Labor Underutilization." In *Labor Force Statistics from the Current Population Survey*, Table A-8. Web site: http://stats.bls.gov/webapps/legacy/opsatab8.htm (August 15, 2000).

———. "Selected Unemployment Indicators, Seasonally Adjusted." In *Labor Force Statistics from the Current Population Survey*, Table A-5. Web site: http://stats.bls.gov/webapps/legacy/cpsatab5.htm (December 4, 2000).

Coase, Ronald. "The Problem of Social Cost." *The Journal of Law and Economics* (October 1960).

Cohen, Joshua, and Rogers, Joel. *On Democracy: Toward a Transformation of American Society*. New York: Penguin Books, 1983.

Cole, Ken; Cameron, John; and Edwards, Chris. *Why Economists Disagree: The Political Economy of Economics*. London and New York: Longman, 1983.

Collins, Chuck; Leondar, Betsy; and Sklar, Holly. *Shifting Fortunes: The Perils of the Growing American Wealth Gap*. Boston: United for a Fair Economy, 1999.

Comanor, William S., and Smiley, Robert H. "Monopoly and the Distribution of Wealth." *Quarterly Journal of Economics* 89 (1975): 177–194.

Cordova, Ramon Vela. "Why Economists Are Wrong about Coops." *Dollars and Sense* 219 (September/October 1998): 44–47.

Council of Economic Advisers. *Economic Report of the President*. Washington, DC: Council of Economic Advisers, February 2000.

Cowling, Keith, and Sugden, Roger. "Control, Markets and Firms." In *Transaction Costs, Markets and Hierarchies*, Christos Pitelis, pp. 66–76. Oxford: Basil Blackwell, 1993.

Dahl, Robert A. *On Democracy*. New Haven: Yale University Press, 1998.

———. *A Preface to Economic Democracy*. Berkeley: University of California Press, 1985.

Danziger, Sheldon, and Gottschalk, Peter. *America Unequal*. New York: Russell Sage Foundation, 1995.

Deutsch, Larry L., ed. *Industry Studies*, 2nd ed. Armonk, NY: M.E. Sharpe, 1998.

Devine, Theresa J., and Kiefer, Nicholas M. *Empirical Labor Economics: The Search Approach*. Oxford: Oxford University Press, 1991.

Domhoff, G. William. *Who Rules America? Power and Politics in the Year 2000*. Mountain View, CO: Mayfield Publishing, 1998.

Dow, Sheila C. "The Post-Keynesian School." In *A Modern Guide to Economic Thought*. Douglas Mair and Anne G. Miller, pp. 176–206. Brookfield, VT: Edward Elgar, 1991.

Dowding, Keith. *Power*. Minneapolis: University of Minnesota Press, 1996.

Driver, David E. *Defending the Left: An Individual's Guide to Fighting for Social Justice, Individual Rights and the Environment*. Chicago: Noble Press, 1992.

Dugger, William M. *Corporate Hegemony*. Westport, CT: Greenwood Press, 1989.

———. "Power: An Institutional Framework of Analysis." *Journal of Economic Issues* 14 (1980): 897–907.

Eatwell, John; Milgate, Murray; and Newman, Peter, eds. *The New Palgrave: A Dictionary of Economics*. New York: Groves Dictionaries, 1987.

Edwards, Richard. *Rights at Work: Employment Relations in the Post-Union Era*. New York: Twentieth Century Fund, 1993.

———. *Contested Terrain*. New York: Basic Books, 1979.

Edwards, Richard C.; Reich, Michael; and Weisskopf, Thomas E. *The Capitalist System*, 3rd ed. Englewood Cliffs, NJ: Prentice-Hall, 1986.

Einstein, Albert. "Why Socialism?" In *Ideas and Opinions*, Albert Einstein, pp. 152–158. New York: Dell Publishing, 1954.

Ellerman, David. *The Democratic Worker-Owned Firm: A New Model for the East and West*. Boston: Unwin-Hyman, 1990.

Faux, Jeff. "The Fed's Unnecessary Assault on Wages." Economic Policy Institute Issue Brief #136. Web site: http://www.epinet.org (March 2000).

Federal Reserve Board. "Large Commercial Banks: Insured U.S. Chartered Commercial Banks That Have Consolidated Assets of $100-Million or More Ranked by

Consolidated Assets," March 31, 2000. Web site: http://www.bog.frb.fed.us/release/lbr/lrg_bnk_lst.pdf (August 2000).

Fischer, Claude S.; Hout, Michael; Jankowski, Martin Sanchez; Lucas, Samuel R.; Swidler, Ann; and Voss, Kim. *Inequality by Design: Cracking the Bell Curve Myth.* Princeton, NJ: Princeton University Press, 1996.

Folbre, Nancy. *Who Pays for the Kids? Gender and the Structures of Constraint.* London and New York: Routledge, 1994.

Fourie, Frederick C.V.N. "In the Beginning There Were Markets?" In *Transaction Costs, Markets and Hierarchies*, Christos Pitelis, pp. 41–65. Oxford, UK: Basil Blackwell, 1993.

Freeman, Richard B., ed. *Working Under Different Rules.* New York: Russell Sage Foundation, 1994.

Friedman, Milton. *Capitalism and Freedom.* Chicago: University of Chicago Press, 1962.

Fromm, Erich. "Marx's Concept of Man." In Erich Fromm, *Marx's Concept of Man*, 1–83, 1992.

———. *Marx's Concept of Man.* New York: The Continuum, 1992.

Galbraith, James K. *Created Unequal: The Crisis in American Pay.* New York: The Free Press, 1998.

Galbraith, John Kenneth. *The Anatomy of Power.* Boston: Houghton Mifflin, 1983.

———. *The New Industrial State*, 3rd ed. Boston: Houghton Mifflin, 1978.

———. *Economics and the Public Purpose.* Boston: Houghton Mifflin, 1973.

Gomes-Casseres, Benjamin. *The Alliance Revolution: The New Shape of Business Rivalry.* Cambridge, MA: Harvard University Press, 1996.

Gordon, David M. *Fat and Mean: The Corporate Squeeze of American Workers and the Myth of Managerial "Downsizing."* New York: The Free Press, 1996.

Gordon, David M.; Weisskopf, Thomas E.; and Bowles, Samuel. "Power, Accumulation, and Crisis: The Rise and Demise of the Postwar Social Structure of Accumulation." In *The Imperiled Economy*, Book I. New York: Union for Radical Political Economics, 1987.

Green, Philip. *Retrieving Democracy: In Search of Civic Equality.* Totowa, NJ: Rowman and Allanheld, 1985.

Greenwald, Bruce, and Stiglitz, Joseph E. "Imperfect Information, Credit Markets and Unemployment." *European Economic Review* 31 (1987): 444–456.

Gunn, Christopher, and Gunn, Hazel Dayton. *Reclaiming Capital: Democratic Initiatives and Community Development.* Ithaca, NY: Cornell University Press, 1991.

Harrison, Bennett. *Lean and Mean: The Changing Landscape of Corporate Power in the Age of Flexibility.* New York: Basic Books, 1994.

Harrison, Bennett, and Bluestone, Barry. *The Great U-Turn: Corporate Restructuring and the Polarizing of America.* New York: Basic Books, 1988.

Hayden, Tom. *The American Future: New Visions beyond Old Frontiers.* Boston: South End Press, 1980.

Held, David. *Models of Democracy.* Stanford, CA: Stanford University Press, 1987.

Henwood, Doug. *Wall Street: How It Works and for Whom.* London and New York: Verso, 1997.

Herman, Edward S. *Corporate Control, Corporate Power.* Cambridge, UK: Cambridge University Press, 1981.

Herman, Edward S., and Chomsky, Noam. *Manufacturing Consent: The Political Economy of the Mass Media.* New York: Pantheon, 1988.

Hewlitt, Sylvia Ann, and West, Cornel. *The War against Parents: What We Can Do for America's Beleaguered Moms and Dads*. Boston: Houghton Mifflin, 1998.

Hodgson, Geoffrey M. "Evolution and Institutional Change: On the Nature of Selection in Biology and Economics." In *Rationality, Institutions and Economic Methodology*, Uskali Maki, Bo Gustafson, and Christian Knudsen, pp. 222–241. London and New York: Routledge, 1993.

_____. *The Democratic Economy: A New Look at Planning, Markets and Power*. New York: Penguin Books, 1984.

Horvat, Branko. "The Theory of the Worker-Managed Firm Revisited." *Journal of Comparative Economics* 10 (1986): 9–25.

Hunt, E.K., and Sherman, Howard J. *Economics: An Introduction to Traditional and Radical Views*, 6th ed. New York: HarperCollins, 1990.

ICA Group. Boston, MA. Web site: http://www.ica-group.org (August 12, 2000).

Inequality.Org, "News, Information and Expertise on the Divide in Income, Wealth and Health." Web site: http://inequality.org (July 16, 2000).

International Health Program, "Health and Income Equity." University of Washington and Health Alliance International. Web site: http://depts.washing-ton.edu/eqhlth (August, 2000).

Jouvenal, Bertrand de. *On Power: The Natural History of Its Growth*. Indianapolis, IN: Liberty Fund, 1993.

Klein, Benjamin; Crawford, Robert; and Alchian, Armen. "Vertical Integration, Appropriable Rents, and the Competitive Process." In *The Economic Nature of the Firm*, Louis Putterman and Randall S. Kroszner, pp. 105–124. Cambridge, UK: Cambridge University Press, 1996.

Klein, Phillip A. "Confronting Power in Economics: A Pragmatic Evaluation." *Journal of Economic Issues* 14 (1980): 871–896.

Korten, David C. *When Corporations Rule the World*. West Hartford, CT: Kumarian Press, 1995.

Kotz, David M. *Bank Control of Large Corporations in the United States*. Berkeley: University of California Press, 1978.

Kuttner, Robert. *Everything for Sale: The Virtues and Limits of Markets*. Chicago: University of Chicago Press, 1996.

Lazonick, William. *Business Organization and the Myth of the Market Economy*. Cambridge, UK: Cambridge University Press, 1991.

Levy, Frank. *The New Dollars and Dreams: American Incomes and Economic Change*. New York: Russell Sage Foundation, 1998.

Lipietz, Alain. *Towards a New Economic Order: Postfordism, Ecology and Democracy*. New York: Oxford University Press, 1992.

Lippman, Steven A., and McCall, John J. "The Economics of Job Search: A Survey." *Economic Inquiry* 14 (June 1976): 155–189.

Logan, J., and Molotch, H. *Urban Fortunes: The Political Economy of Place*. Berkeley: University of California Press, 1987.

Lukes, Steven. *Power: A Radical View*. London: Macmillan, 1974.

_____, ed. *Power*. New York: New York University Press, 1986.

Lydall, Harold. *Yugoslavia in Crisis*. Oxford, UK: Clarendon, 1989.

Lynch, John W.; Kaplan, George A.; and Shema, Sarah J. "Cumulative Impact of Sustained Economic Hardship on Physical, Cognitive, Psychological, and Social Functioning." *New England Journal of Medicine* 337 (December 25, 1997): 1889–1895.

McChesney, Robert W. *Rich Media, Poor Democracy: Communication Politics in Dubious Times*. Urbana and Chicago: University of Illinois Press, 1999.

———. *Corporate Media and the Threat to Democracy*. New York: Seven Stories Press, 1997.

Mair, Douglas, and Miller, Anne G. *A Modern Guide to Economic Thought: An Introduction to Comparative Schools of Thought in Economics*. Brookfield, VT: Edward Elgar, 1991.

Maki, Uskali; Gustafson, Bo; and Knudsen, Christian. *Rationality, Institutions and Economic Methodology*. London and New York: Routledge, 1993.

Mander, Jerry. *In the Absence of the Sacred: The Failure of Technology and the Survival of the Indian Nations*. San Francisco: Sierra Club Books, 1991.

Mankiw, N. Gregory. *Principles of Economics*. New York: Dryden, 1997.

Marglin, Stephen. "What Do Bosses Do? The Origins and Functions of Hierarchy in Capitalist Production." *Review of Radical Political Economics* 6 (Summer 1974): 60–112.

Marshall, Ray, ed. *Back to Shared Prosperity: The Growing Inequality of Wealth and Income in America*. Armonk, NY: M.E. Sharpe, 2000.

Martin, Stephen. *Industrial Economics: Economic Analysis and Public Policy,* 2nd ed. New York: Macmillan, 1994.

Marx, Karl. "Economic and Philosophical Manuscripts of 1844." In Erich Fromm, *Marx's Concept of Man*, 90–196. New York: Continuum, 1992.

———. *Capital*, Vol. 1. New York: Vintage Books, 1977.

Mintz, Beth, and Schwartz, Michael. "Capital Flows and Financial Hegemony." In *Structures of Capital: The Social Organization of the Economy*, Sharon Zhukin and Paul DiMaggio, pp. 203–226. Cambridge, UK: Cambridge University Press, 1990.

———. "Corporate Interlocks, Financial Hegemony, and Intercorporate Coordination." In *The Structure of Power in America*, Michael Schwartz, chapter 3. New York: Holmes and Meier, 1987.

———. "Sources of Intercorporate Unity." In *The Structure of Power in America*, Michael Schwartz, chapter 2. New York: Holmes and Meier, 1987.

———. *The Power Structure of American Business*. Chicago: University of Chicago Press, 1985.

Mishel, Lawrence; Bernstein, Jared; and Schmitt, John. *The State of Working America 1998–99*. Armonk, NY: M.E. Sharpe, 1999.

———. "Finally, Real Wage Gains: Lower Unemployment, Higher Minimum Wage Spur Recent Wage Growth." Economic Policy Institute Issue Brief #127 (July 1998). Web site: http://www.epinet.org (August 2000).

Munkirs, John R. *The Transformation of American Capitalism*. Armonk, NY: M.E. Sharpe, 1984.

Munnell, Alicia H.; Tootell, Geoffrey M.B.; Browne, Lynn E.; and McEnearney, James. "Mortgage Lending in Boston: Interpreting HMDA Data," *American Economic Review* 86 (March 1996): 25–53.

Nightingale, Demetra Smith, and Pindus, Nancy. "Privatization of Public Social Services: A Background Paper." *The Urban Institute* (1998). Web site: http://www.urban.org/pub-man/privitiz.html (August 16, 2000).

O'Hara, Phillip Anthony, ed. *The Encyclopedia of Political Economy*. London and New York: Routledge, 1999.

Ollman, Bertell. *Alienation: Marx's Conception of Man in Capitalist Society*, 2nd ed. Cambridge, UK: Cambridge University Press, 1976.

Olson, Mancur. *Power and Prosperity: Outgrowing Communist and Capitalist Dictatorships*. New York: Basic Books, 2000.

Osberg, Lars. *Economic Inequality in the U.S.* Armonk, NY: M.E. Sharpe, 1984.

Parenti, Michael. *Land of Idols: Political Mythology in America*. New York: St. Martin's, 1994.

———. *Make Believe Media: The Politics of Entertainment*. New York: St. Martin's, 1992.

———. *Democracy for the Few*, 5th ed. New York: St. Martin's, 1988.

———. *Inventing Reality: The Politics of the Mass Media*. New York: St. Martin's, 1986.

Pearce, David W., ed. *The MIT Dictionary of Modern Economics*, 4th ed. Cambridge, MA: MIT Press, 1992.

Pechman, Joseph A. *Tax Reform, the Rich and the Poor*, 2nd ed. Washington, DC: Brookings Institution, 1989.

Pepall, Lynn; Richards, Daniel J.; and Norman, George. *Industrial Organization: Contemporary Theory and Practice*. Cincinnati, OH: South-Western, 1999.

Perrow, Charles. "Economic Theories of Organization." In *Structures of Capital: The Social Organization of the Economy*, Sharon Zukin and Paul DiMaggio, pp. 121–152. Cambridge, UK: Cambridge University Press.

Pitelis, Christos. *Market and Non-Market Hierarchies*. Cambridge, UK: Basil Blackwell, 1991.

———, ed. *Transaction Costs, Markets and Hierarchies*. Oxford, UK: Basil Blackwell, 1993.

Powell, Irene. "The Effect of Reductions in Concentration on Income Redistribution." *Review of Economics and Statistics* 69 (February 1987): 75–82.

Prychitko, David L., ed. *Why Economists Disagree: An Introduction to the Alternative Schools of Thought*. Albany, NY: SUNY Press, 1998.

Rebitzer, James. "Radical Political Economy and the Economics of Labor Markets." *Journal of Economic Literature* 31 (1993): 1394–1434.

Rhoades, Stephen A. "Retail Commercial Banking: An Industry in Transition." In *Industry Studies*, Larry L. Deutsch, pp.176–199. Armonk, NY: M.E. Sharpe, 1998.

Riddell, Tom; Shackelford, Jean; and Stamos, Steve. *Economics: A Tool for Critically Understanding Society*, 5th ed. Reading, MA: Addison Wesley, 1998.

Robinson, Joan. *The Economics of Imperfect Competition*. London: Macmillan, 1933.

Rock, Charles. "Workplace Democracy in the United States." In *Worker Empowerment*, Jon D. Wisman, pp. 37–58. New York: Bootstrap Press, 1991.

Roemer, John E. *Free to Lose*. Cambridge: Harvard University Press, 1988.

Rosen, Corey, and Somayaji, Chitra. "Economy in Numbers: ESOP's and Coop's." *Dollars and Sense* 219 (September/October 1998): 48–49.

Ryscavage, Paul. *Income Inequality in America: An Analysis of Trends*. Armonk, NY: M.E. Sharpe, 1999.

Sackrey, Charles, and Schneider, Geoffrey. *Introduction to Political Economy*. Somerville, MA: Economic Affairs Bureau of *Dollars and Sense*, 2000.

Samuels, Warren J. *The Economy as a System of Power*, Vols. 1 and 2. New Brunswick, NJ: Transaction Books, 1979.

Sawyer, Malcolm C. *The Challenge of Radical Political Economy: An Introduction to the Alternatives to Neo-Classical Economics*. Savage, MD: Barnes and Noble Books, 1989.

Schor, Juliet B. "Class Struggle and the Macroeconomy: The Cost of Job Loss." In *The Imperiled Economy* 1. New York: Union for Radical Political Economics, 1987.

Schutz, Eric. "Markets and Power." *Journal of Economic Issues* 29 (December 1995): 1147–1170.

———. "Social Power in Neo-Marxist Analyses." *Review of Radical Political Economics* 26 (1994): 95–102.

Schwartz, Michael, ed. *The Structure of Power in America*. New York: Holmes and Meier, 1987.

Schweickart, David. *Against Capitalism*. Boulder, CO: Westview Press, 1996.

Sexton, Patricia Cayo. *The War on Labor and the Left: Understanding America's Unique Conservatism*. Boulder, CO: Westview Press, 1991.

Shenk, Joshua Wolf. "Hidden Kingdom: Disney's Political Blueprint." *The American Prospect Online* Issue 21 (Spring, 1995). Web site: http://www.prospect.org/archives/21/21shen.html (August 14, 2000).

Shepherd, William G. *The Economics of Industrial Organization*, 4th ed. Englewood Cliffs, NJ: Prentice-Hall, 1997.

———. "Contestability vs. Competition." *American Economic Review* 74 (September 1984): 572–587.

Sherman, Howard J. *The Business Cycle: Growth and Crisis Under Capitalism*. Princeton, NJ: Princeton University Press, 1991.

Shy, Oz. *Industrial Organization*. Cambridge, MA: MIT Press, 1995.

Slimrod, Joel, ed. *Tax Progressivity and Income Inequality*. Cambridge, UK: Cambridge University Press, 1996.

Smithin, John. *Macroeconomic Policy and the Future of Capitalism: The Revenge of the Rentiers and the Threat to Prosperity*. Brookfield, VT: Edward Elgar, 1996.

Stearns, Linda Brewster. "Capital Market Effects on External Control of Corporations." *Theory and Society* 15 (1986): 47–75.

Stone, C. *Regime Politics: Governing Atlanta 1946–1988*. Lawrence: University of Kansas Press, 1989.

Stretton, Hugh. *Economics: A New Introduction*. London and Sterling, VA: Pluto Press, 1999.

Terkel, Studs. *Working: People Talk about What They Do All Day and How They Feel about What They Do*. New York: Pantheon, 1974.

Tregarthen, Timothy, and Rittenberg, Libby. *Economics*. New York: Worth Publishers, 2000.

Tucker, Robert C. *The Marx-Engels Reader*, 2nd ed. New York: W.W. Norton, 1978.

Union for Radical Political Economics. *The Imperiled Economy, Book 1: Macroeconomics from a Left Perspective*. New York: Union for Radical Political Economics, 1987.

U.S. Census Bureau. *Historical Statistics of the United States, Colonial Times to 1970, Bicentennial Edition on CD-Rom*, ed. Susan B. Carter et al. Cambridge, UK: Cambridge University Press, 1997.

———. *Money Income in the United States 1998* (P60–206). 1999.

———. *Statistical Abstract of the United States 1999*.

———. *Poverty in the United States 1998* (P60–207). 1999.

———. *Statistical Abstract of the United States 1998*.

———. *1992 Census of Manufacturers: Concentration Ratios in Manufacturing* (MC92–S-2).

————. *1982 Census of Manufacturers: Concentration Ratios in Manufacturing* (MC82–5–7).

Veblen, Thorstein B. *The Theory of the Leisure Class*. New York: Augustus M. Kelly, 1975.

Vianello, Fernando. "Labor Theory of Value." In *The New Palgrave: Marxian Economics*, John Eatwell, Murray Milgate, and Peter Newman, pp. 233–246. New York: W.W. Norton, 1990.

Voos, Paula. "Employee Involvement and Representation: Economic and Policy Implications." In *Back to Shared Prosperity*, Ray Marshall, pp. 332–340. Armonk, NY: M.E. Sharpe, 2000.

Wachtel, Howard M. *Labor and the Economy*, 3rd ed. New York: Harcourt Brace Jovanovich, 1992.

Wartenberg, Thomas E. *The Forms of Power: From Domination to Transformation*. Philadelphia: Temple University Press, 1990.

————, ed. *Rethinking Power*. Albany, NY: SUNY Press, 1992.

Weisskopf, Walter A. *Alienation and Economics*. New York: Dell, 1971.

Whyte, William Foote, and Whyte, Kathleen King. *Making Mondragon: The Growth and Dynamics of the Worker Cooperative Complex*. Ithaca, NY: Cornell University Press, 1988.

Wisman, Jon D., ed. *Worker Empowerment: The Struggle for Workplace Democracy*. New York: Bootstrap Press, 1991.

Wolff, Edward N. *Economics of Poverty, Inequality and Discrimination*. Cincinnati, OH: Southwestern, 1997.

————. *Top Heavy: A Study of the Increasing Inequality of Wealth in America*. New York: Twentieth Century Fund Press, 1995.

————. "Recent Trends in Wealth Ownership, 1983–1998," Working Paper 300 (April 2000) Jerome Levy Economics Institute. Web site: http://www.levy.org/docs/wrkpap/papers/300.html (August 15, 2000).

Wrong, Dennis H. *Power: Its Forms, Bases, and Uses*. New York: Harper and Row, 1979.

Zukin, Sharon, and DiMaggio, Paul. *Structures of Capital: The Social Organization of the Economy*. Cambridge, UK: Cambridge University Press, 1990.

Index

About the Author

Eric A. Schutz has contributed articles to the *Journal of Economic Issues*, the *Review of Radical Political Economics*, and the *Encyclopedia of Political Economy*. He is active in the U.S. Green Party, and lives with his family in Winter Park, Florida, where he is a professor of economics at Rollins College.